MENtality
& MONSTERS

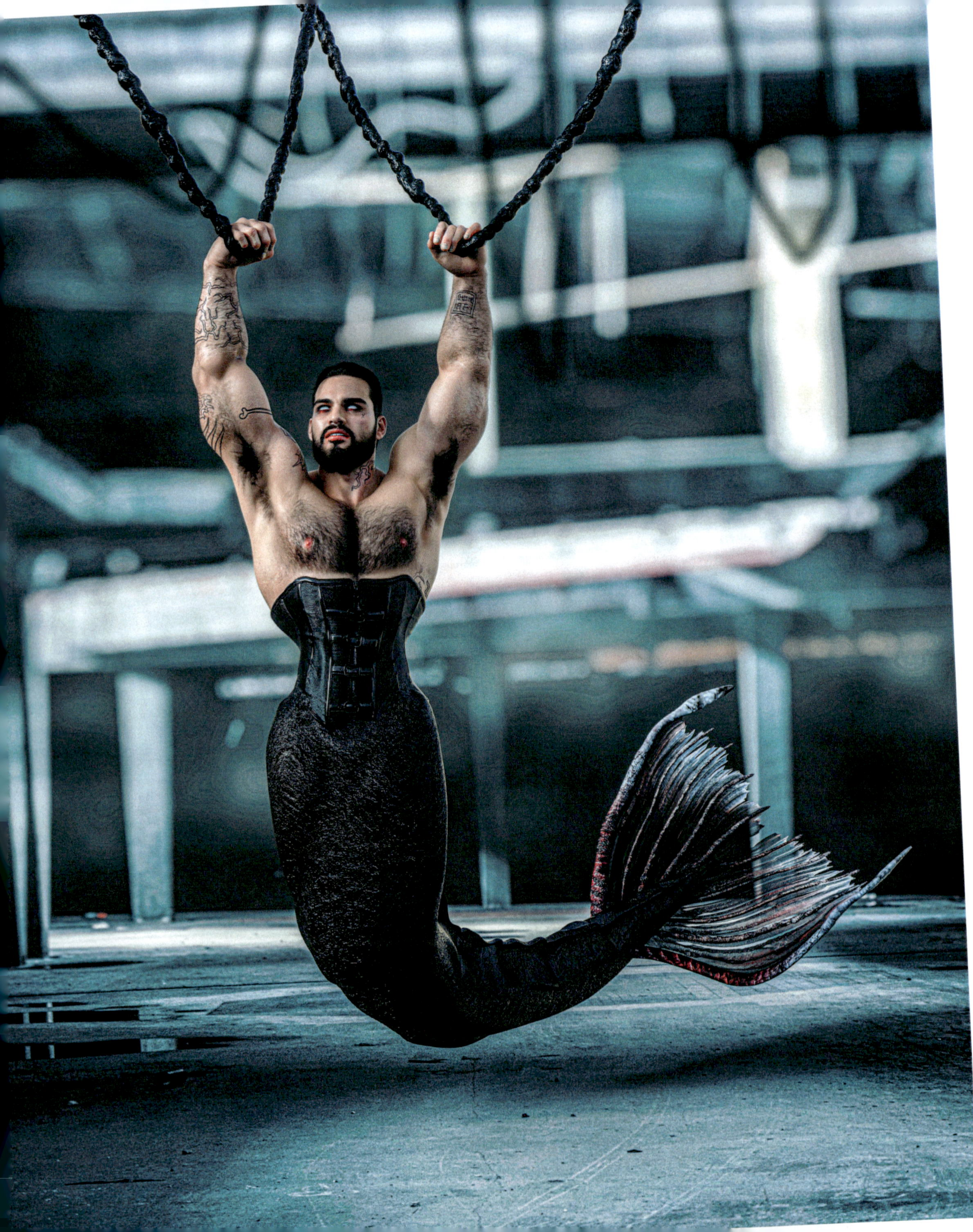

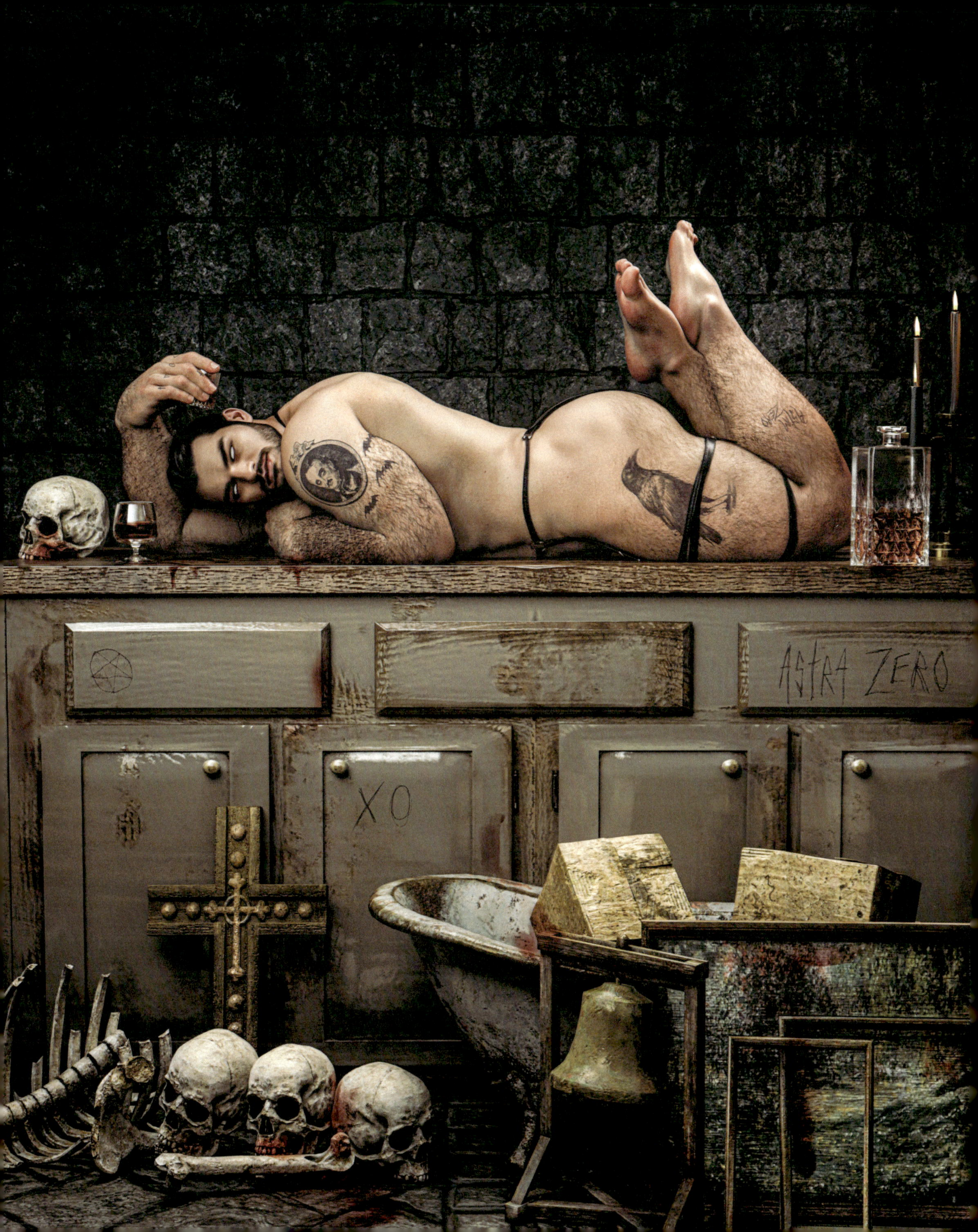

ASTRA ZERO
XO

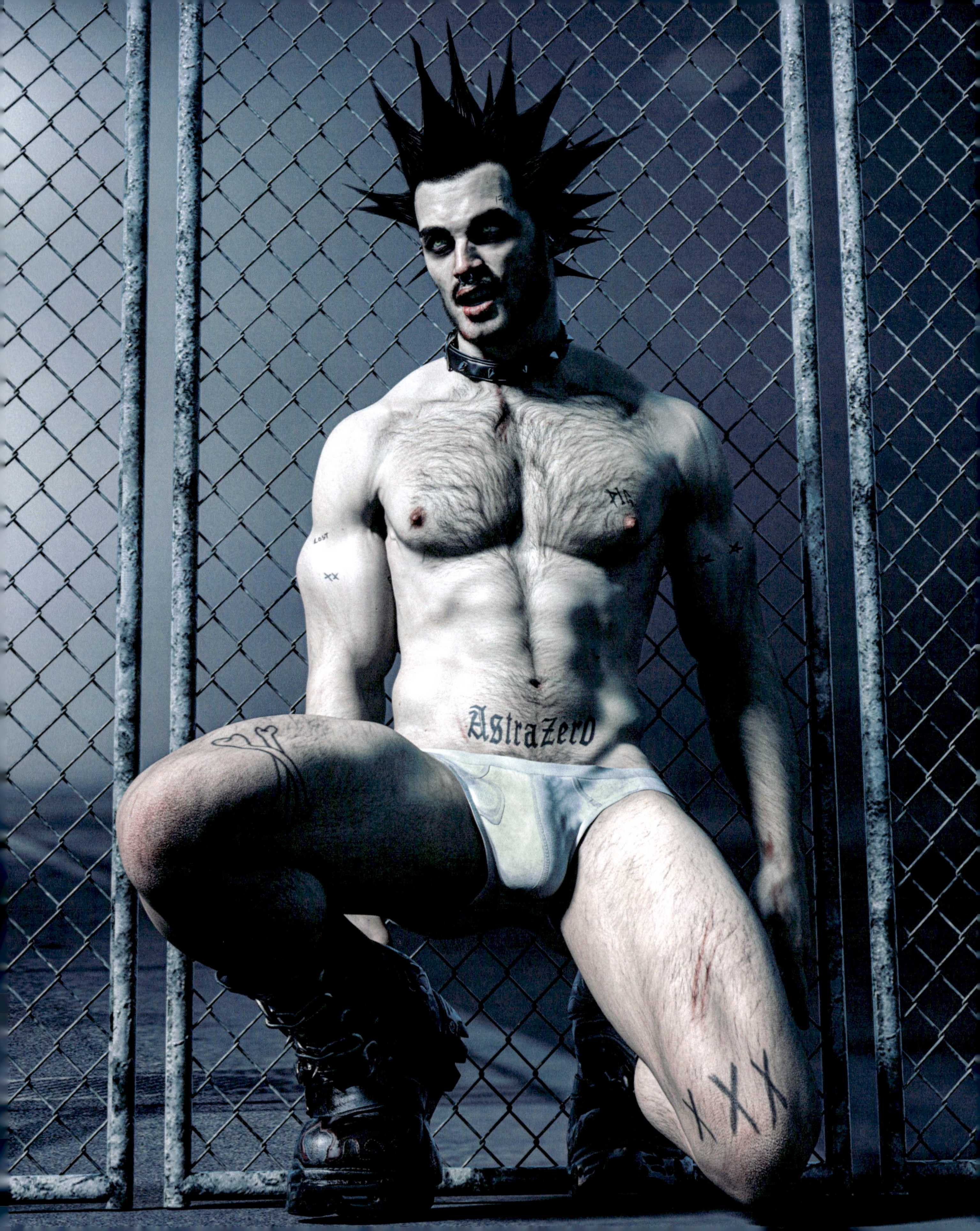

AstraZero
XXX

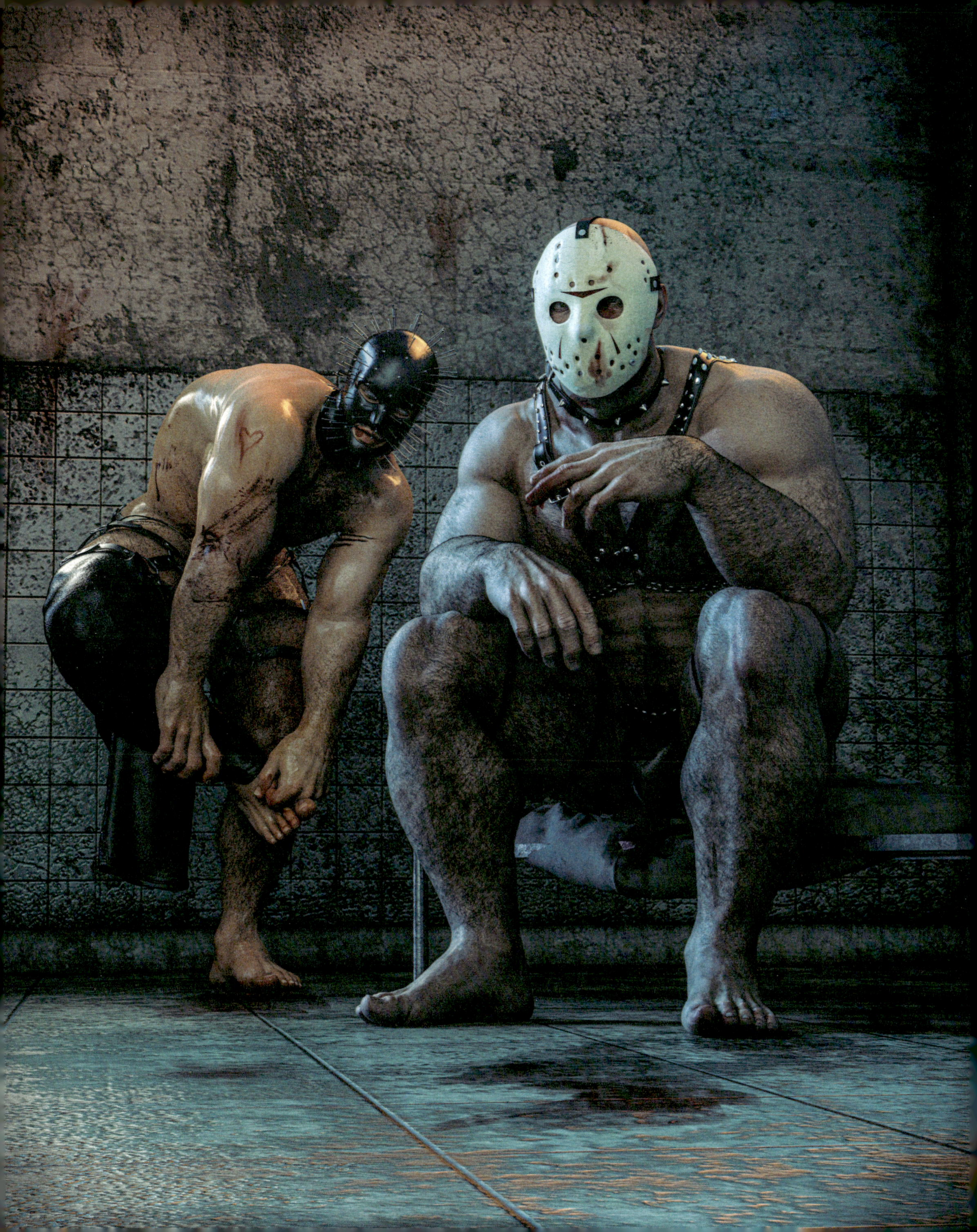

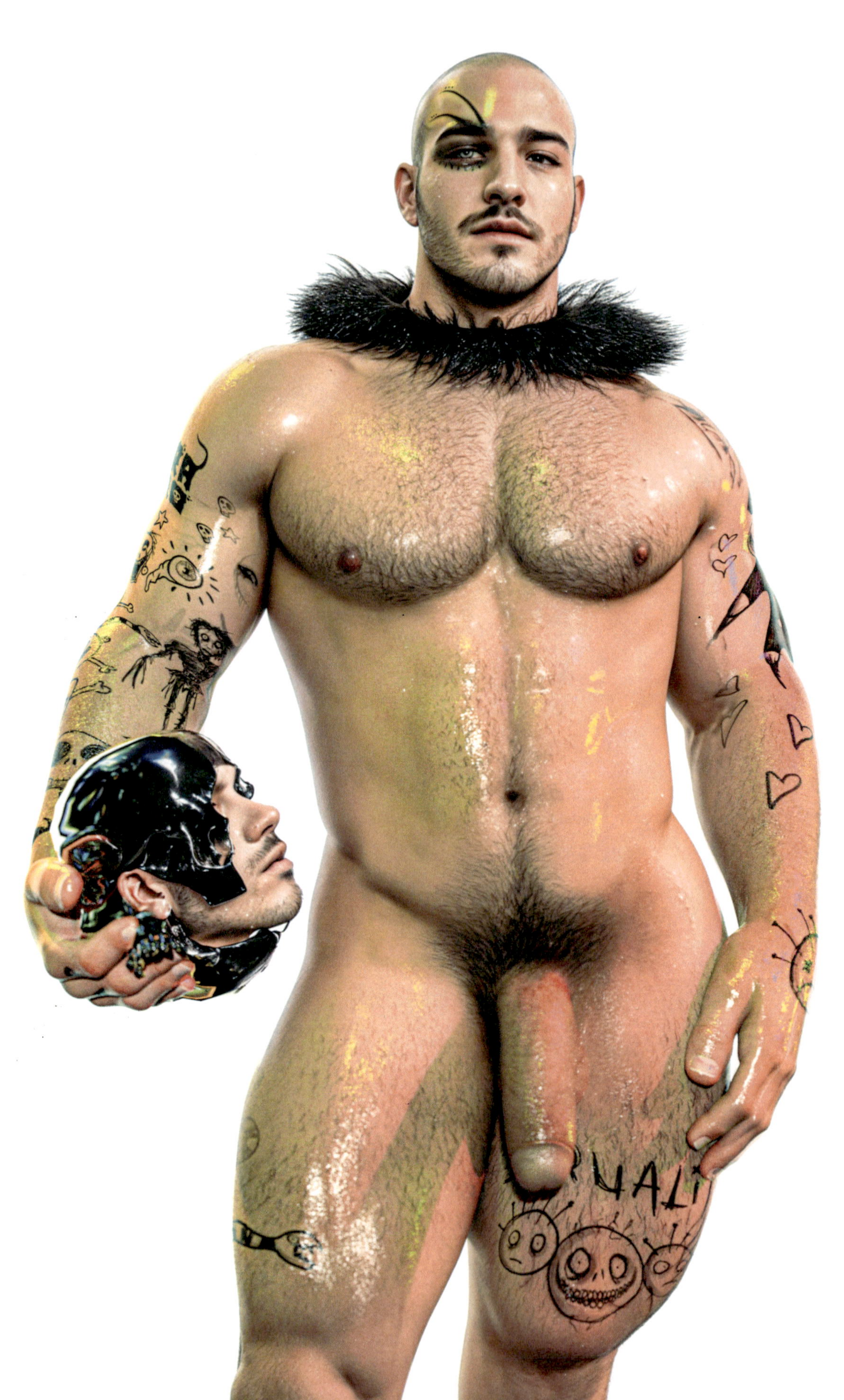

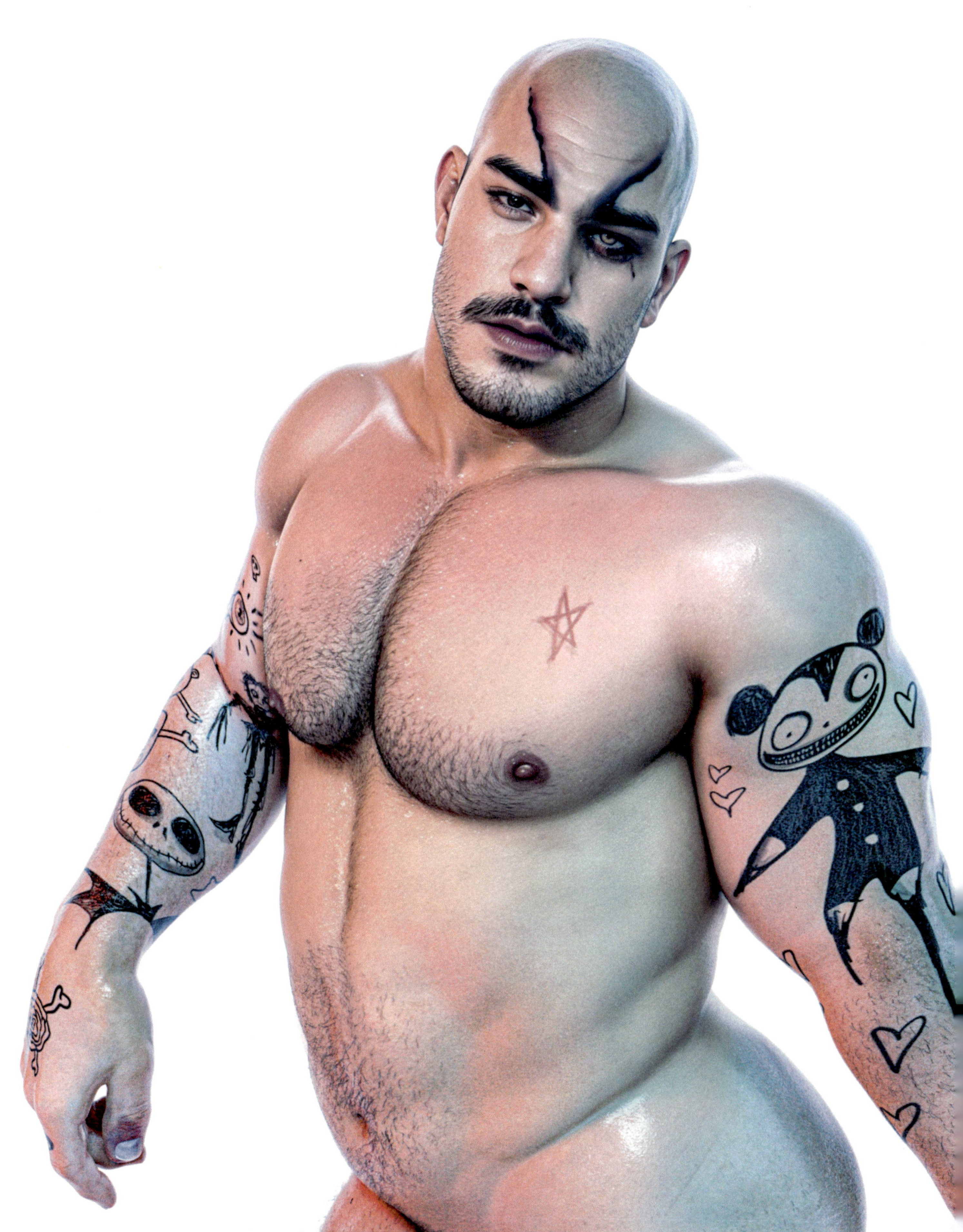

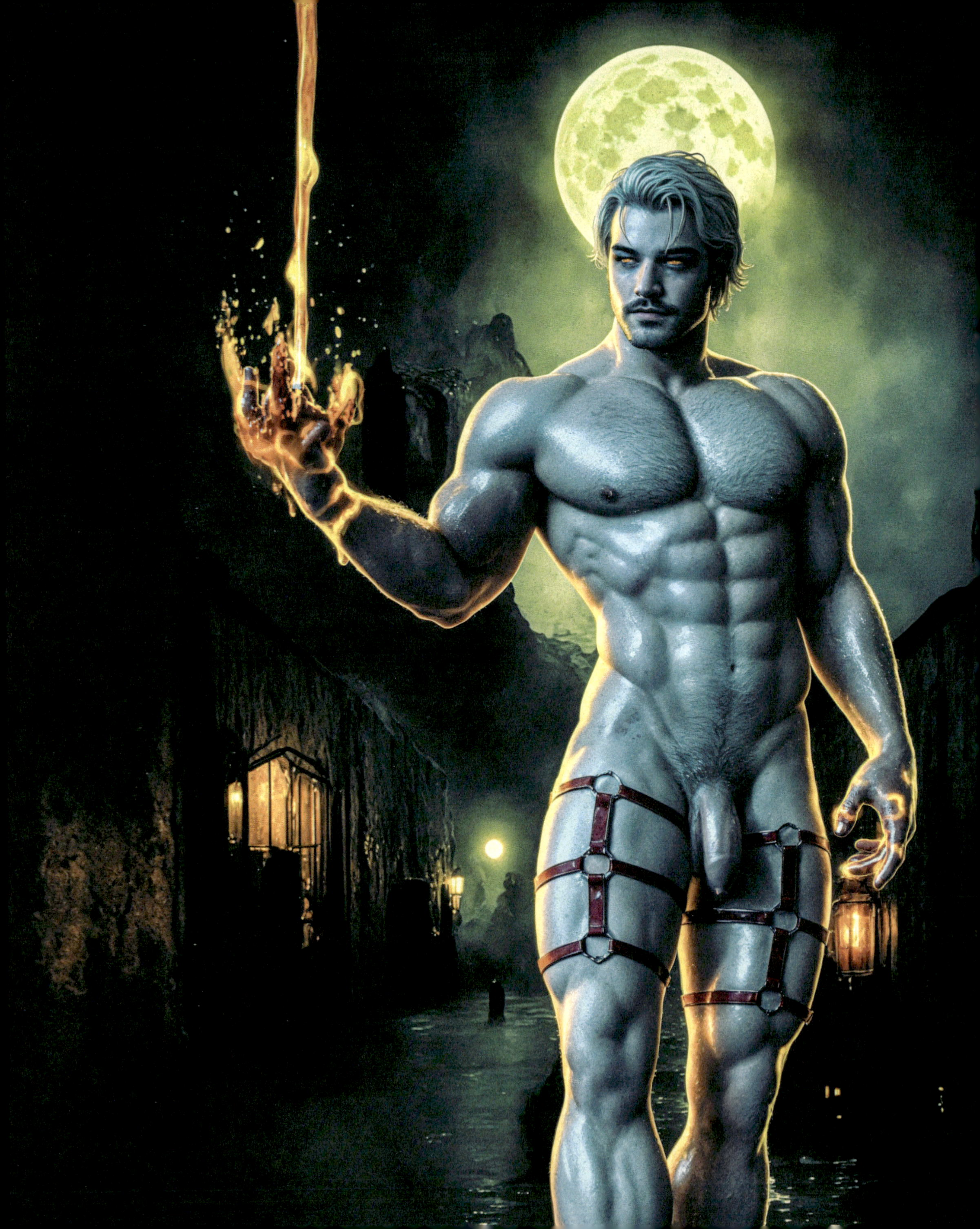

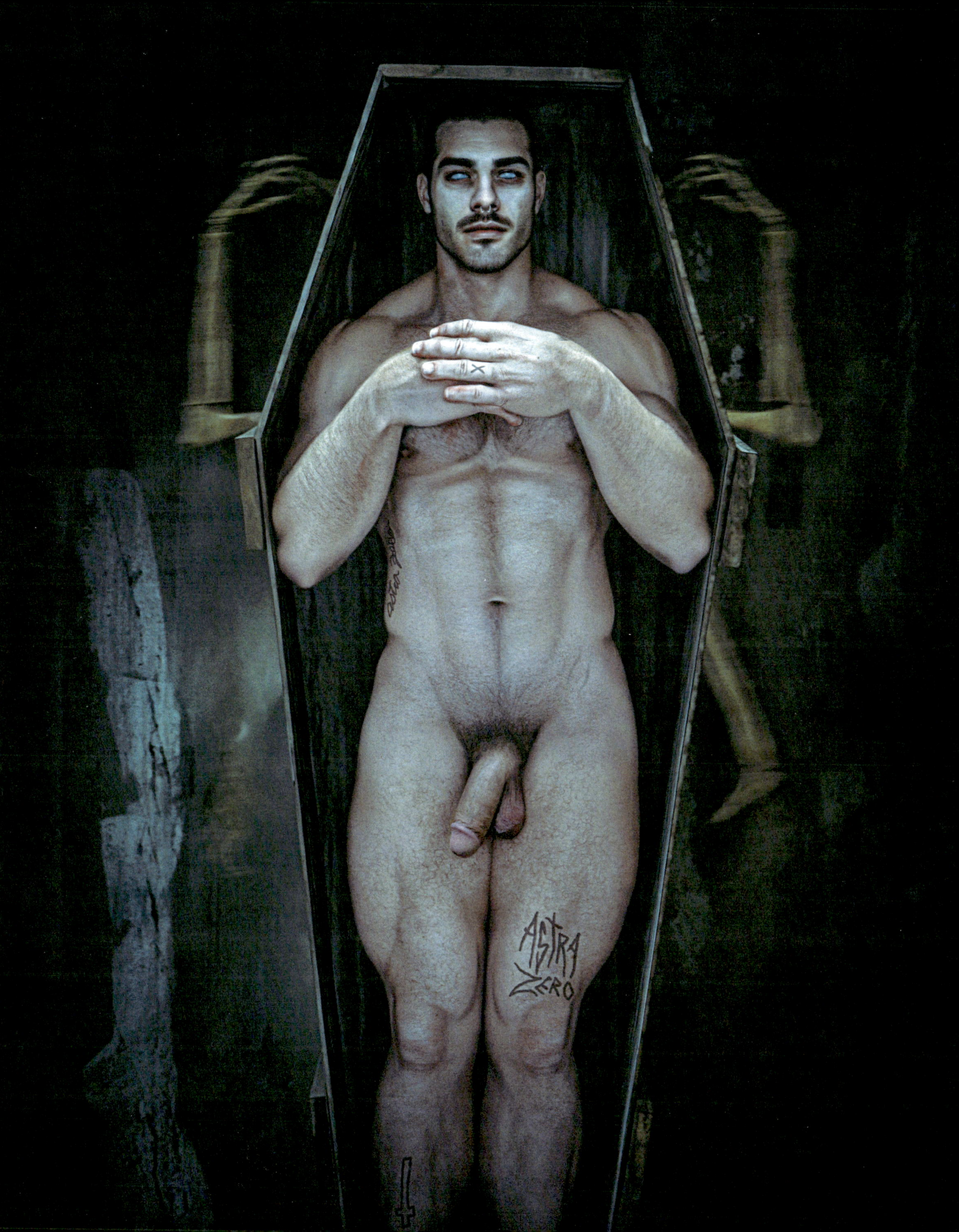

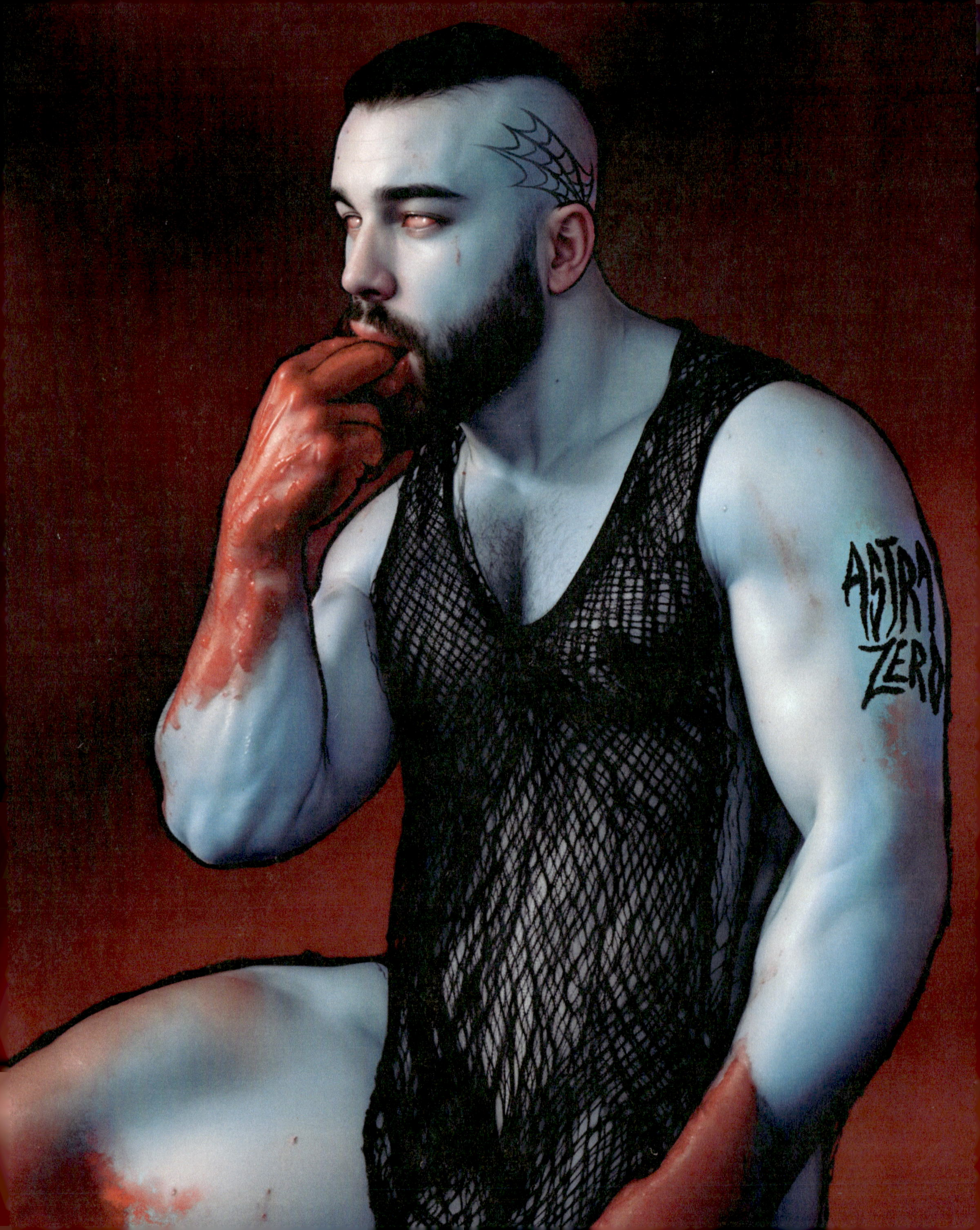

ASTRA
ZERO

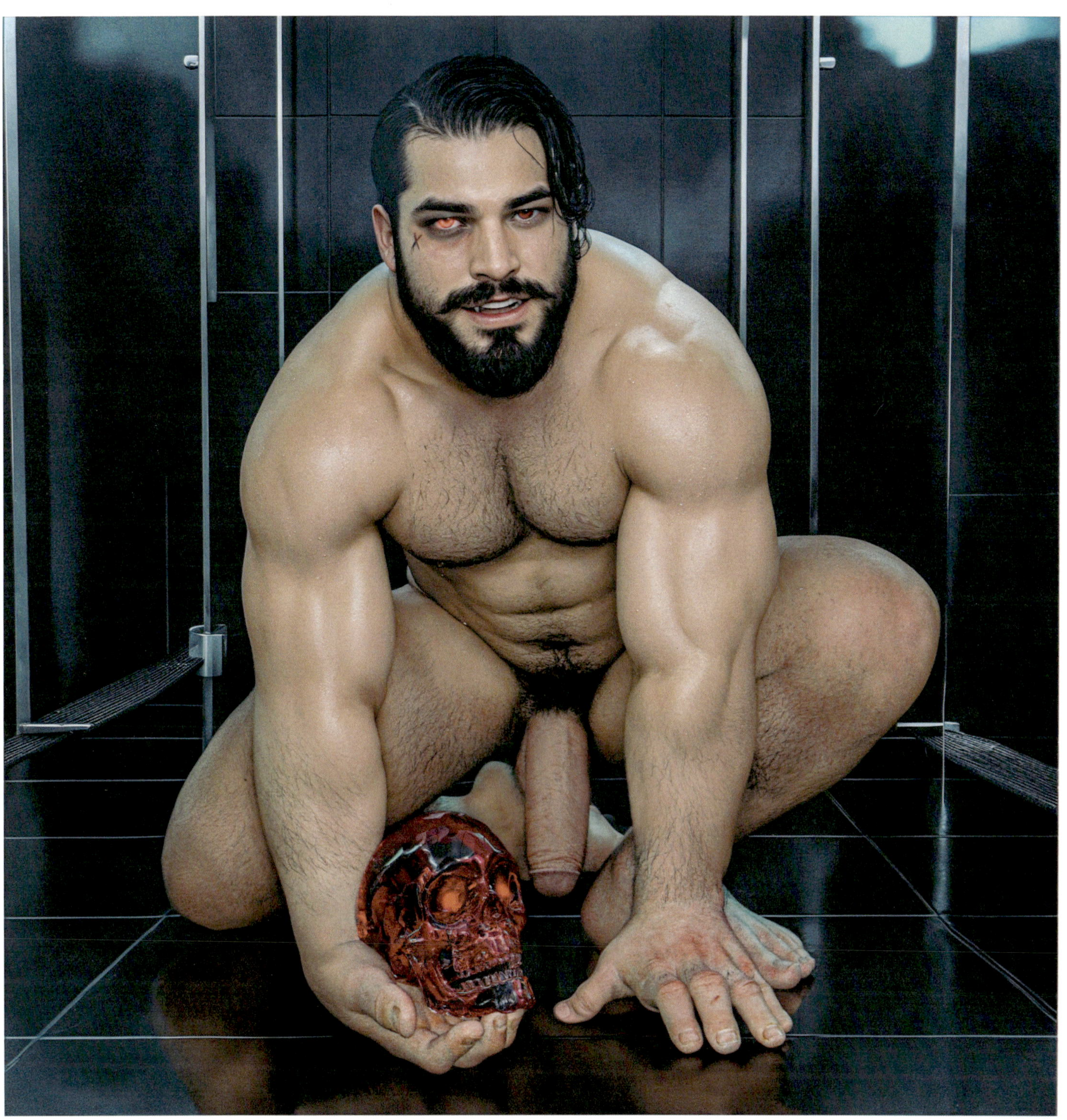

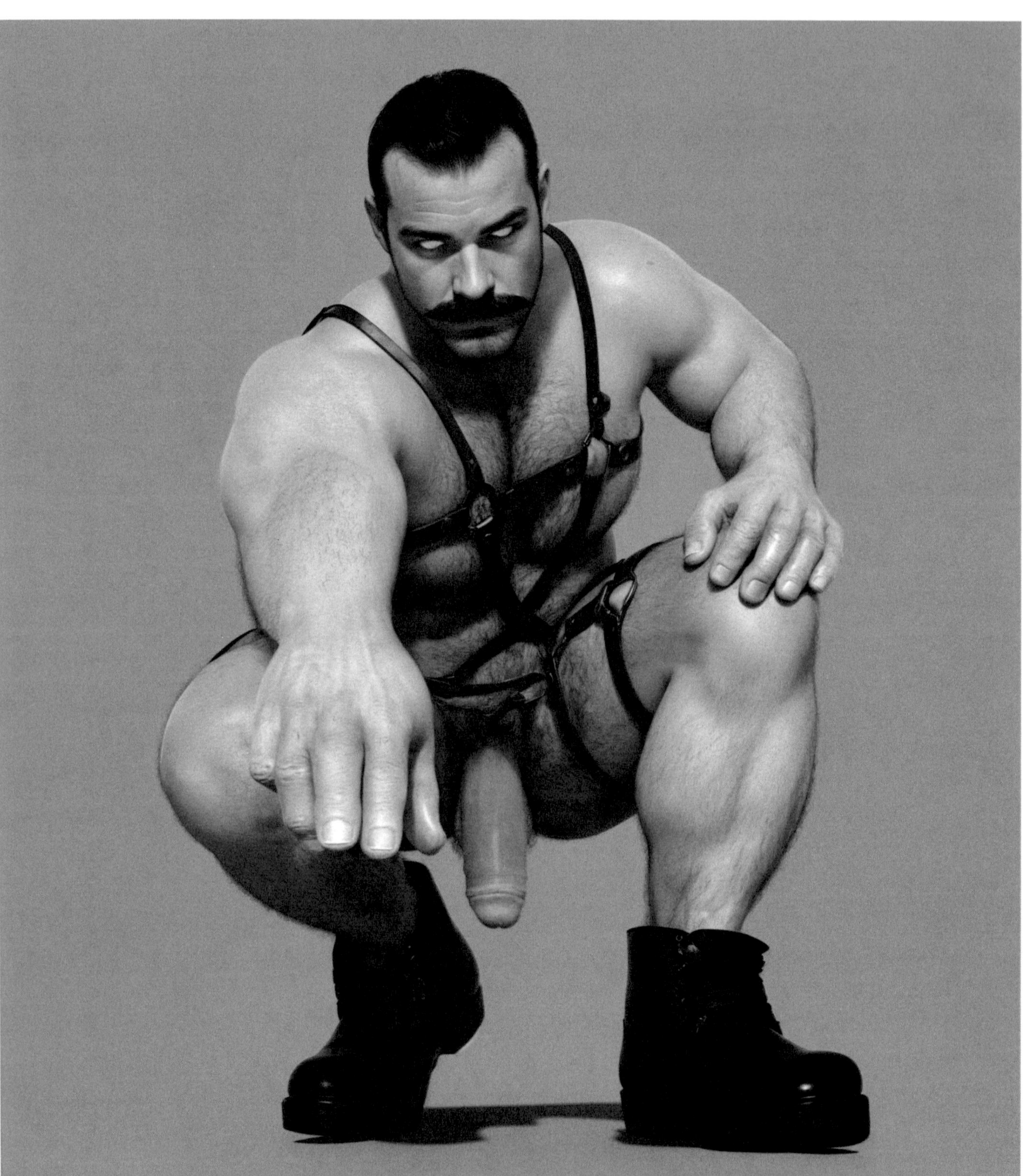

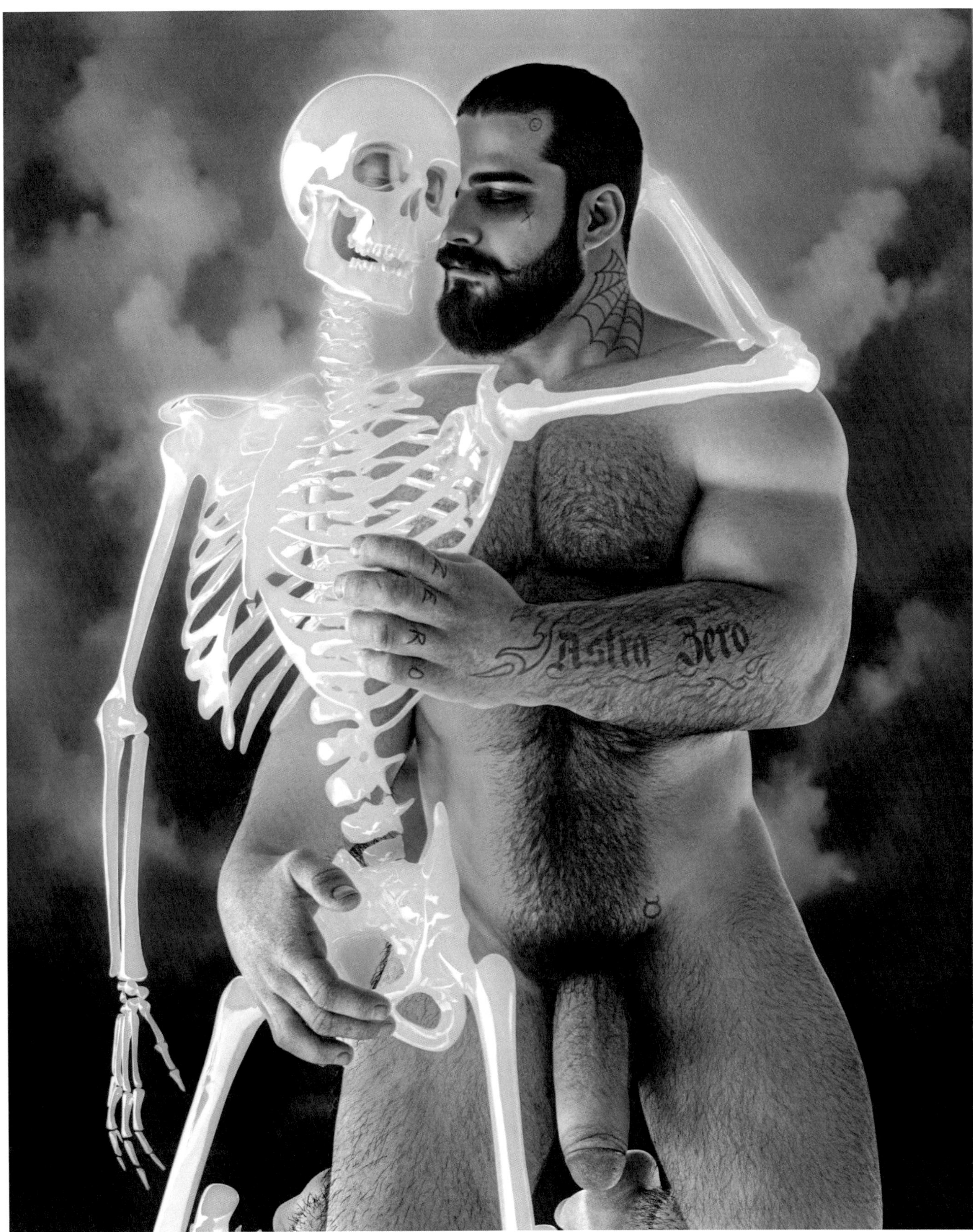
Astra Zero

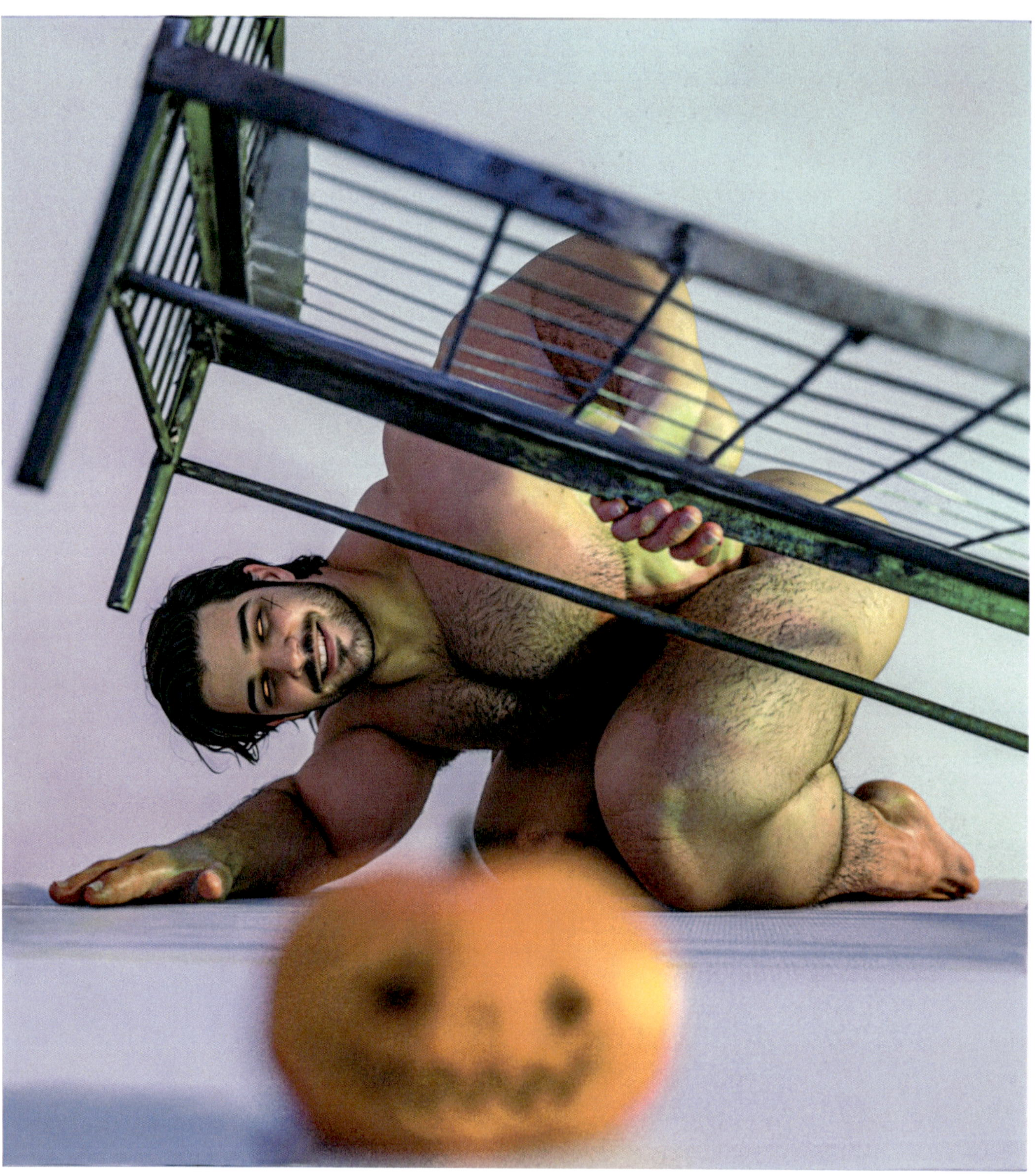

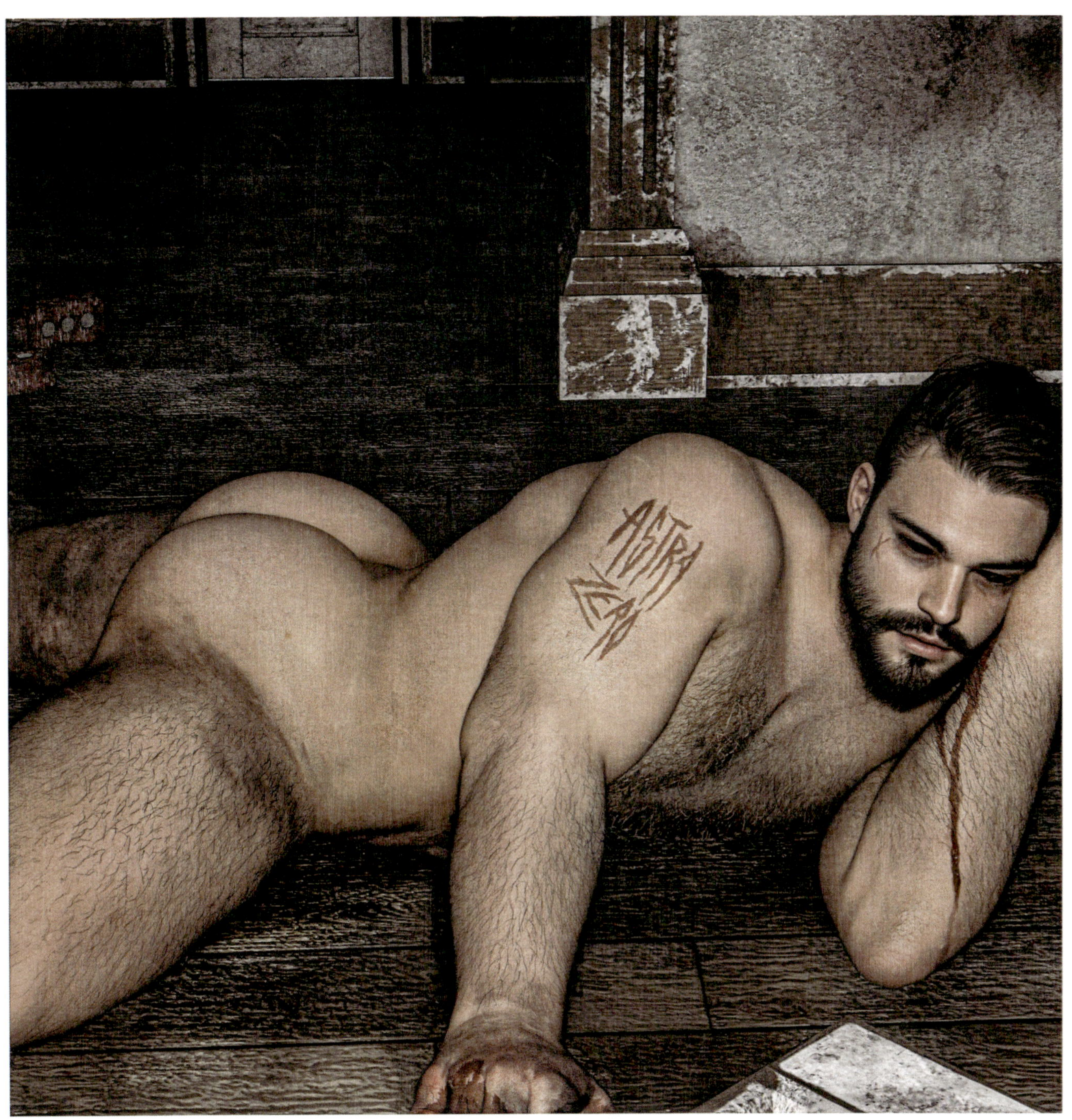

Limited Interactions With the Outside World

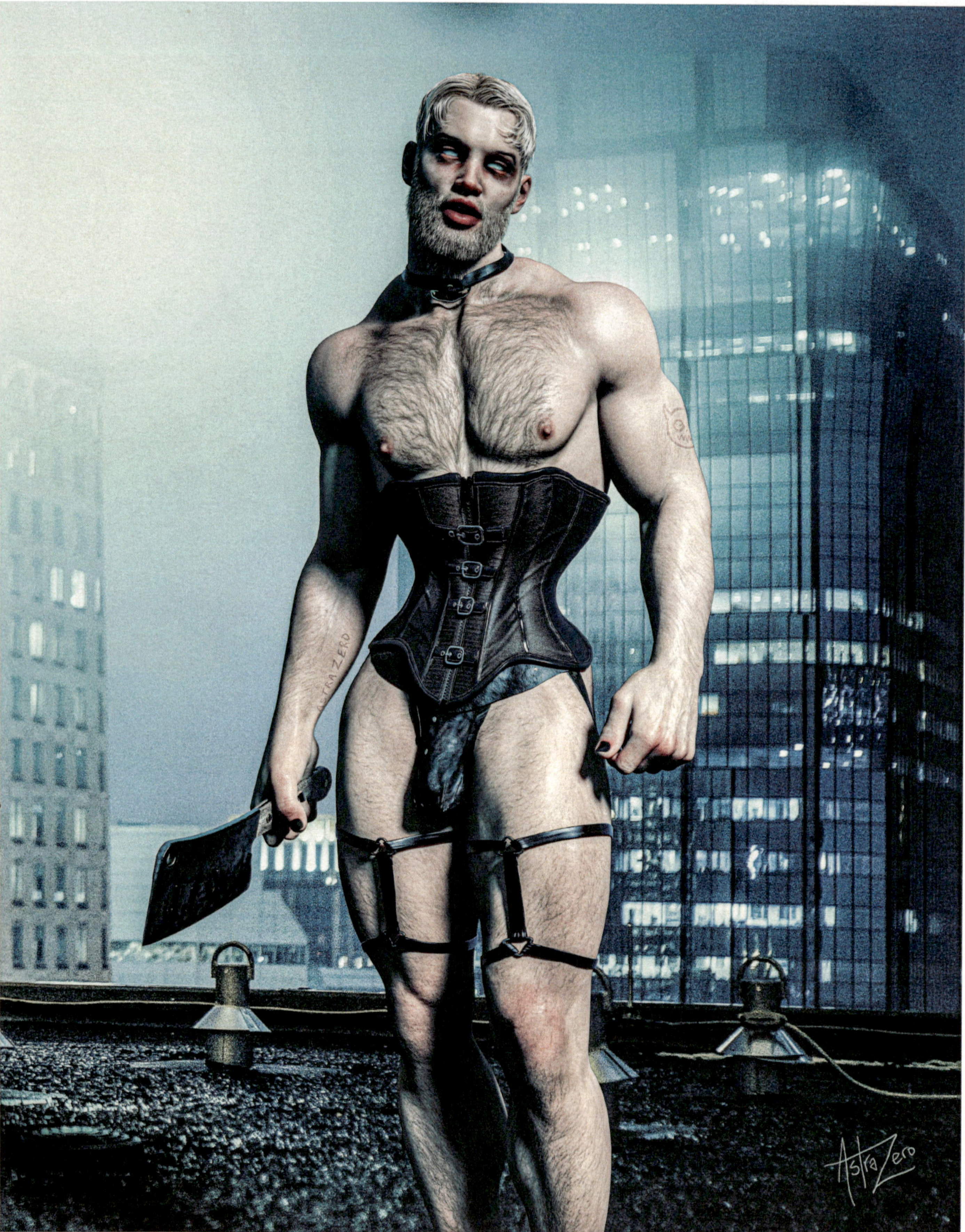

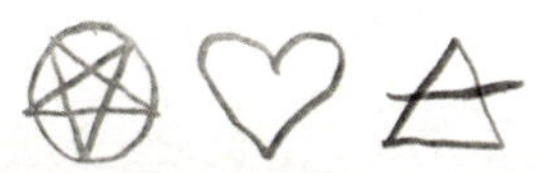

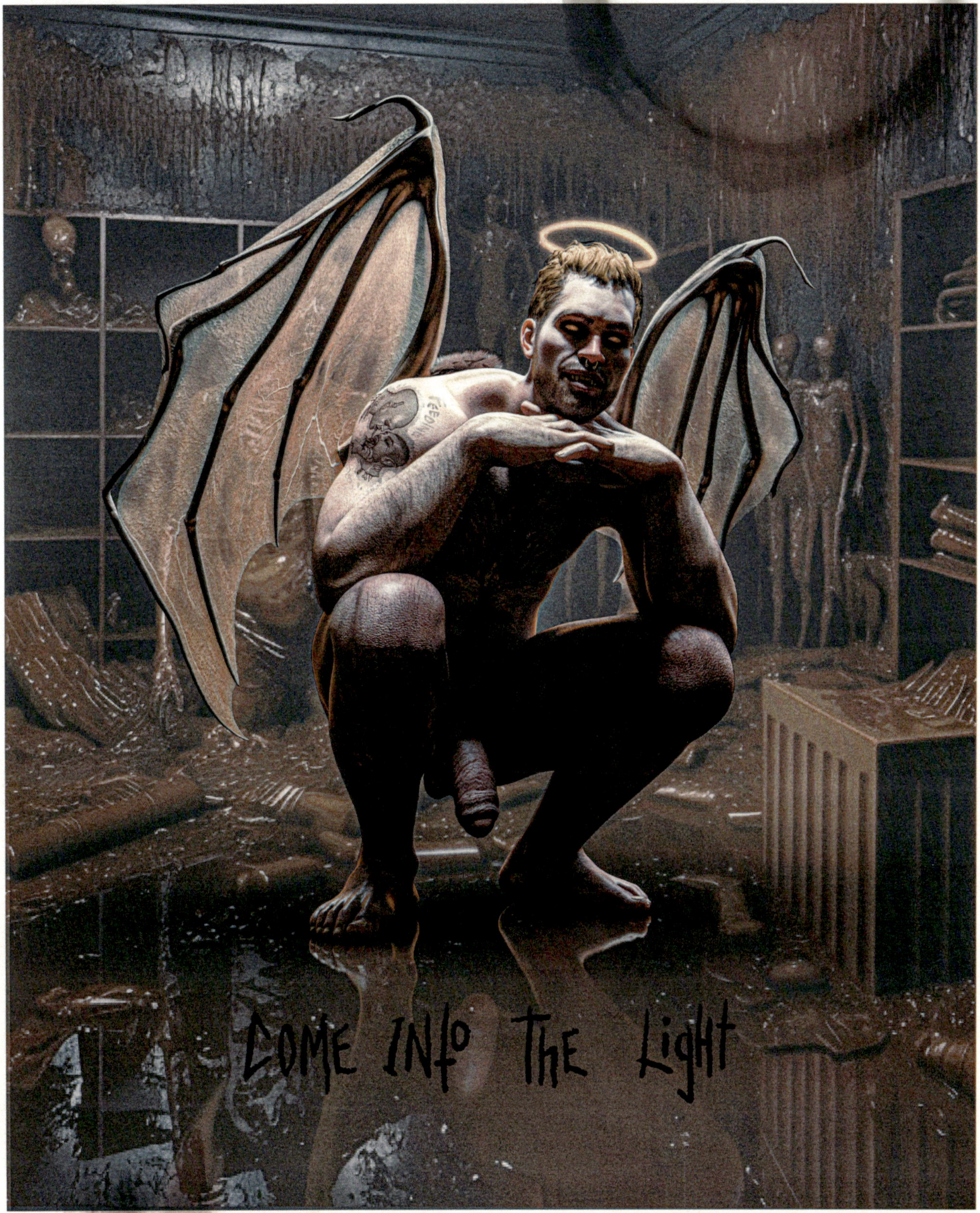

COME INTO THE LIGHT

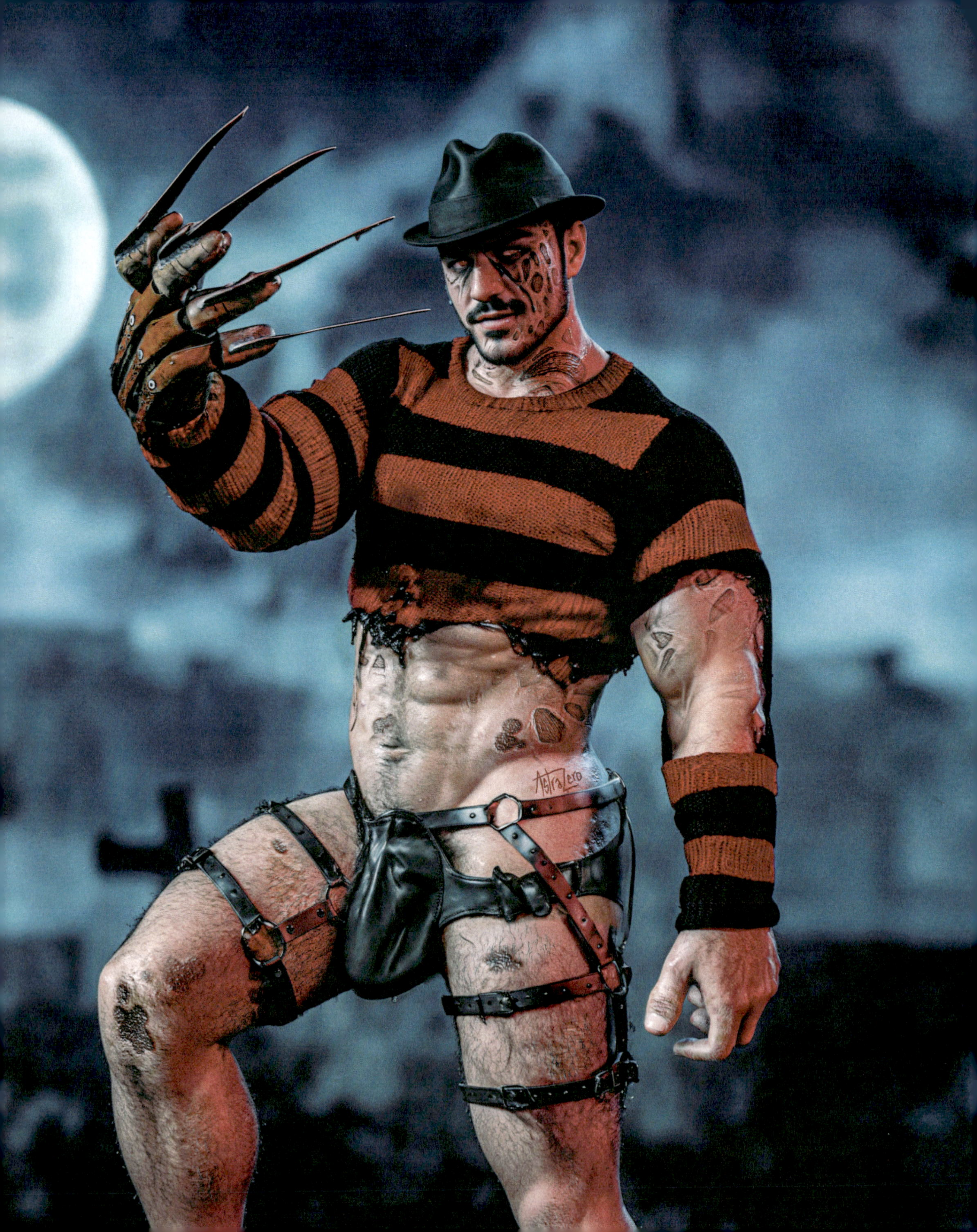

AstraZero

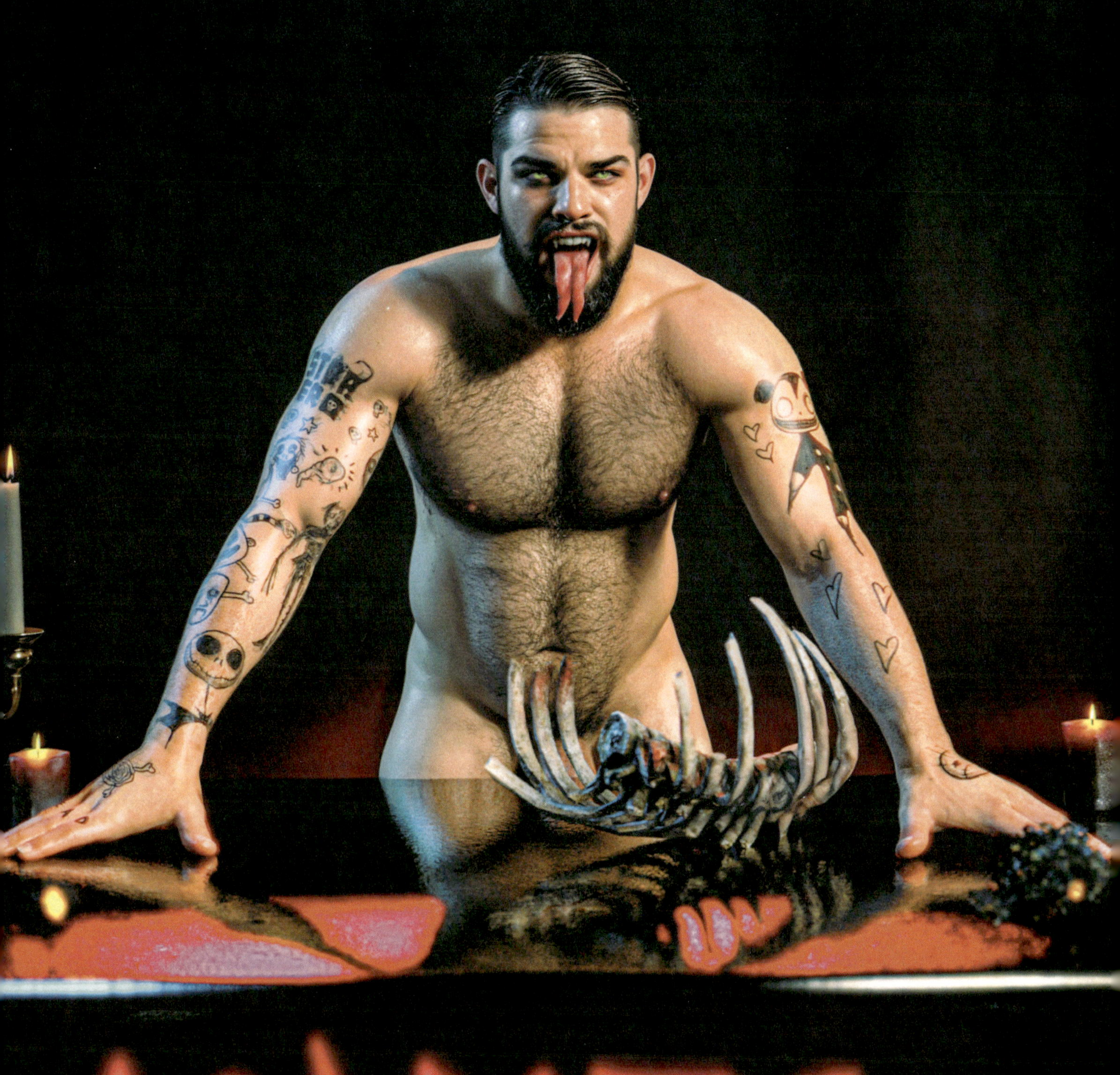

ASTRAZERO

THE GAY AGENDA?
IS IT TO LATE TO SAVE THEM FROM DAMNATION?
SINNERS
POSESSION
EVIL?
HOMO EROTIC?
?
?
?
?
SATAN?
DEMON-STRATION
NO SOUL?
DEVIL WORSHIP?
WE MUST PROTECT THE INODENT FROM THEIR PERVERZION!

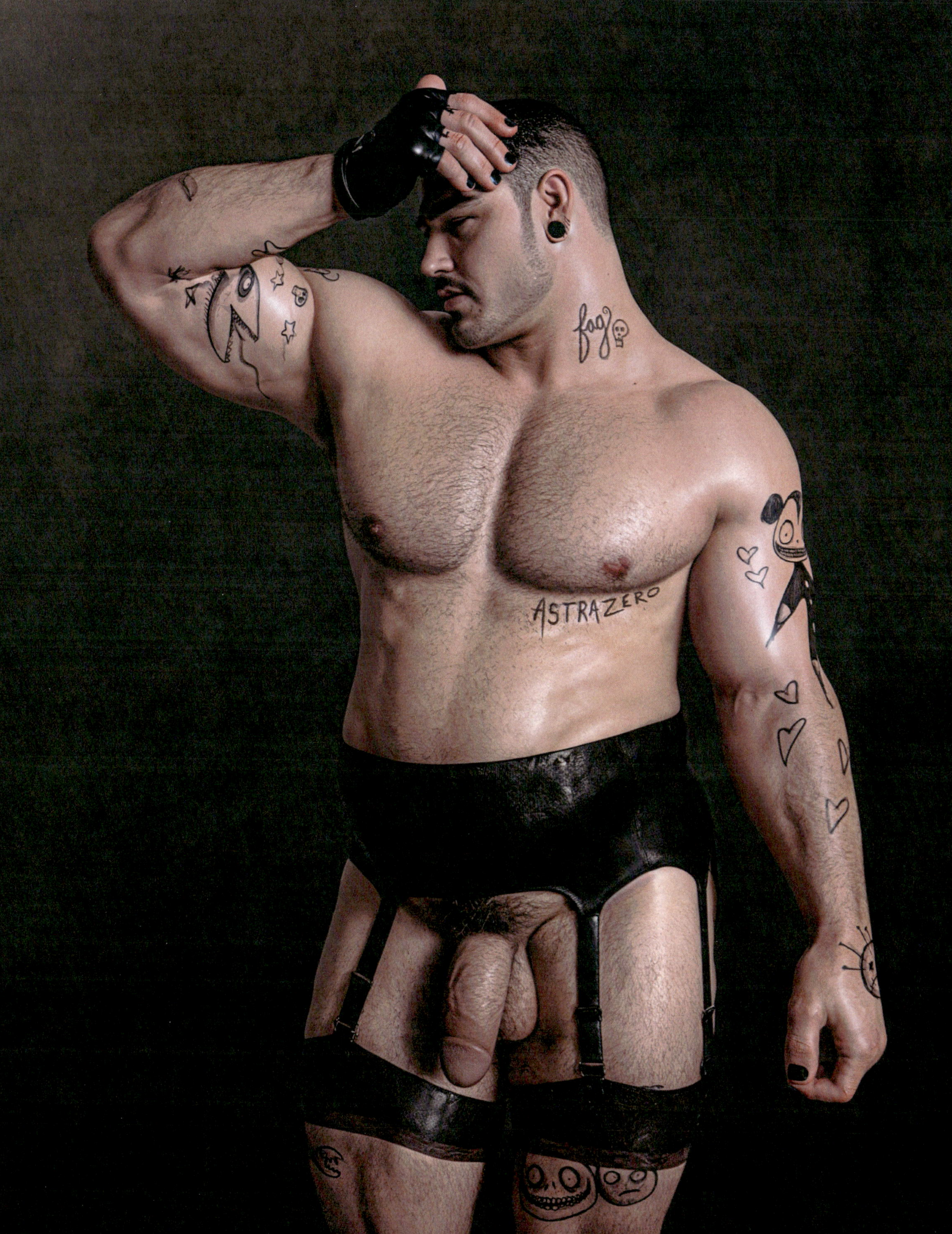

fag
ASTRAZERO

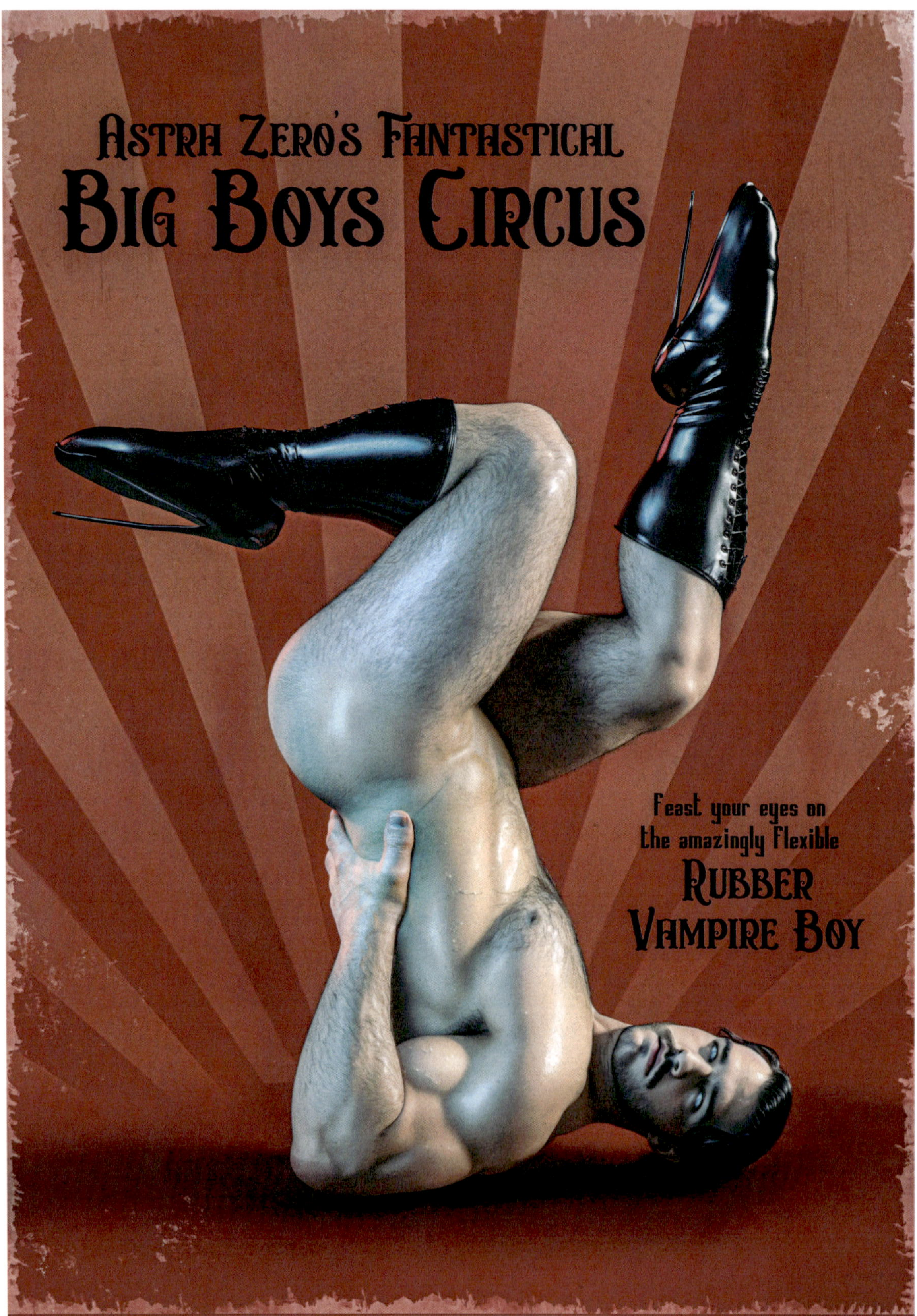

Astra Zero's Fantastical
Big Boys Circus
Feast your eyes on
the amazingly flexible
Rubber
Vampire Boy

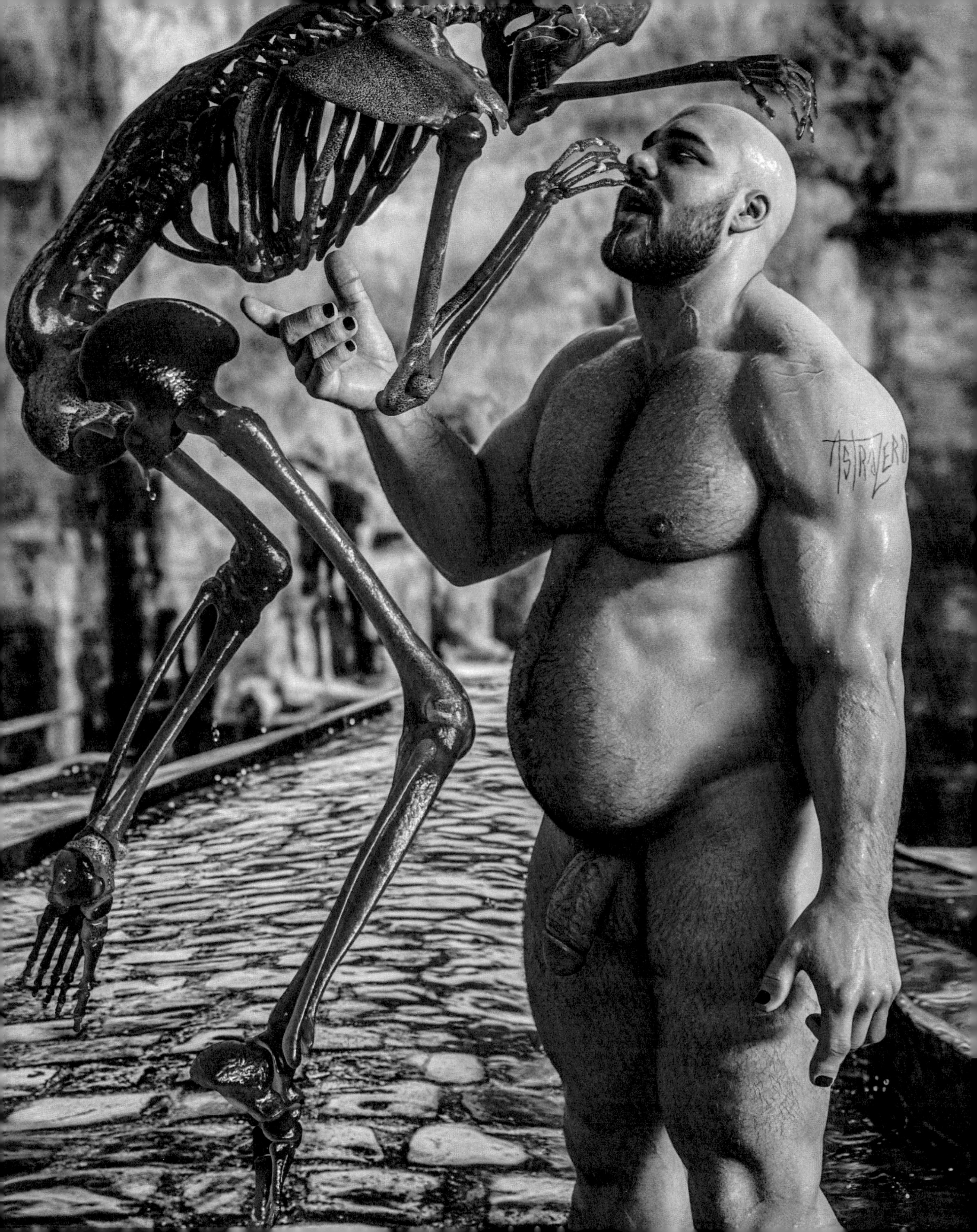

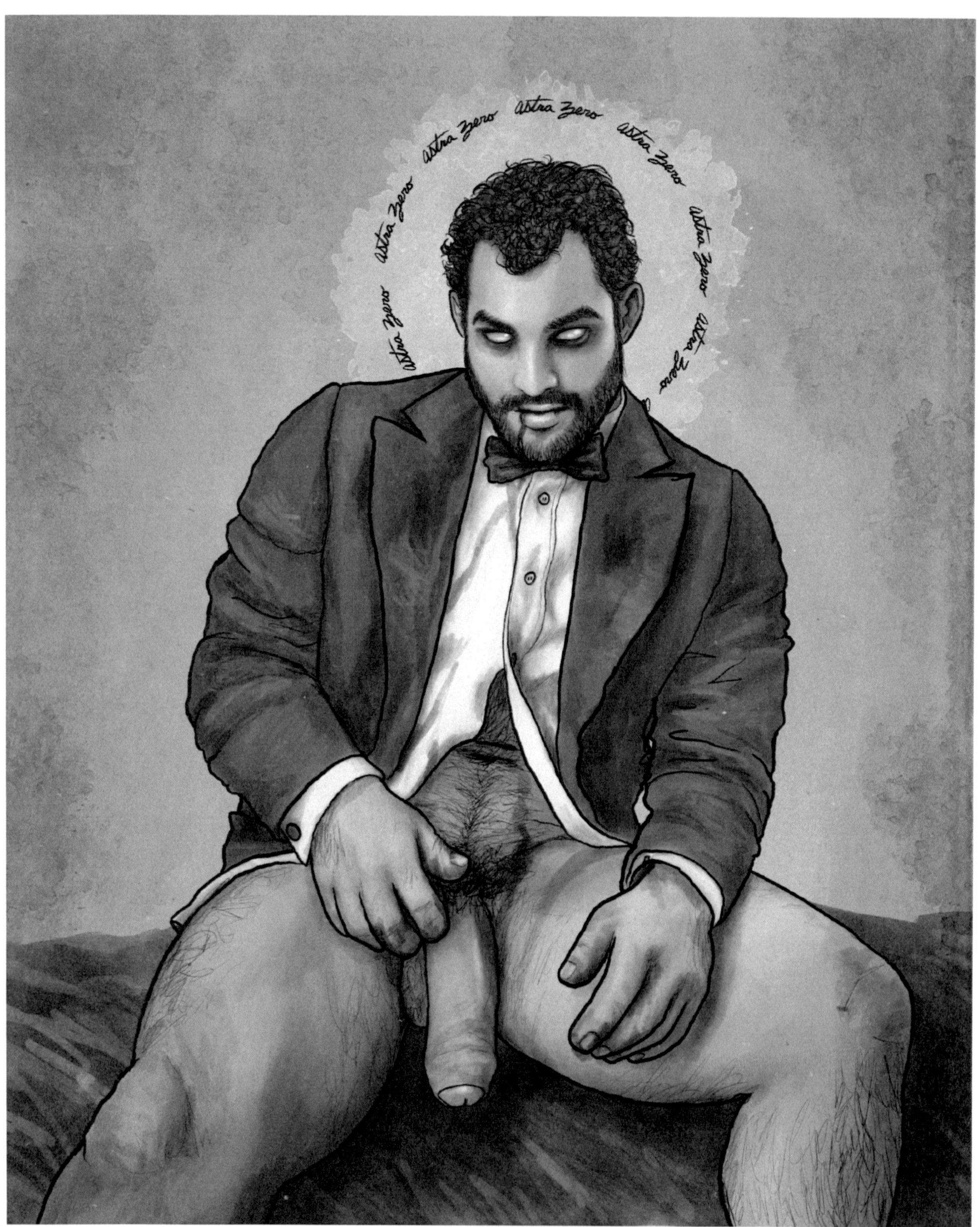

Astra Zero
Astra Zero
Astra Zero
Astra Zero
Astra Zero
Astra Zero
Astra Zero

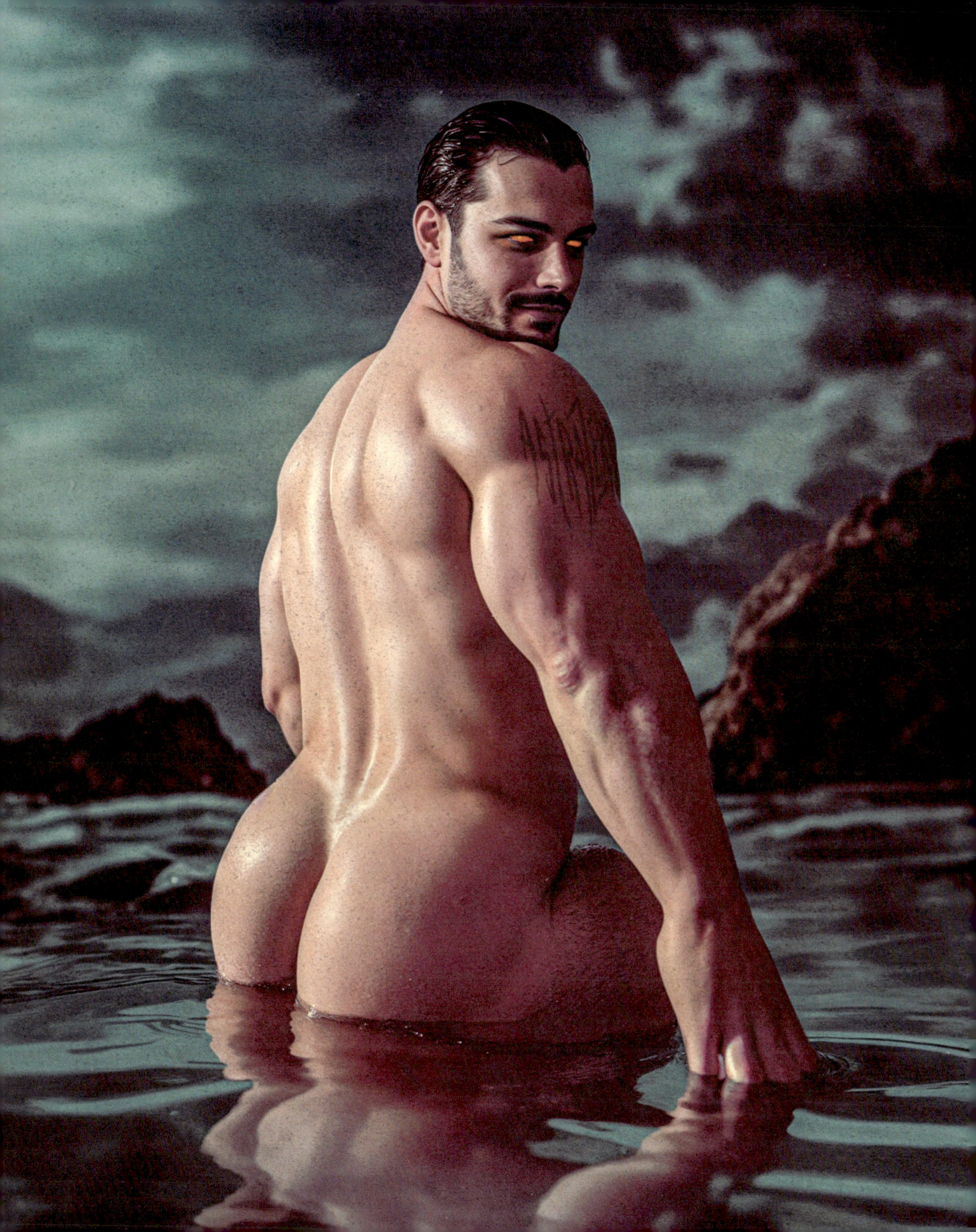

PIG
ZOMBIE
The
CUDDLE
MONSTER
ASTRA
ZERO
DO WHATEVER you want to me

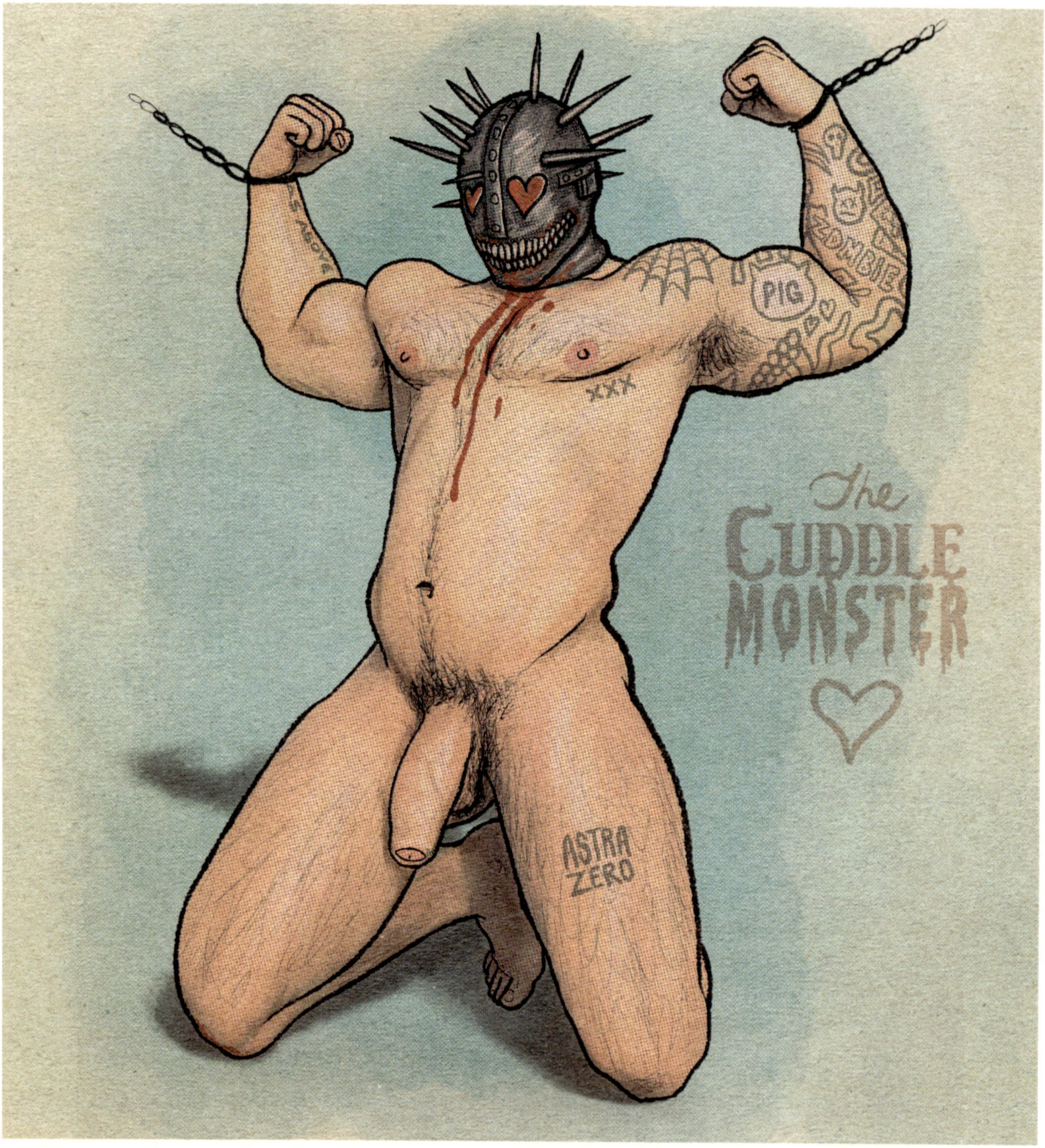

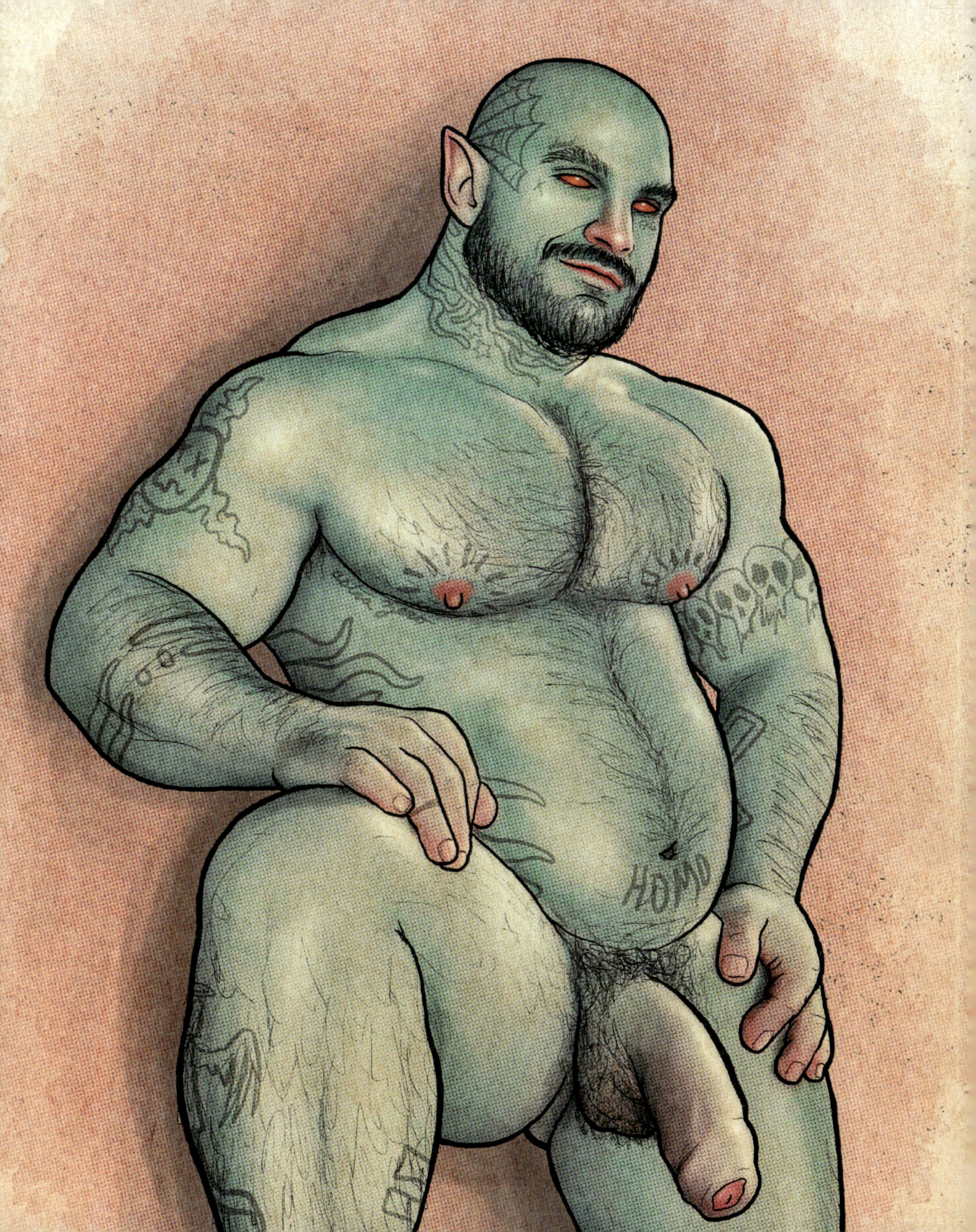
HOMO

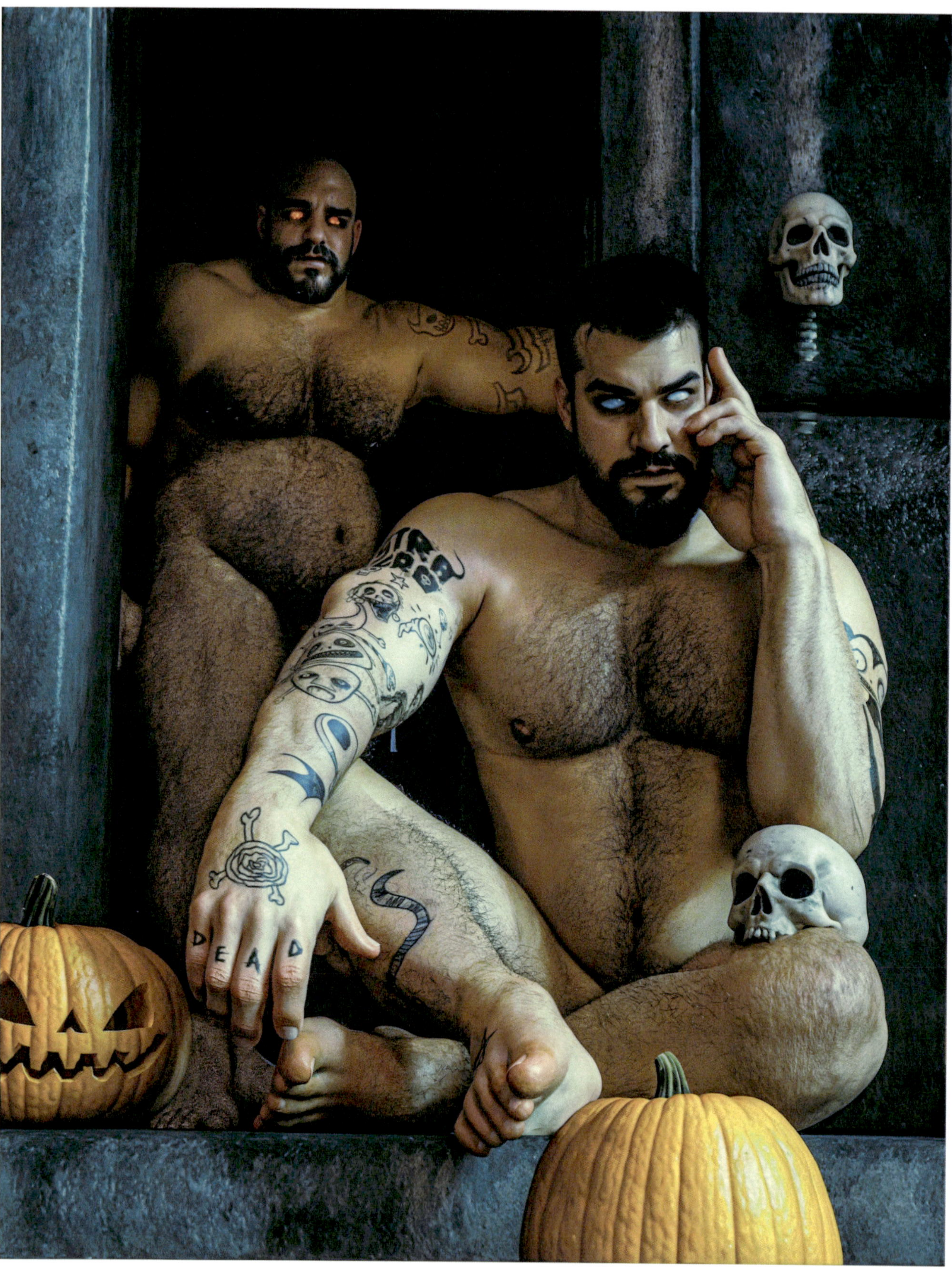

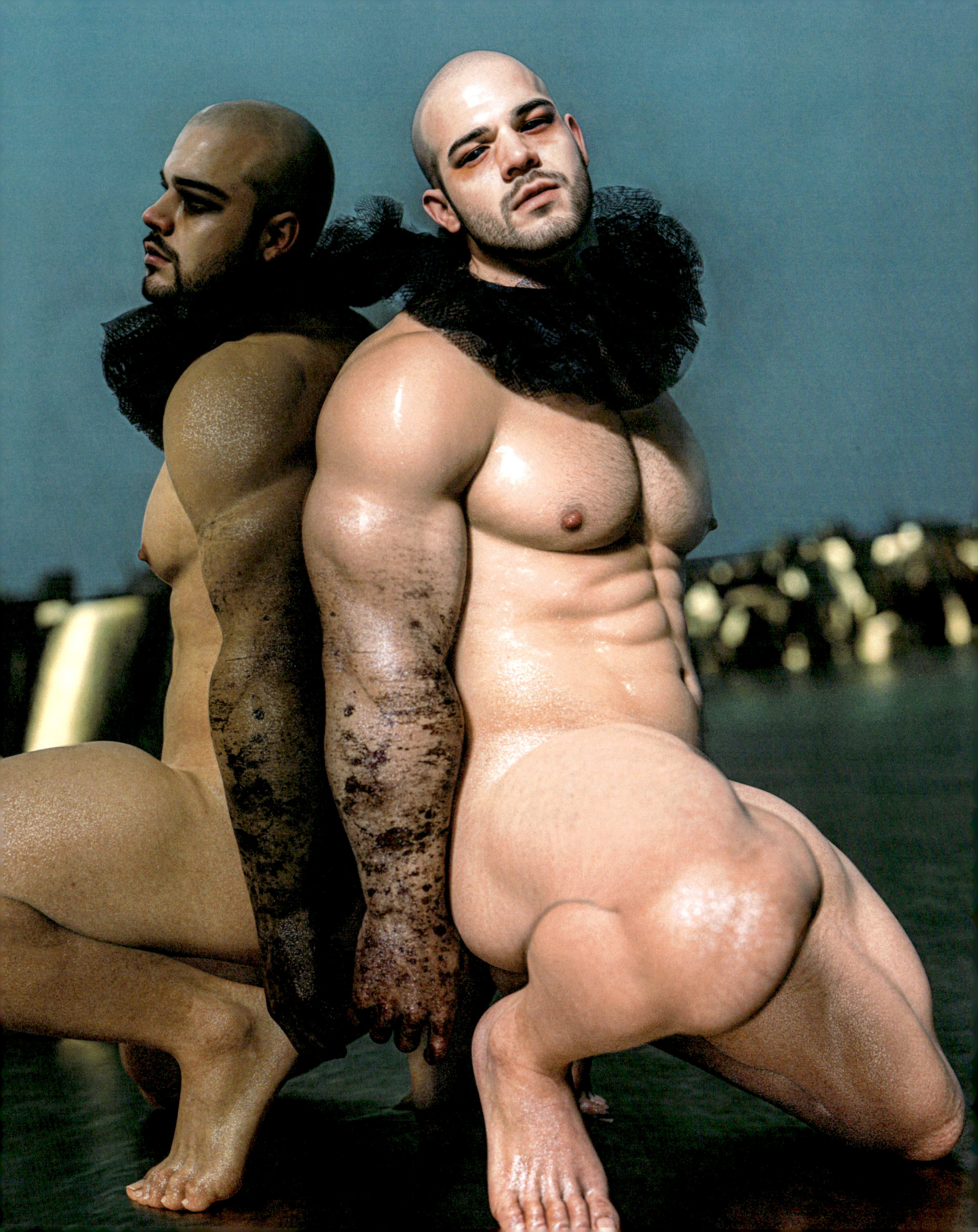

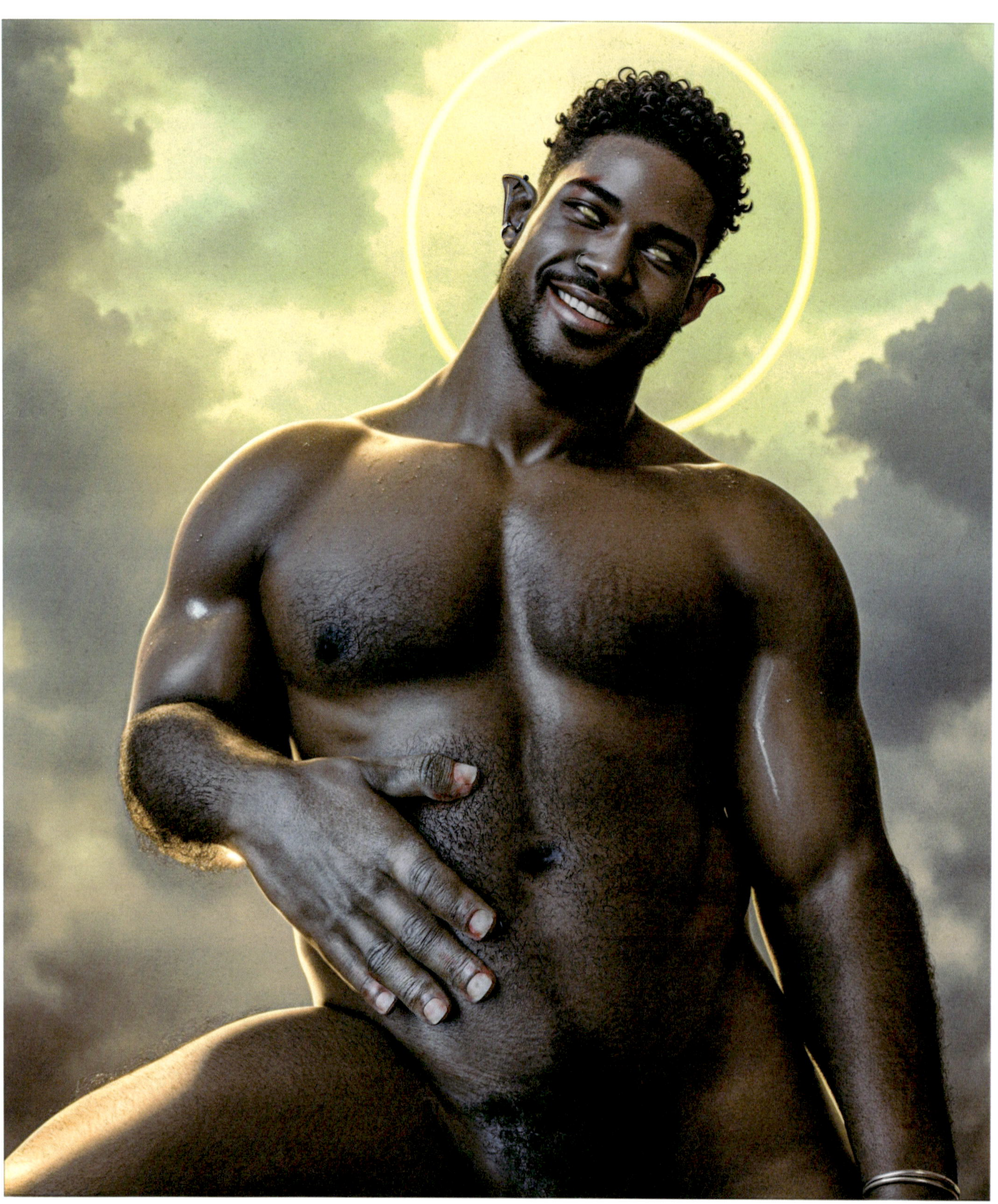

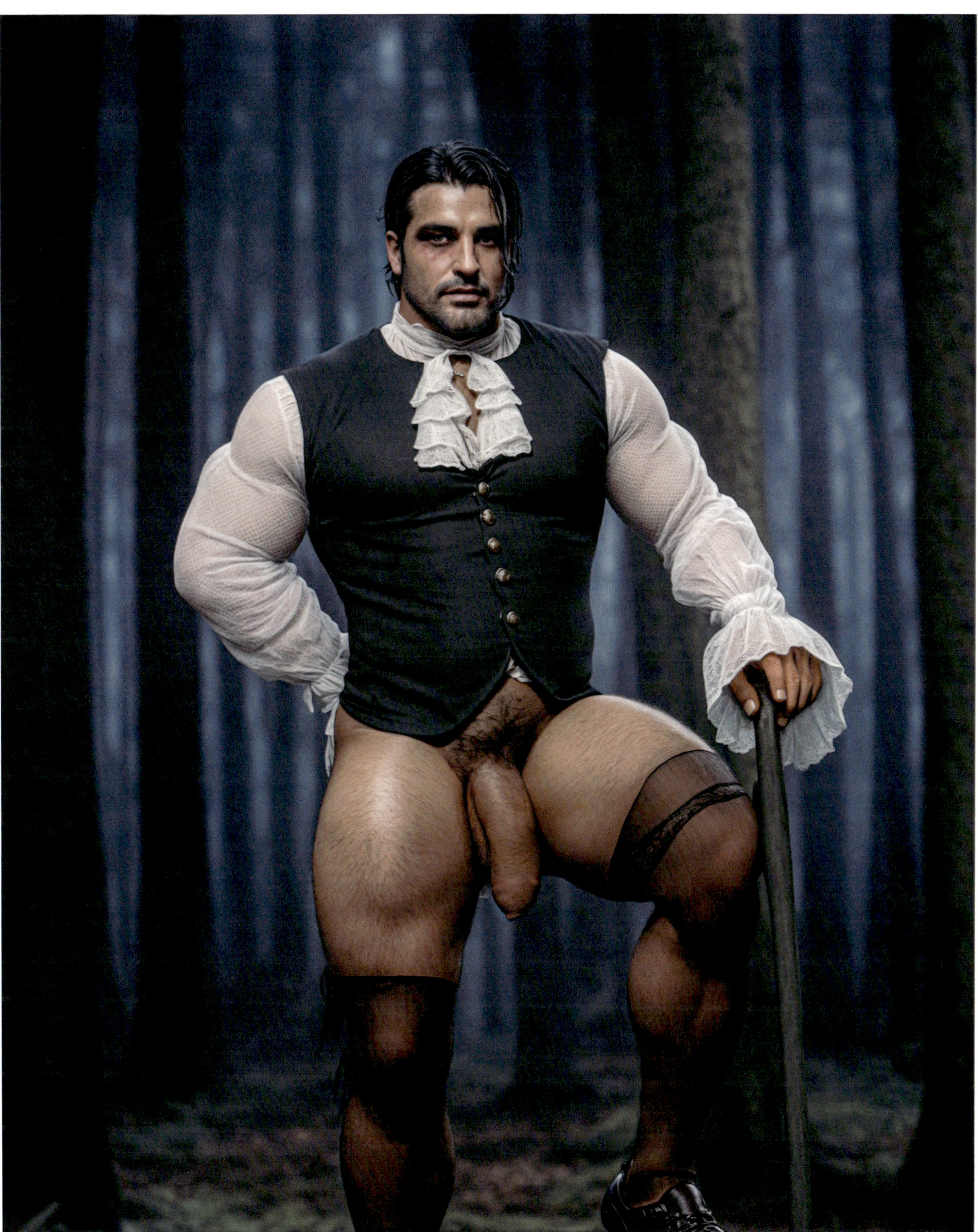

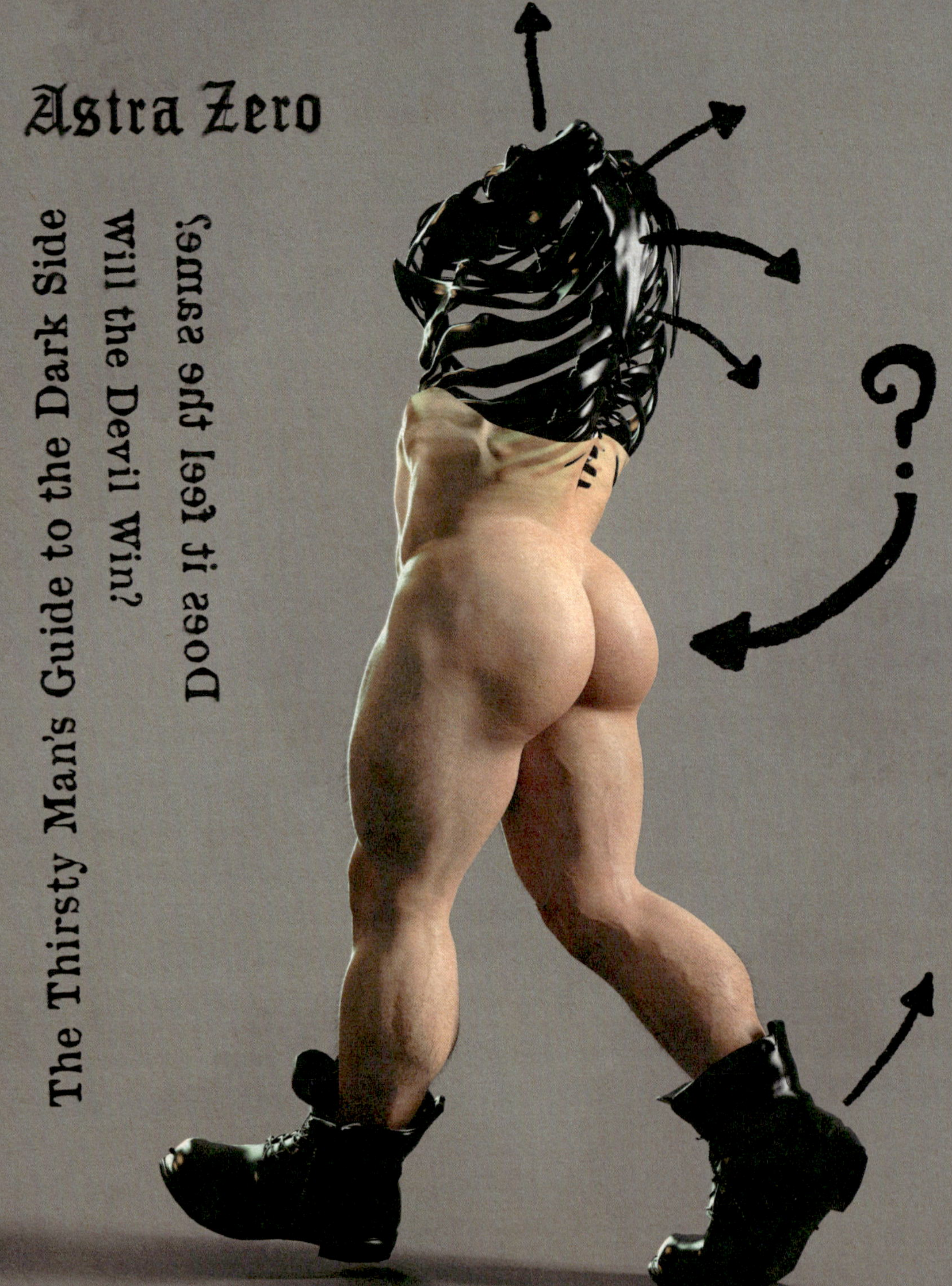

Astra Zero
The Thirsty Man's Guide to the Dark Side
Will the Devil Win?
Does it feel the same?

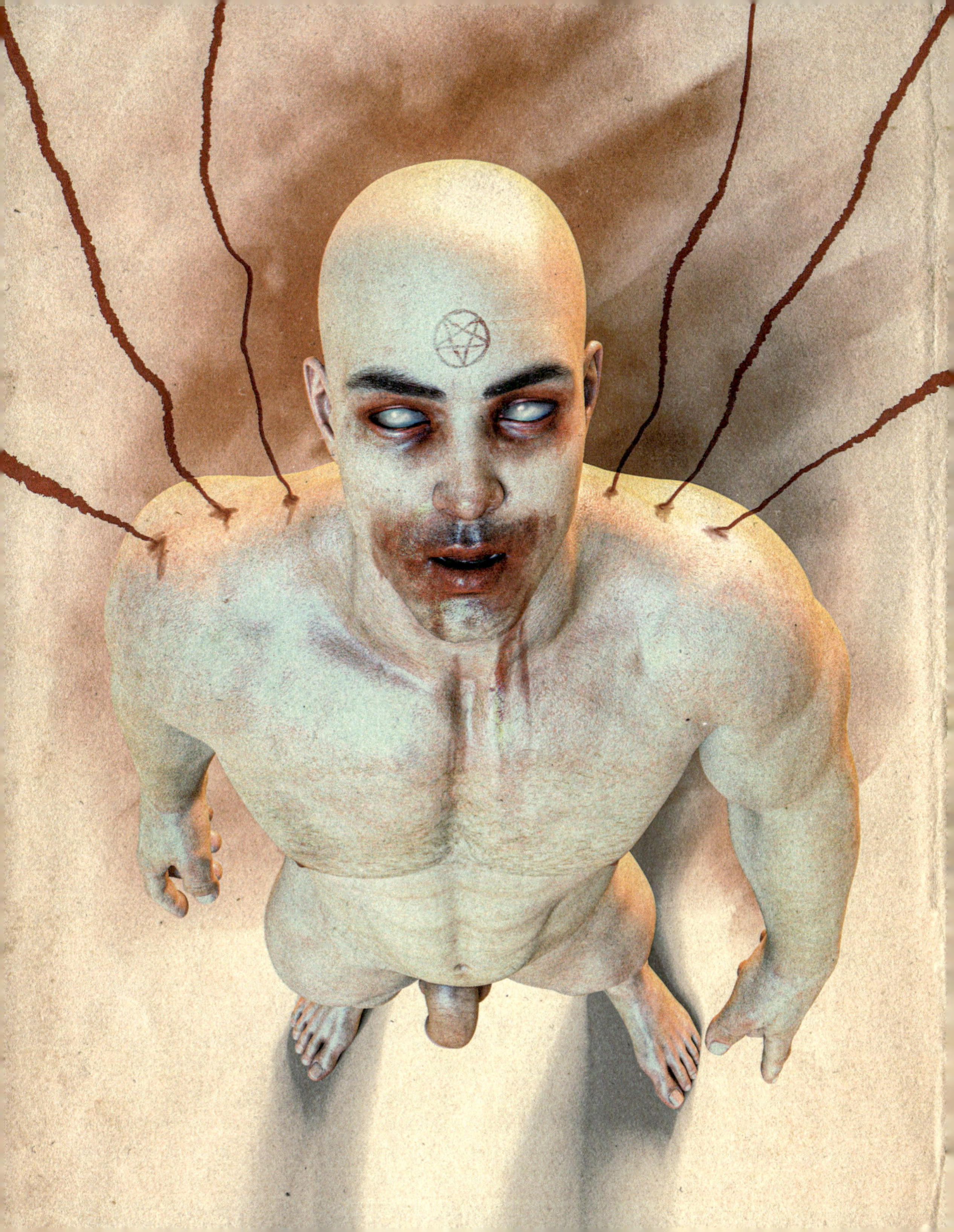

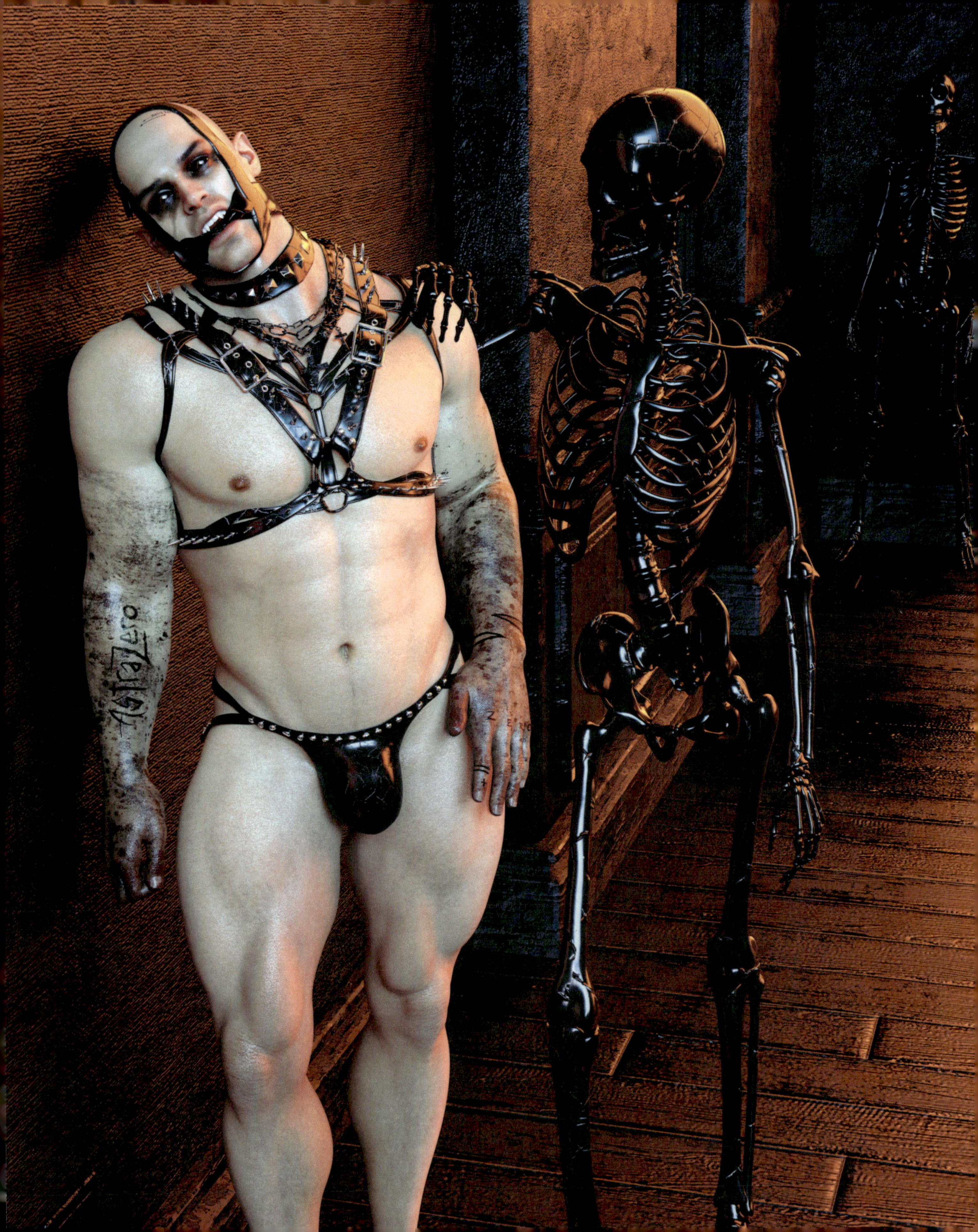

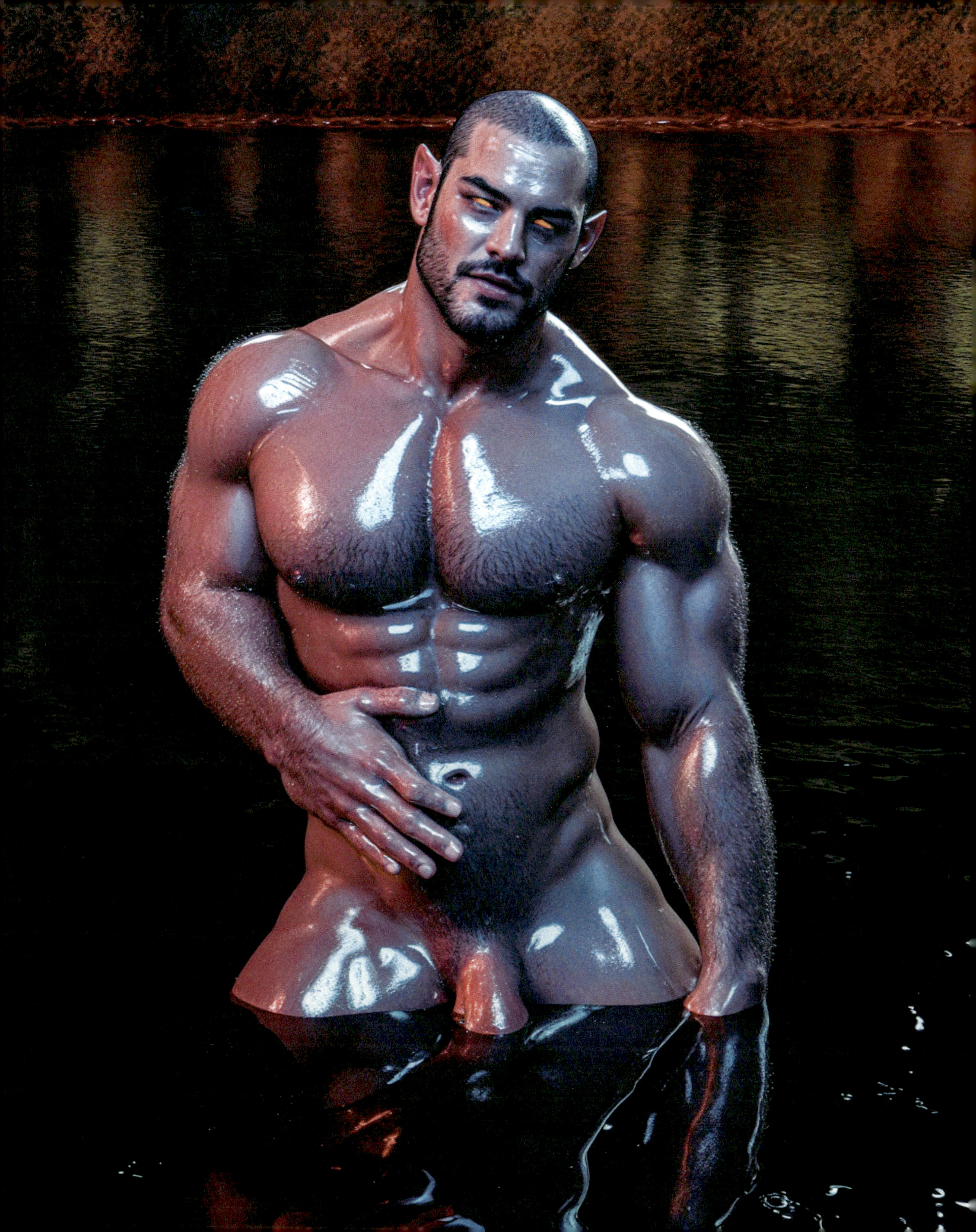

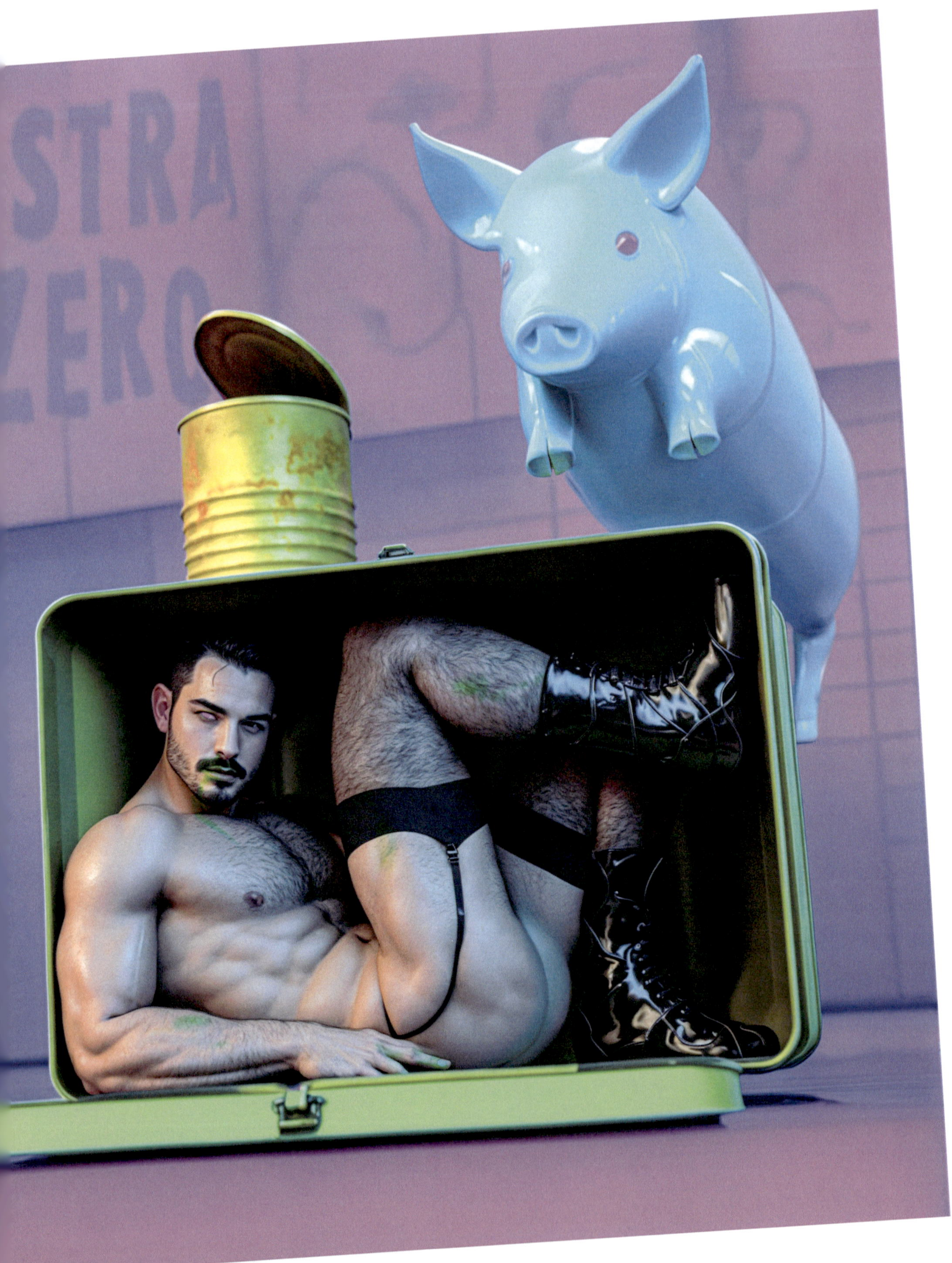
STRA
ZERO

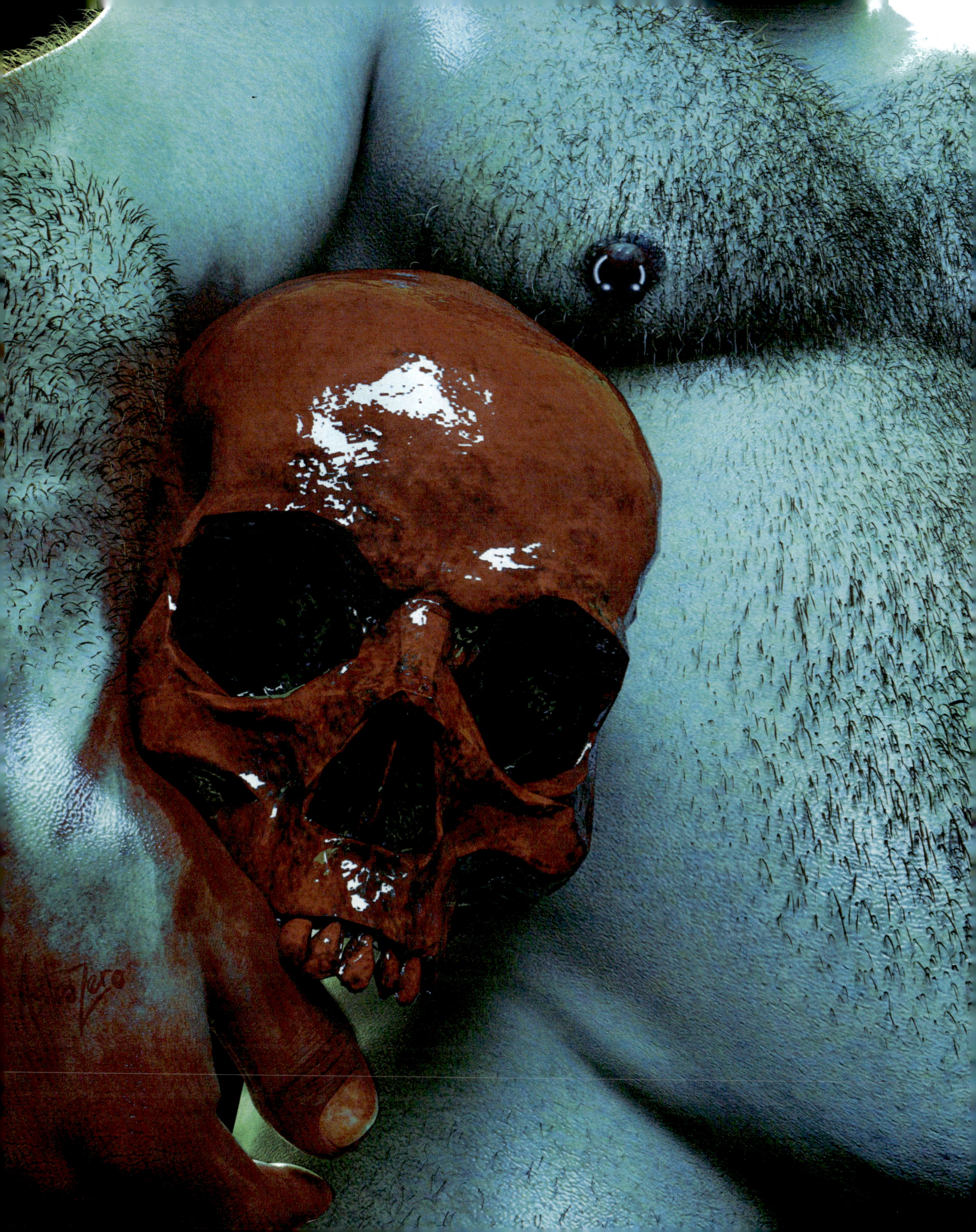

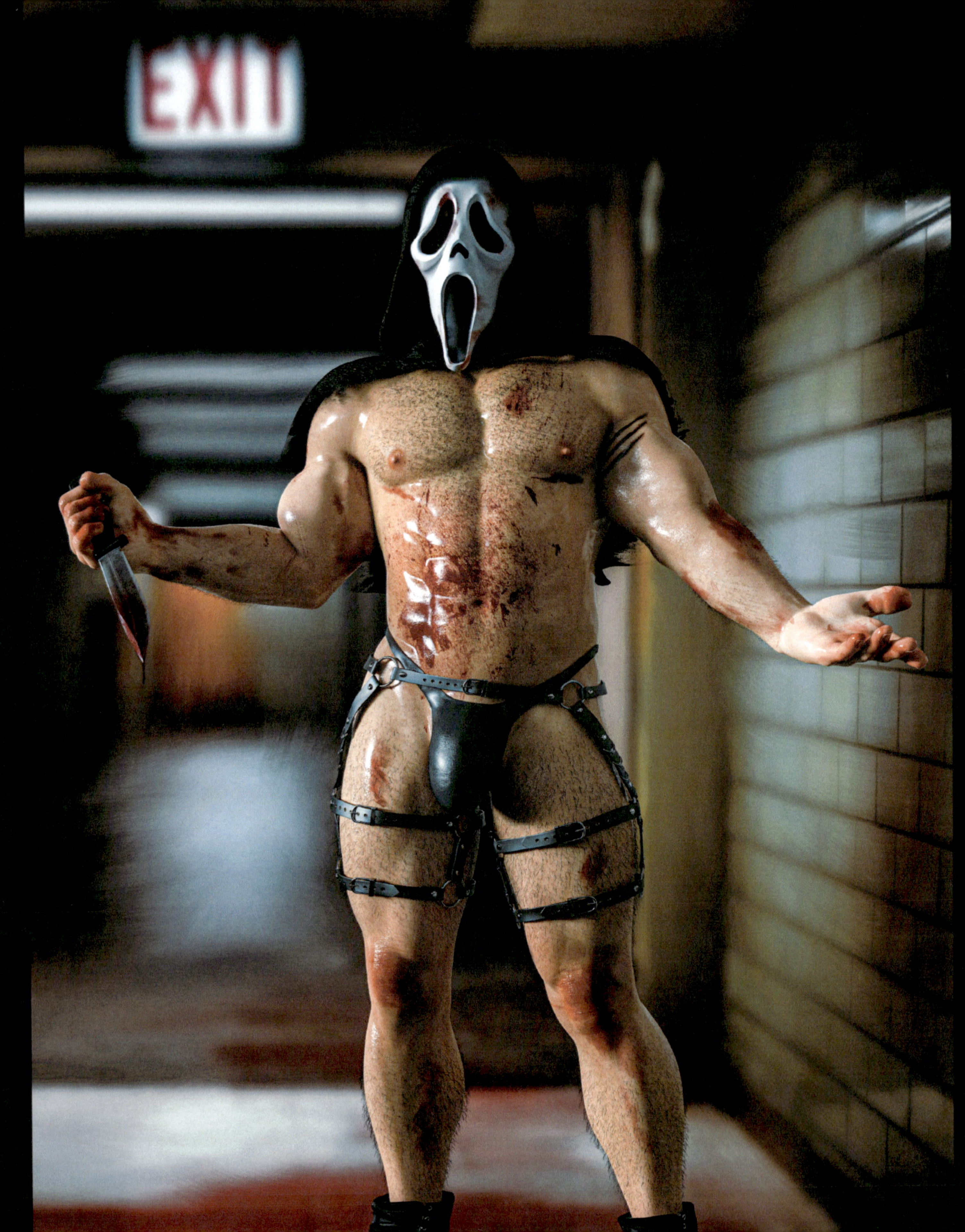

EXIT

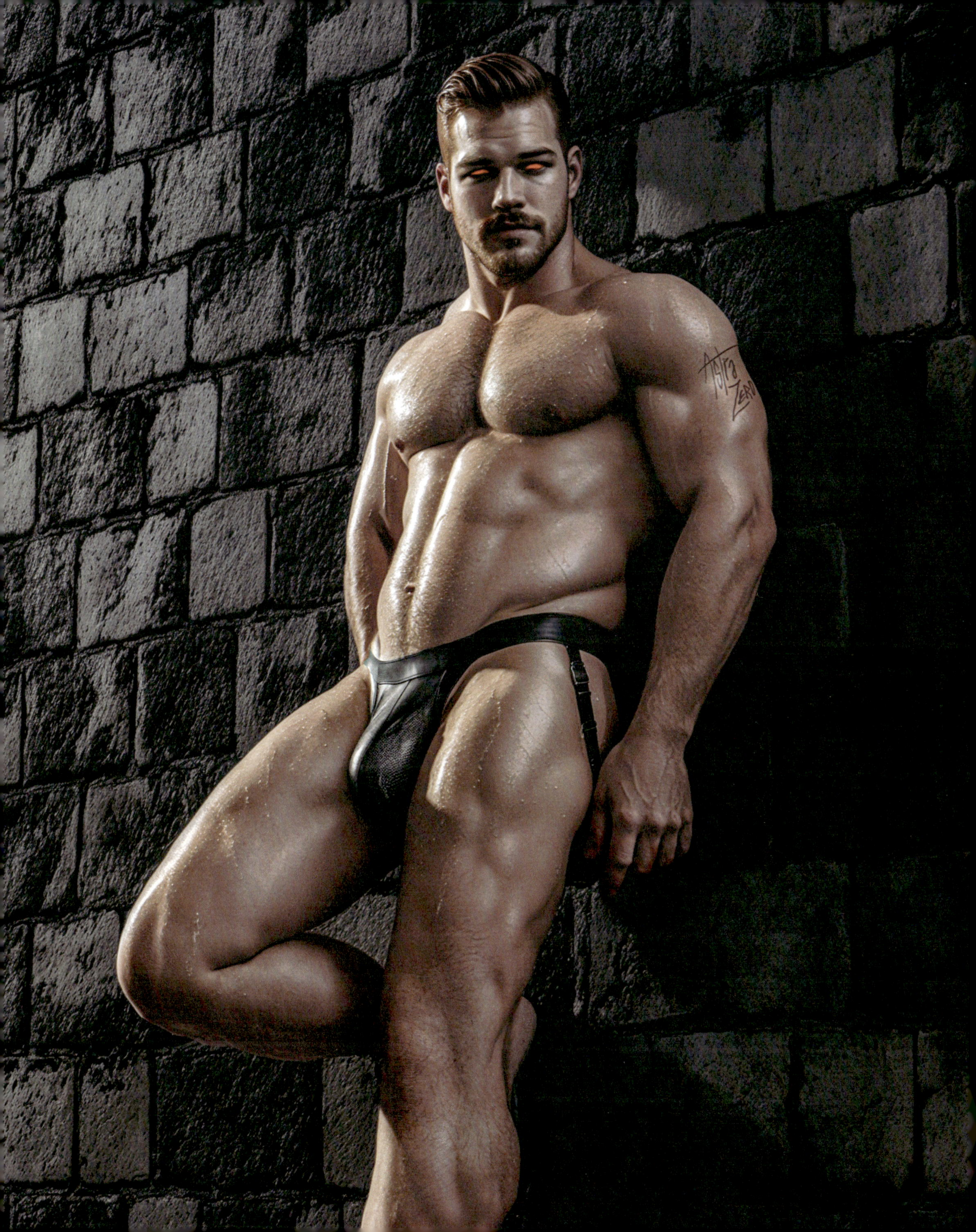
Astra Zero

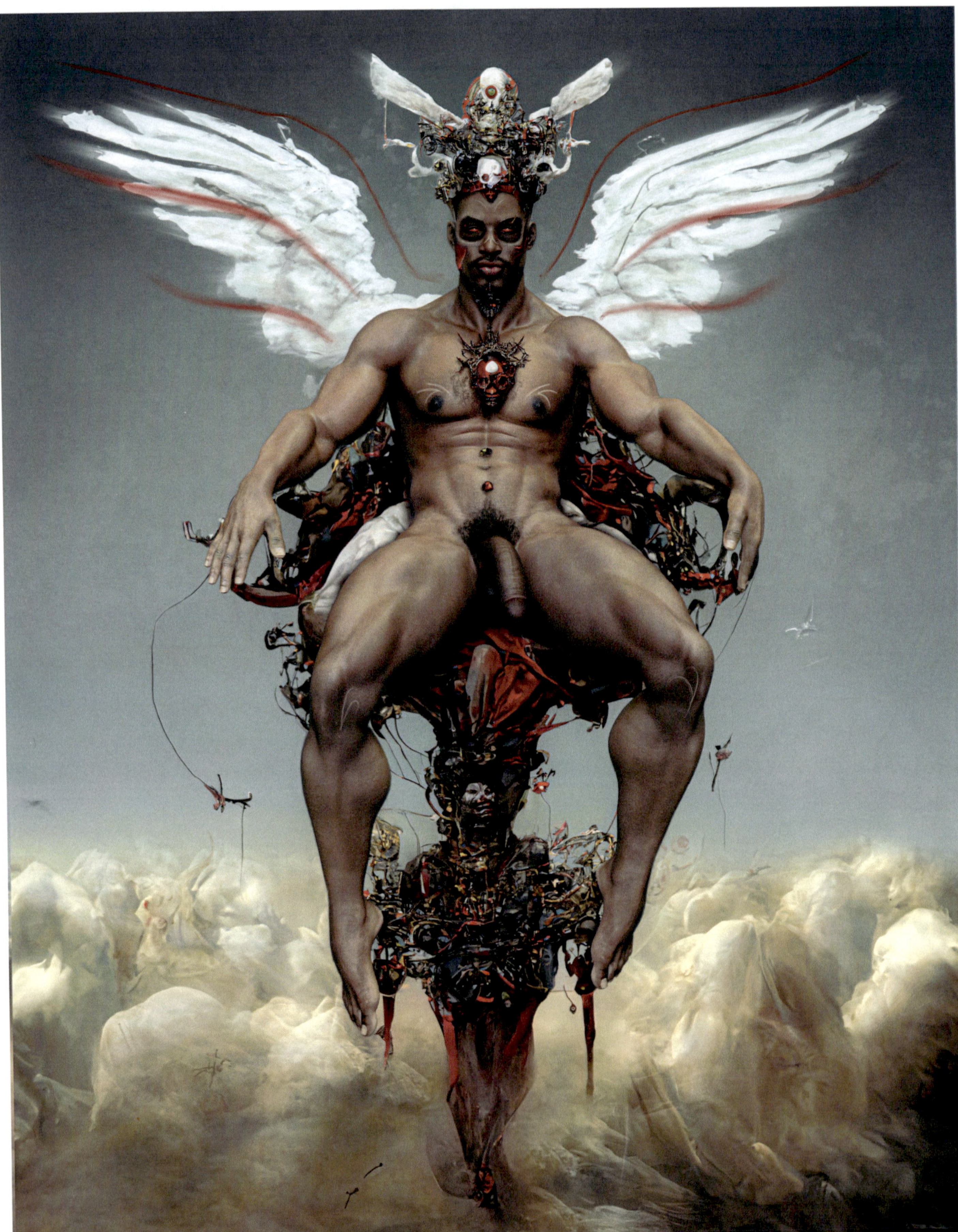

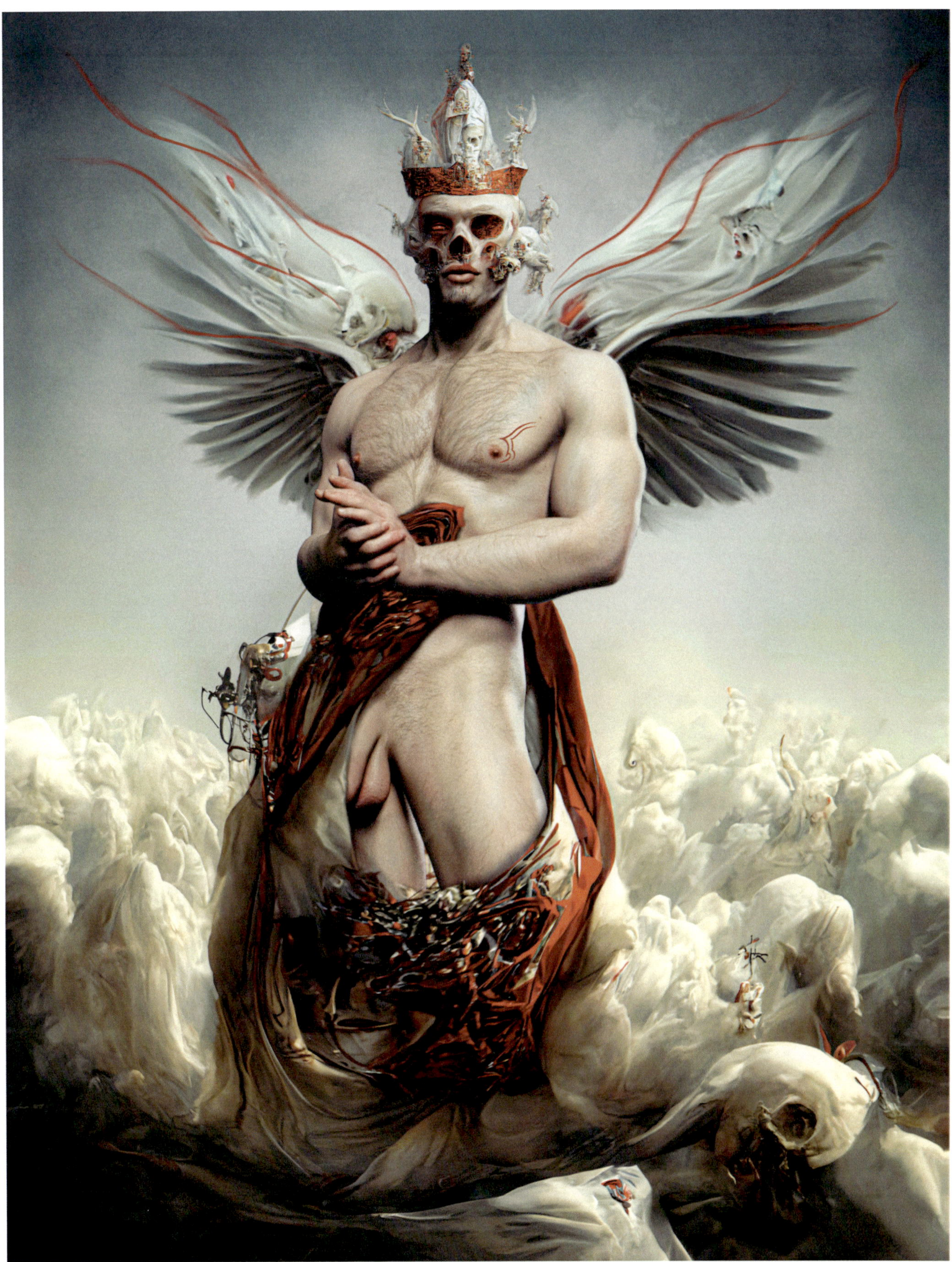

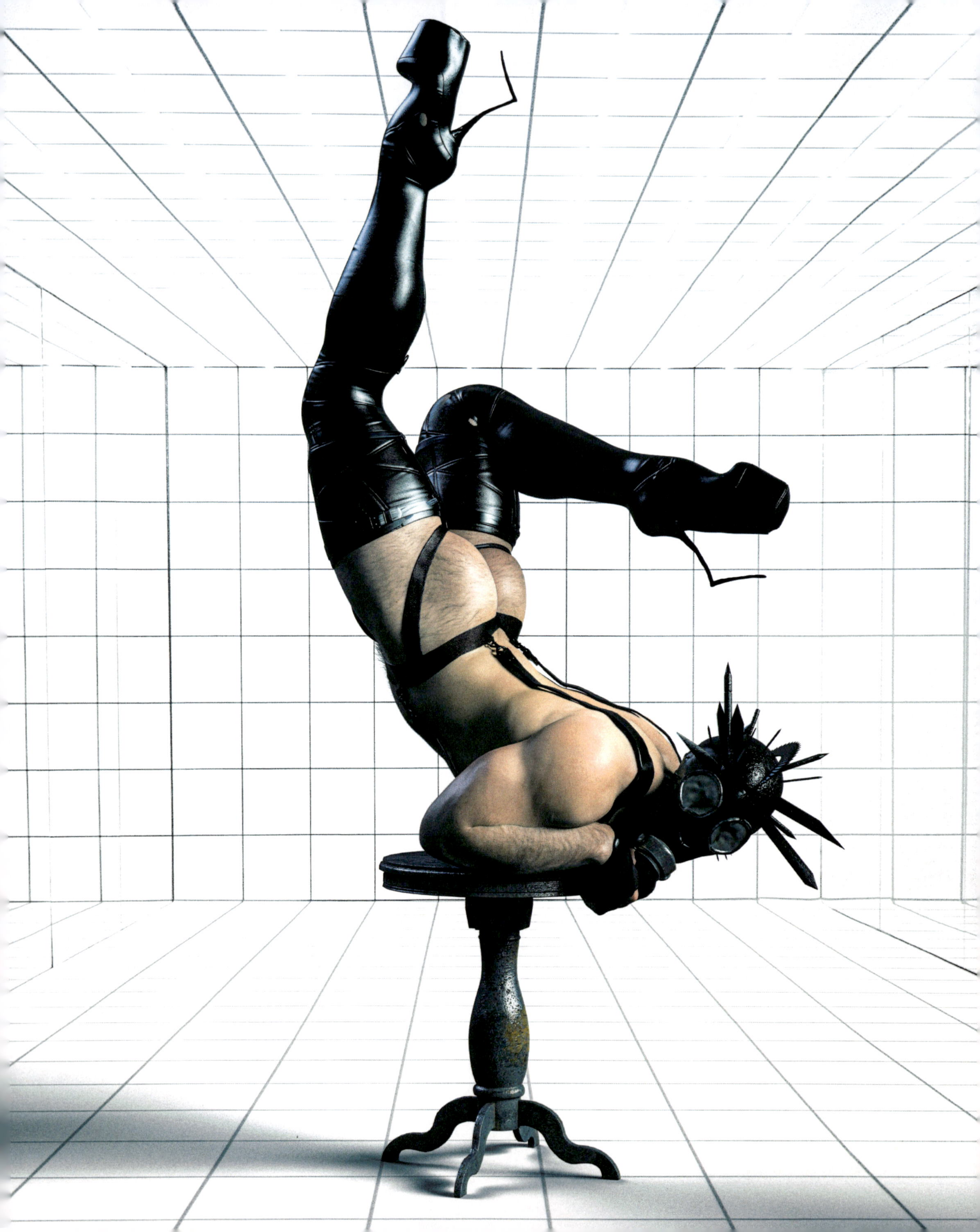

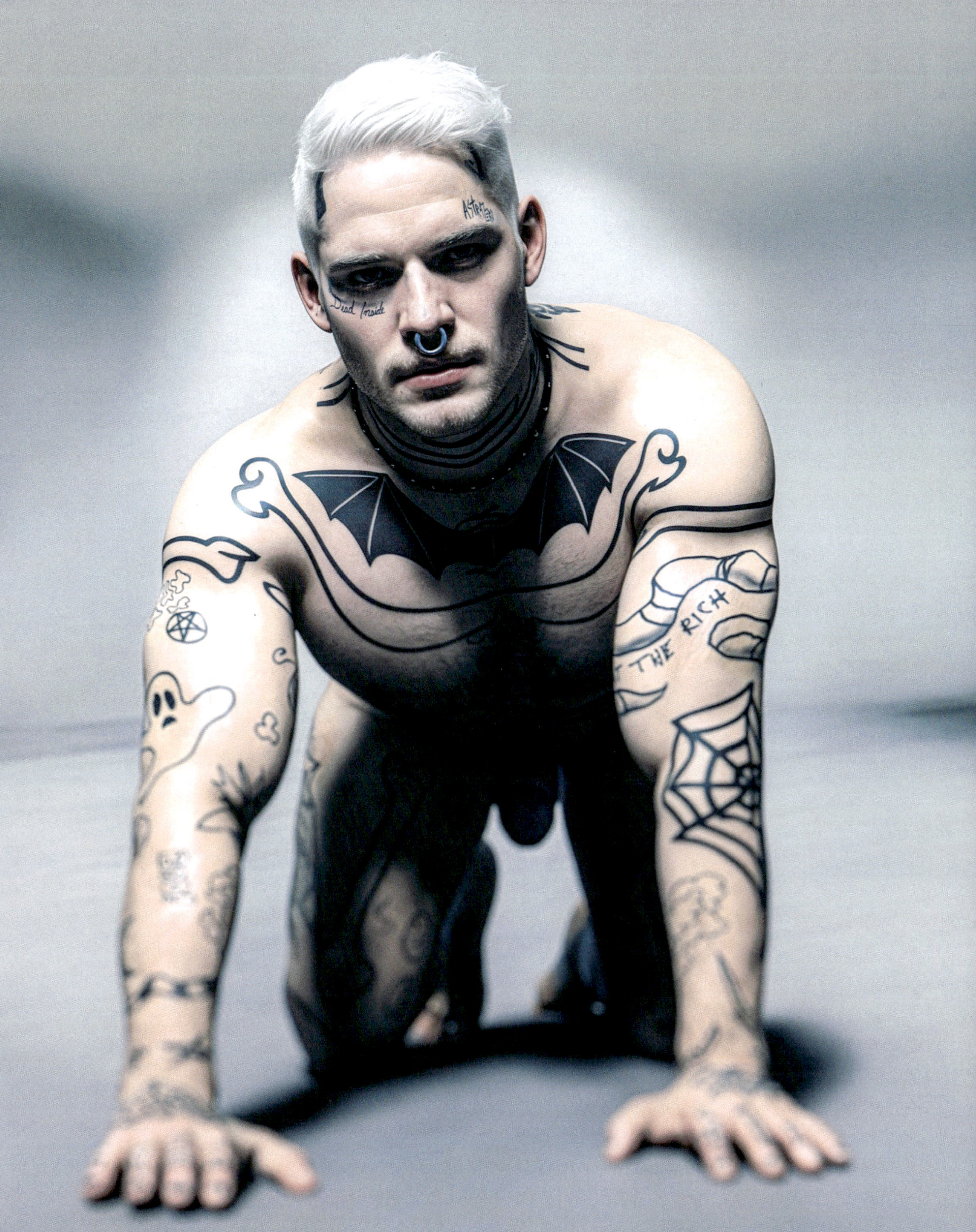
Dead Inside
THE RICH

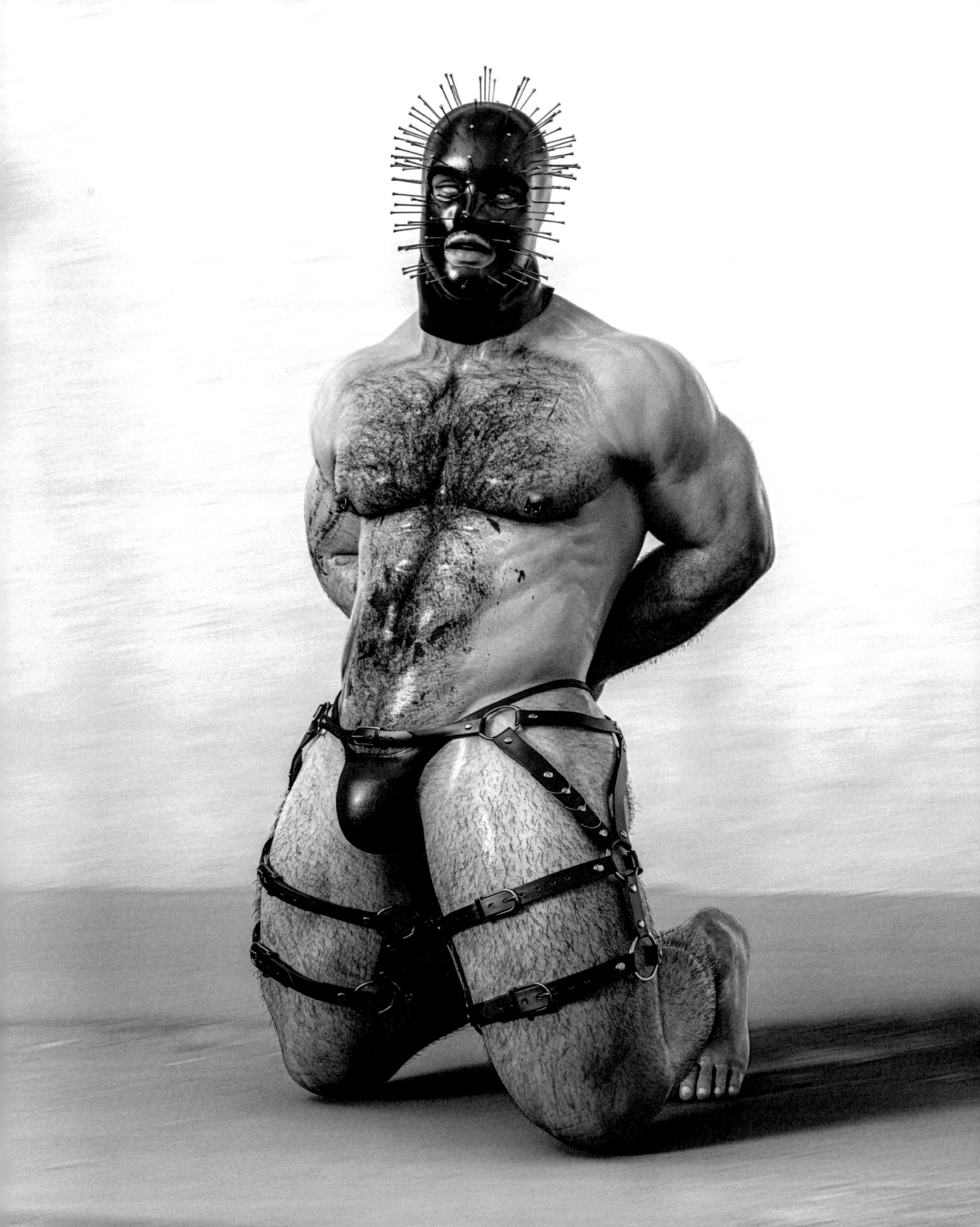

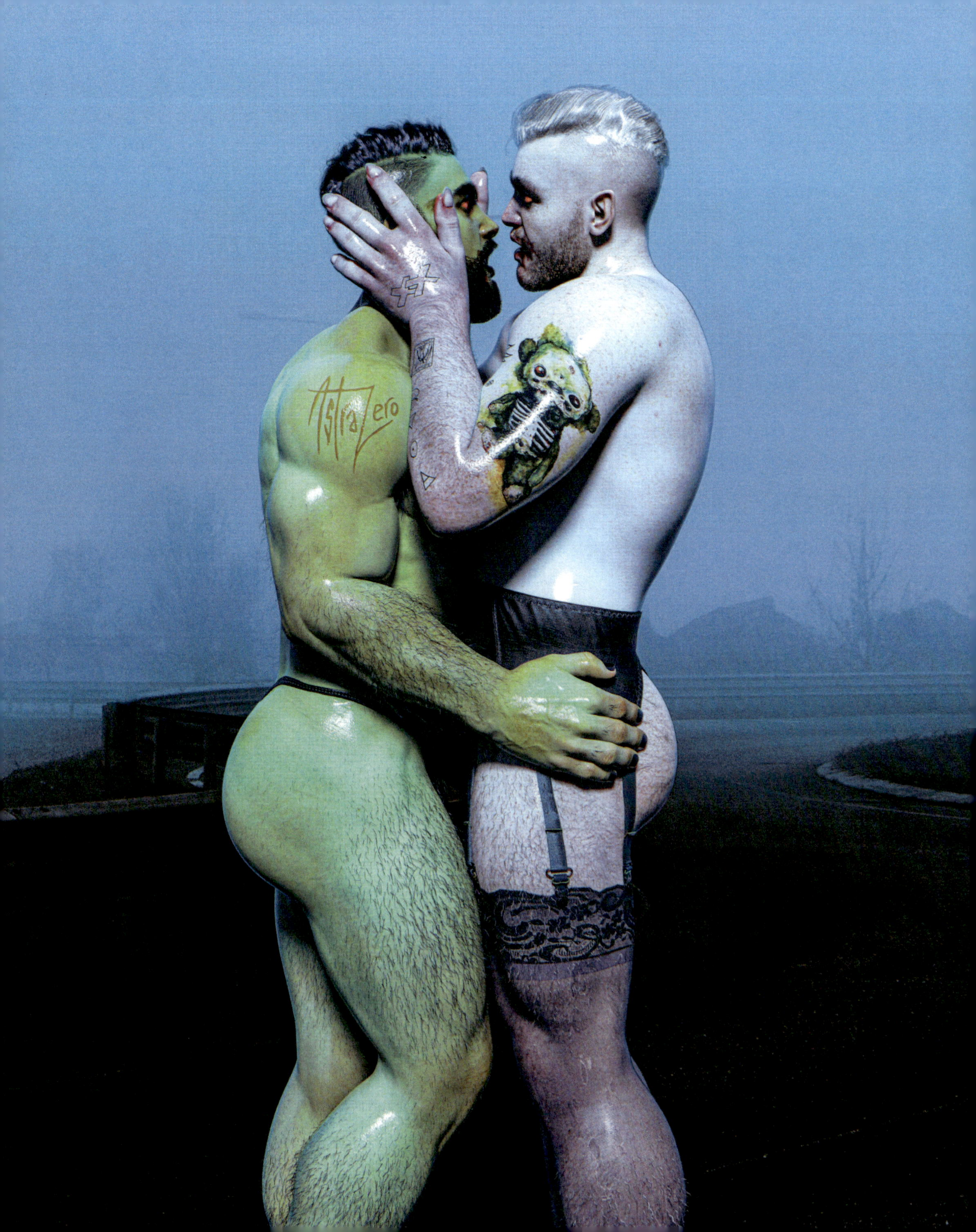

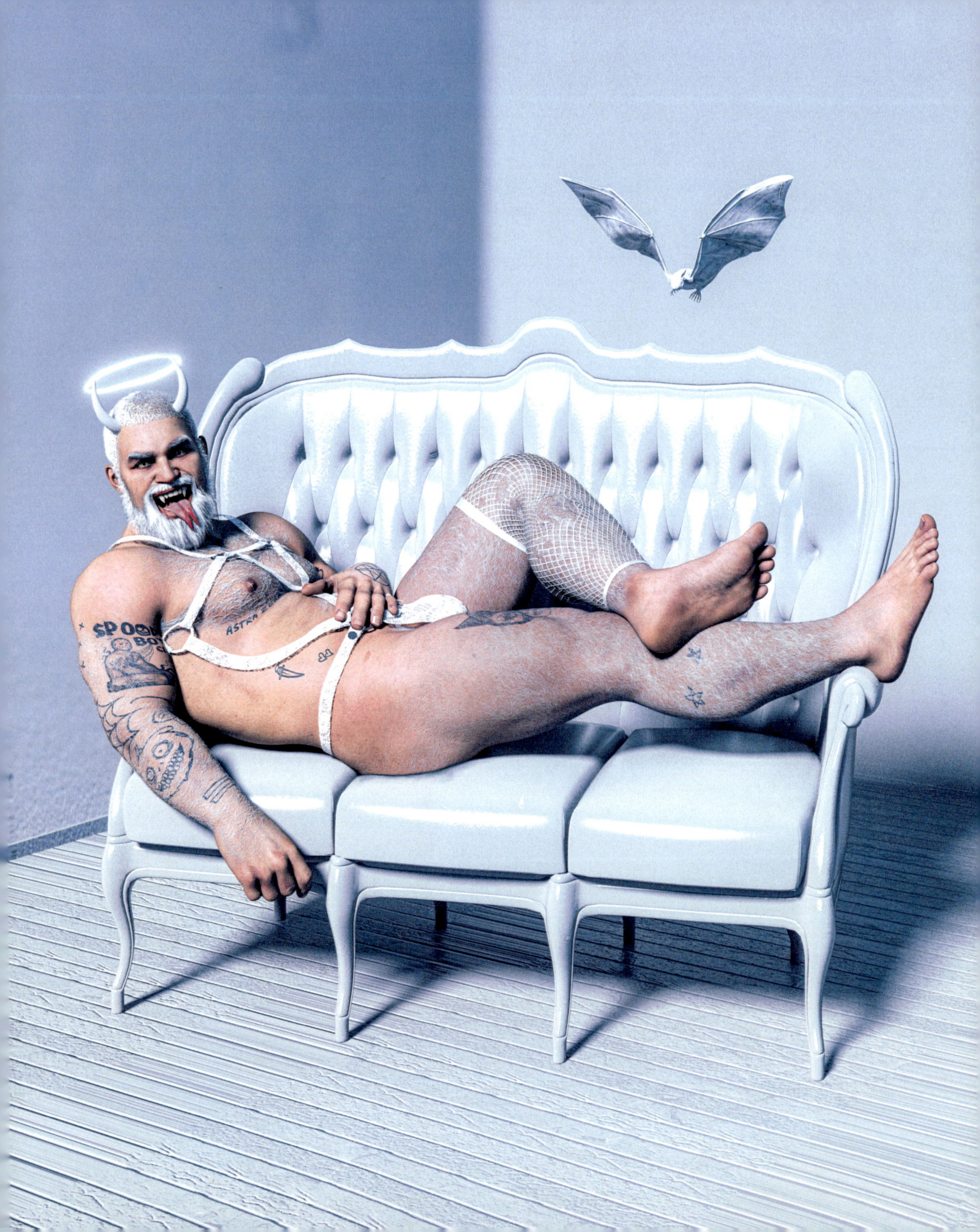

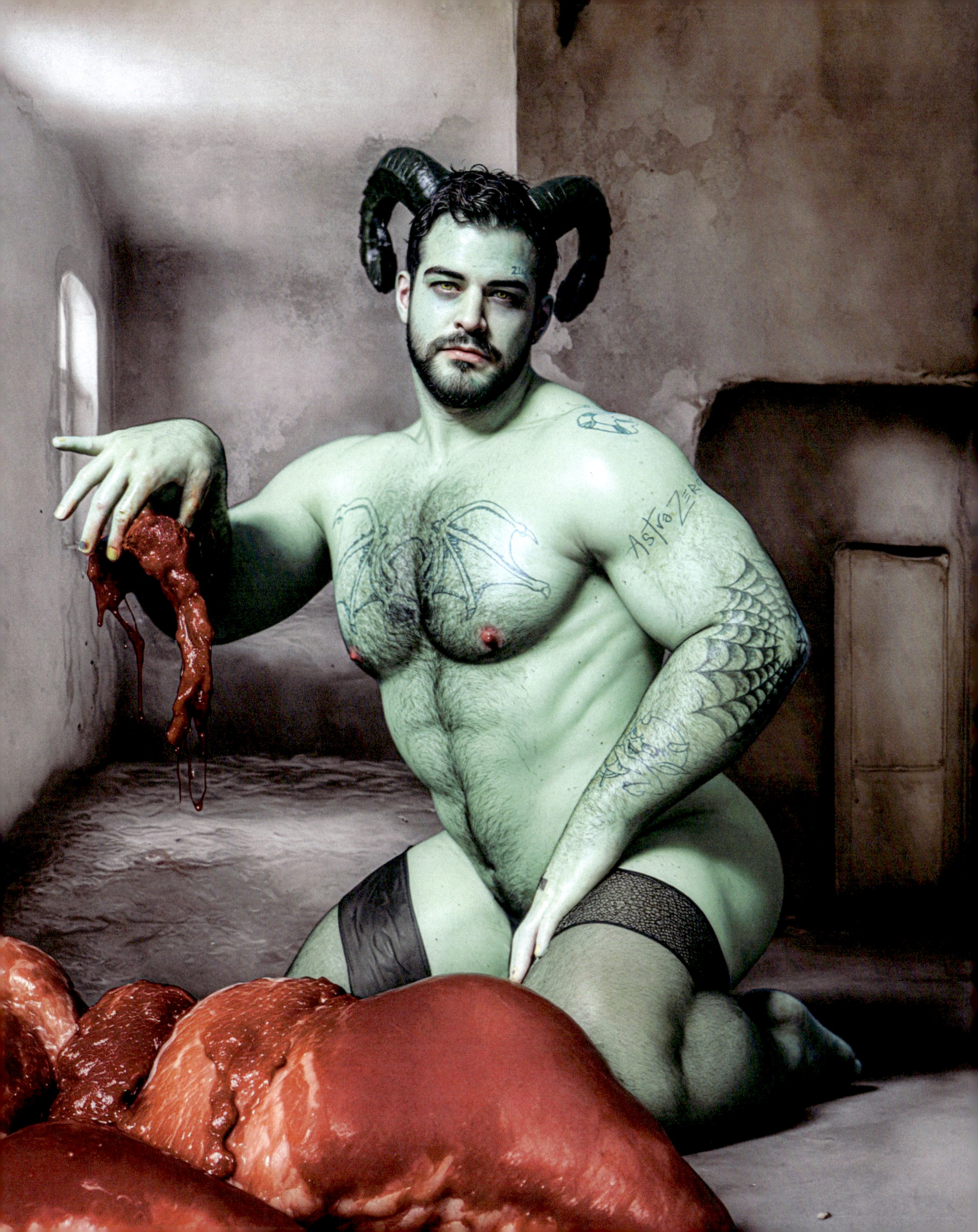

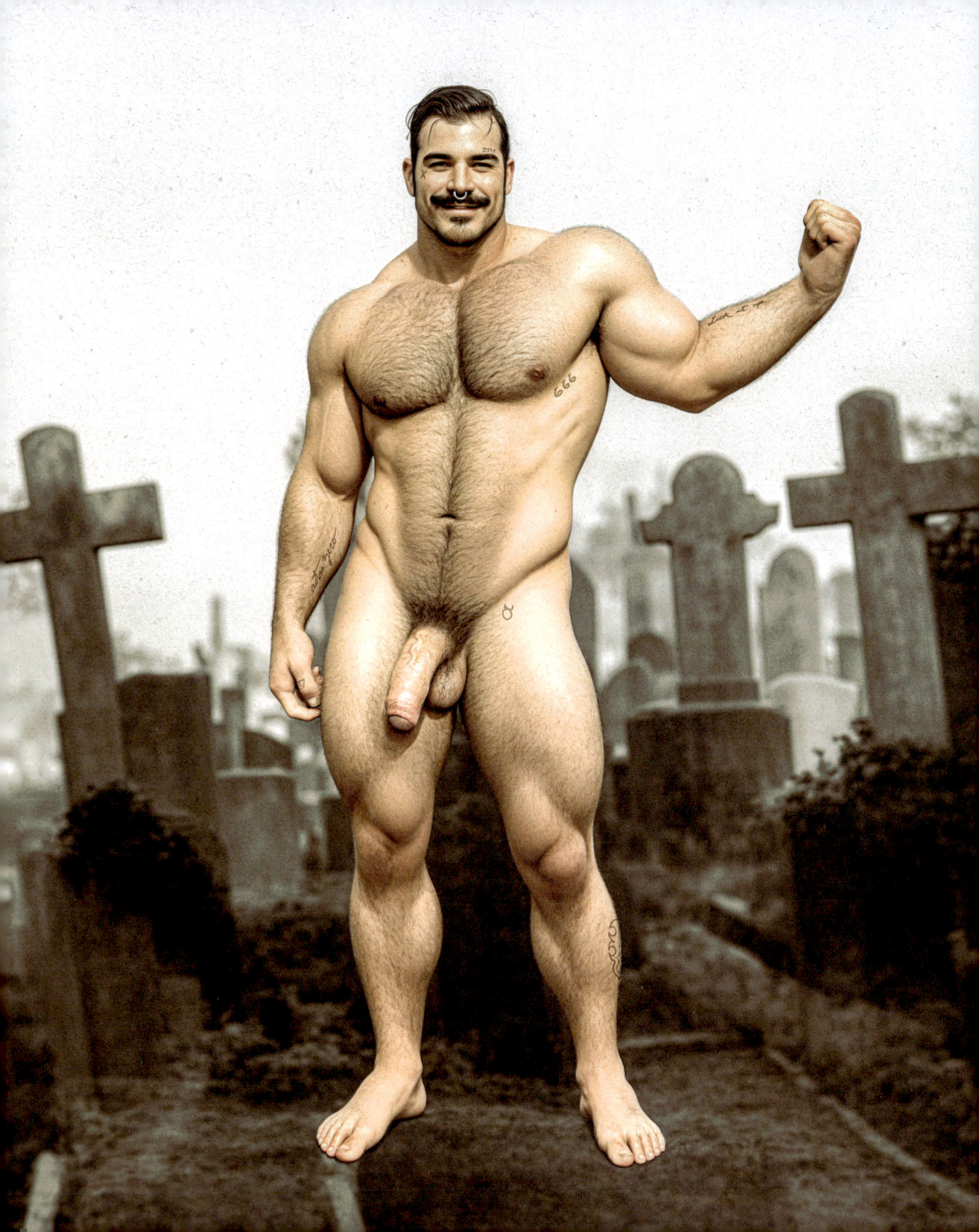

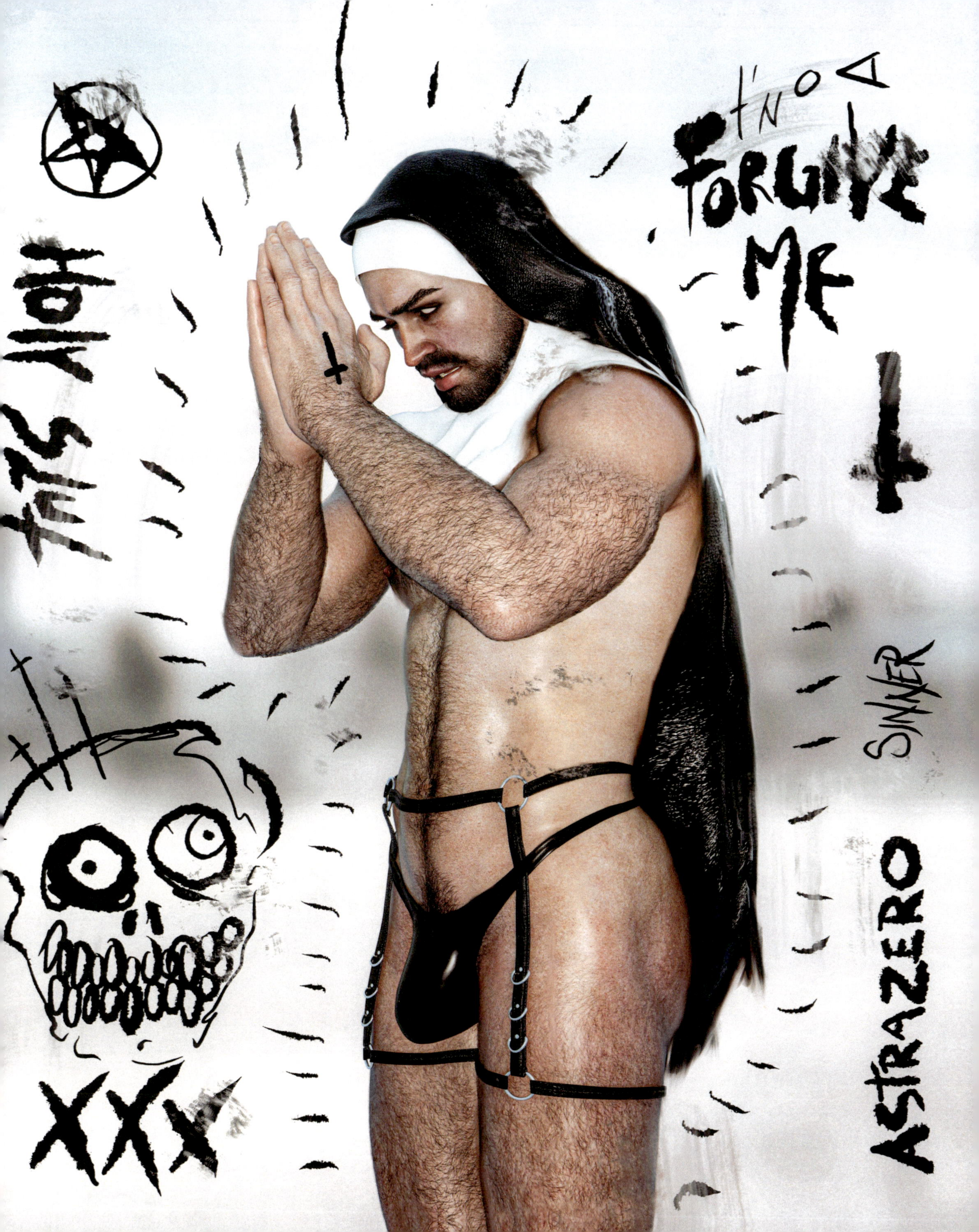
DON'T
FORGIVE ME
HOLY SHIT
SINNER
ASTRAZERO
XXX

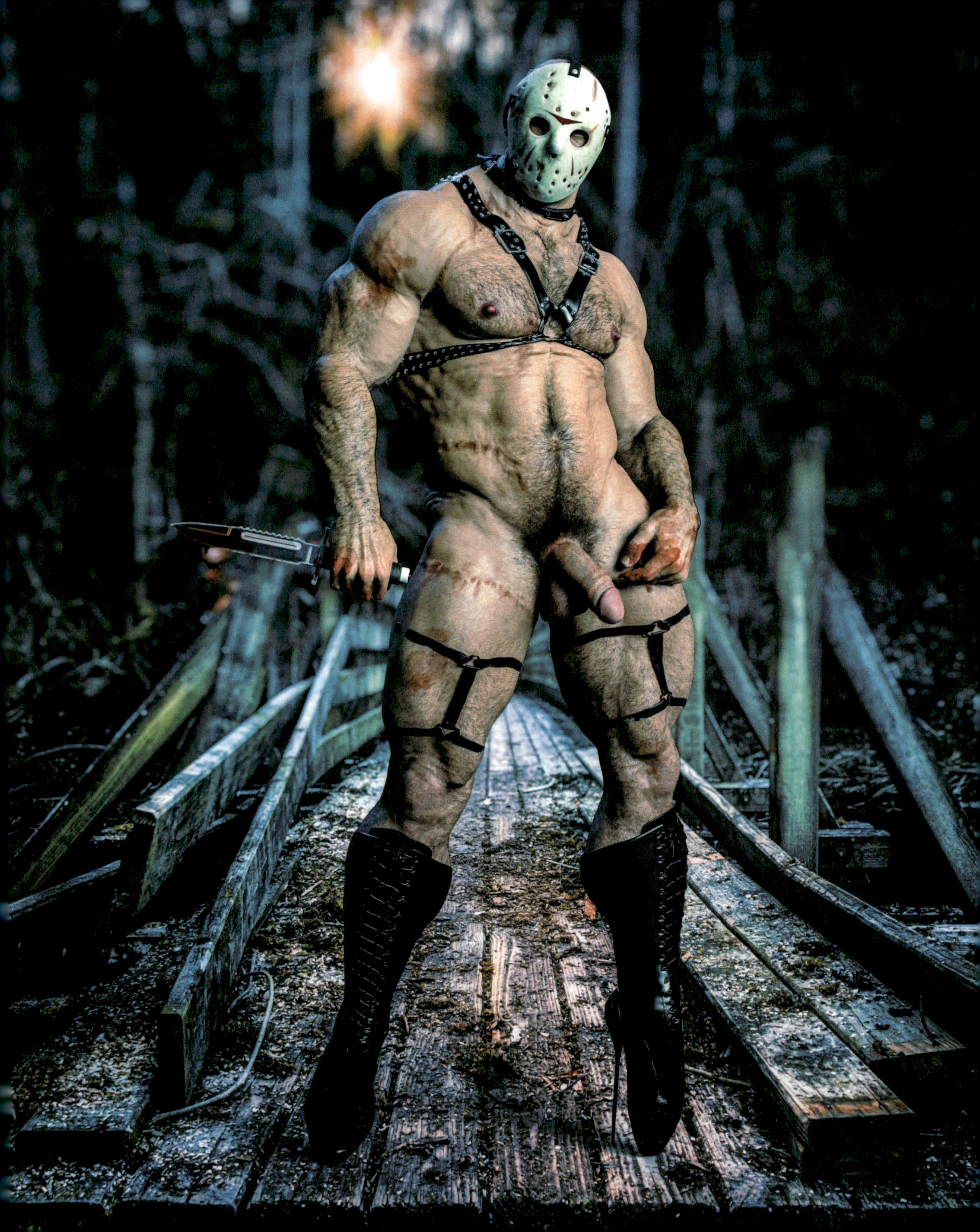

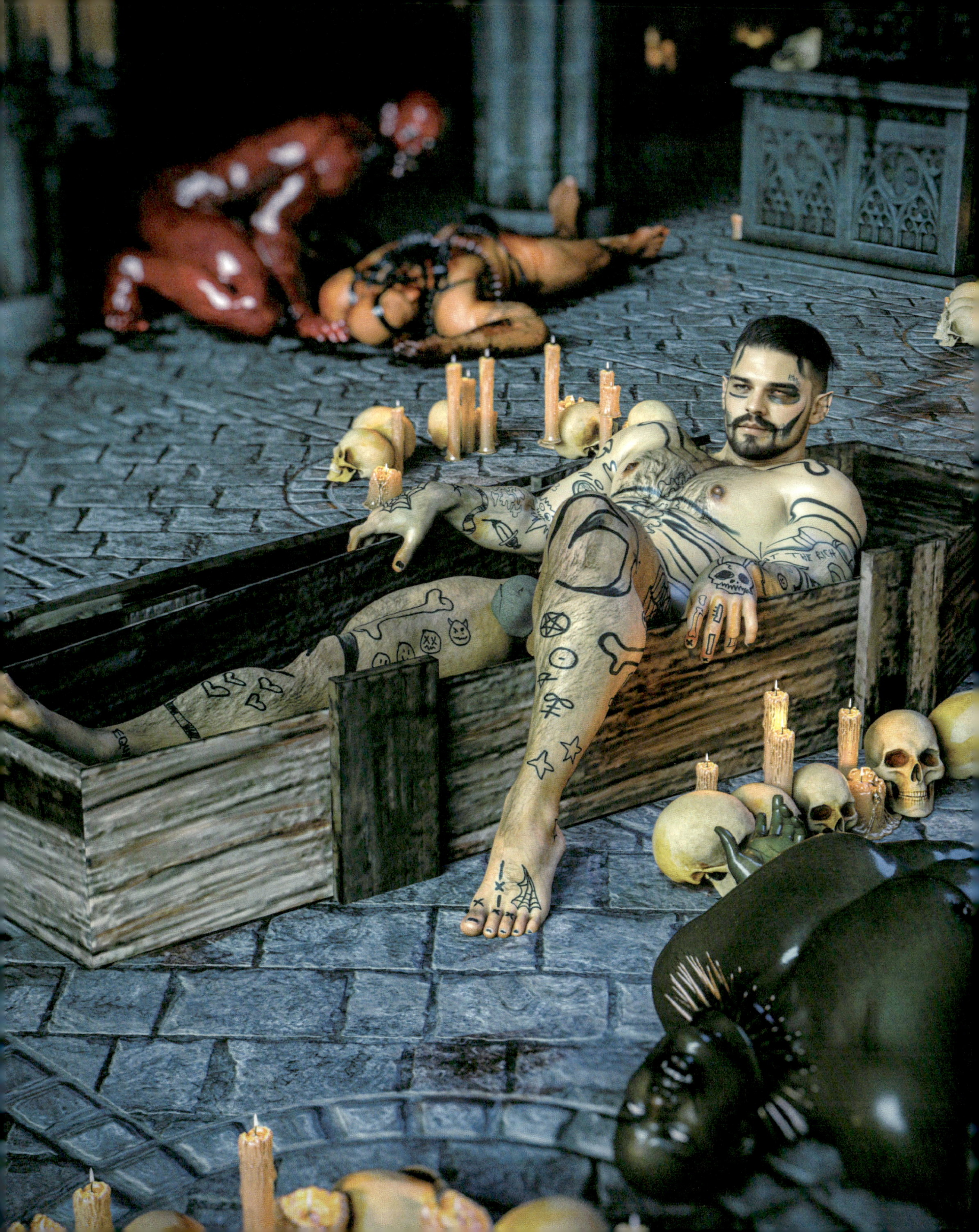

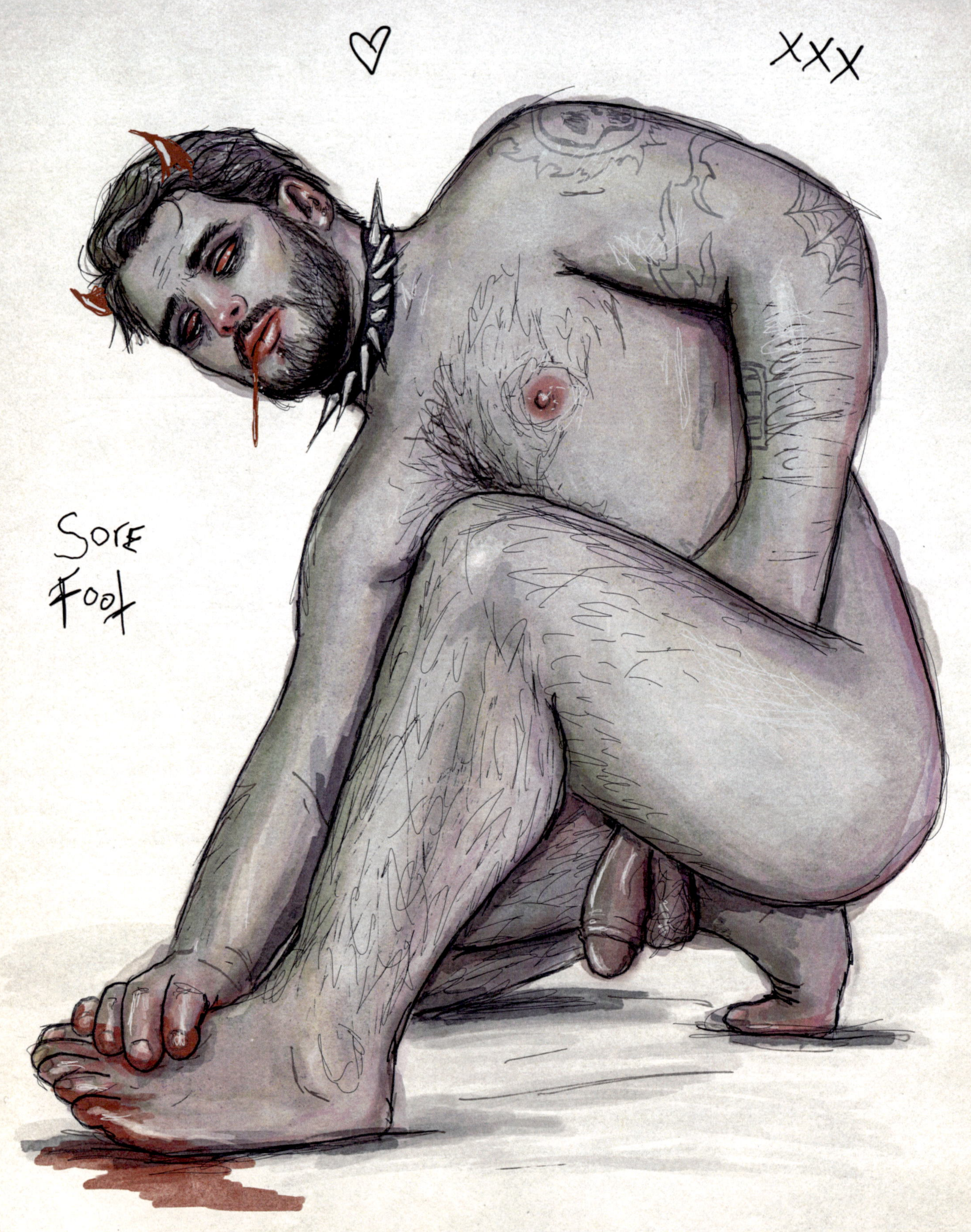
♡
XXX
Sore
Foot

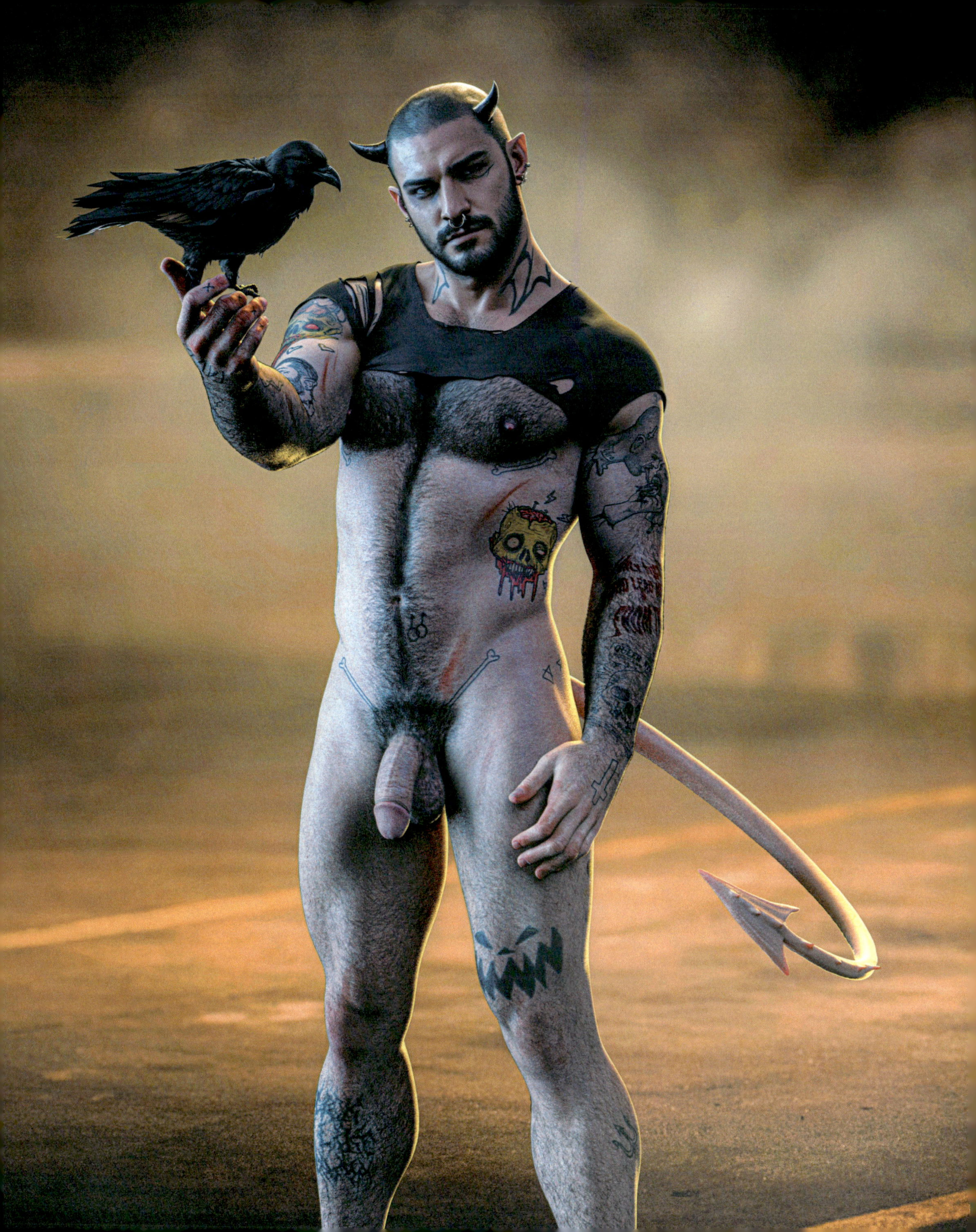

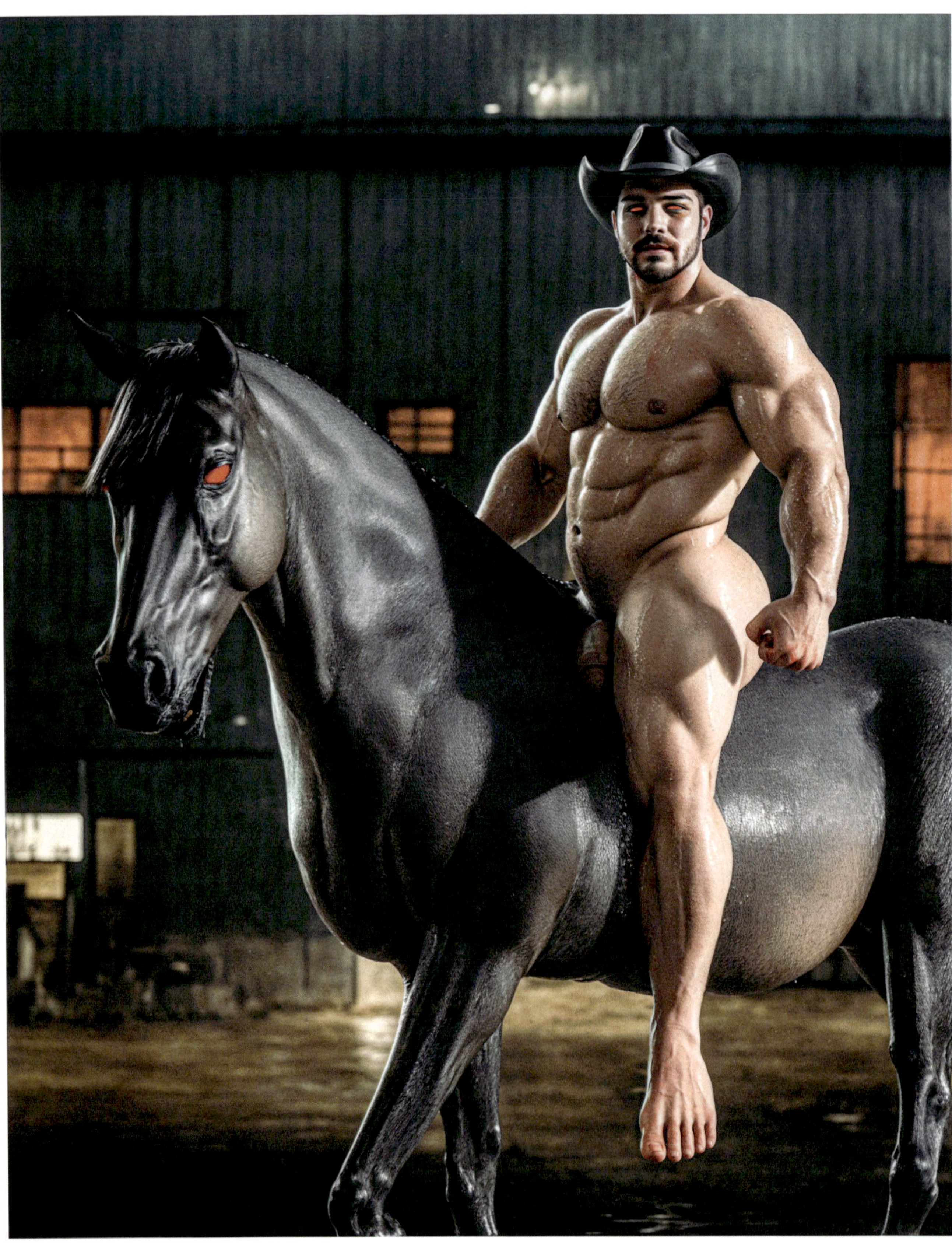

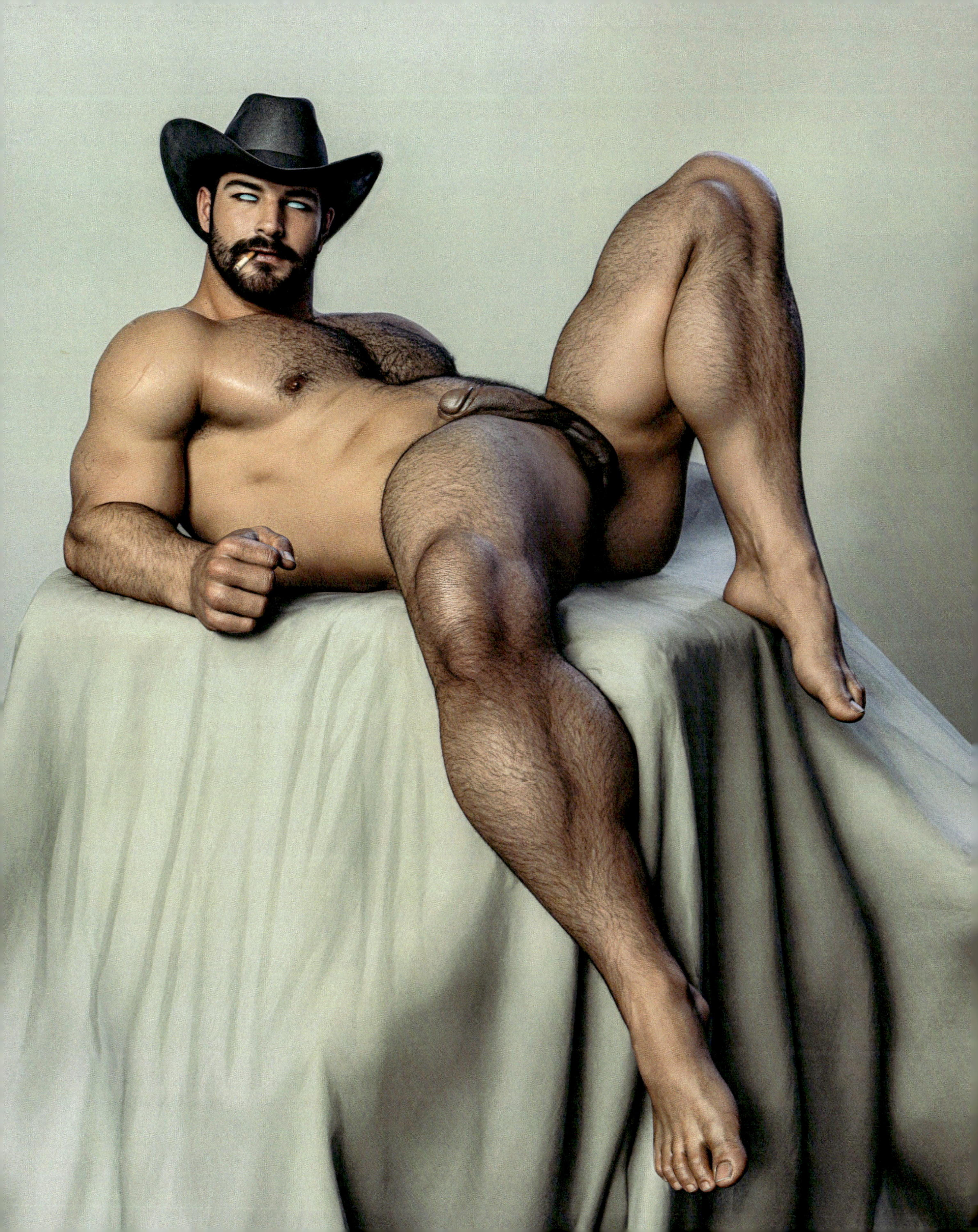

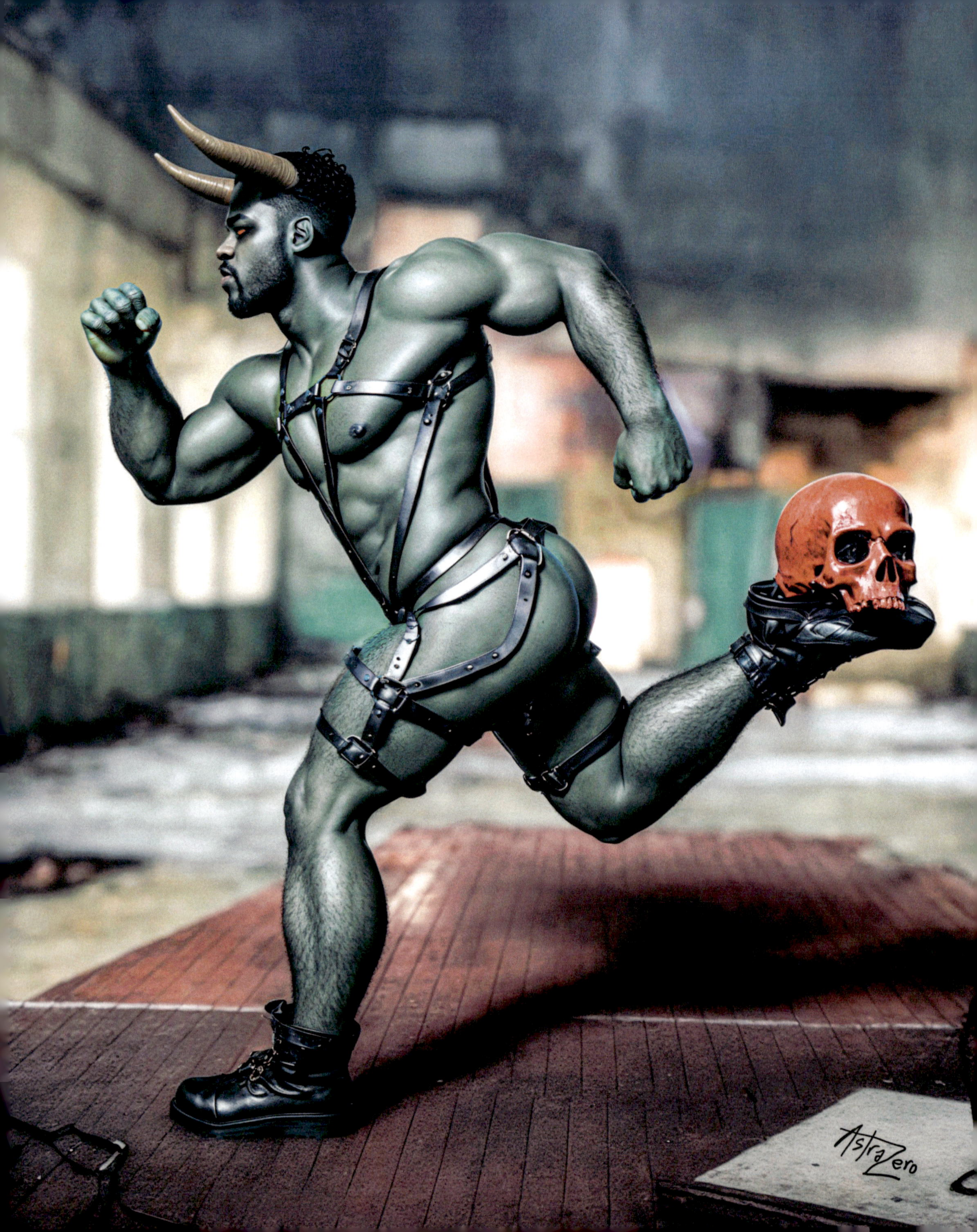

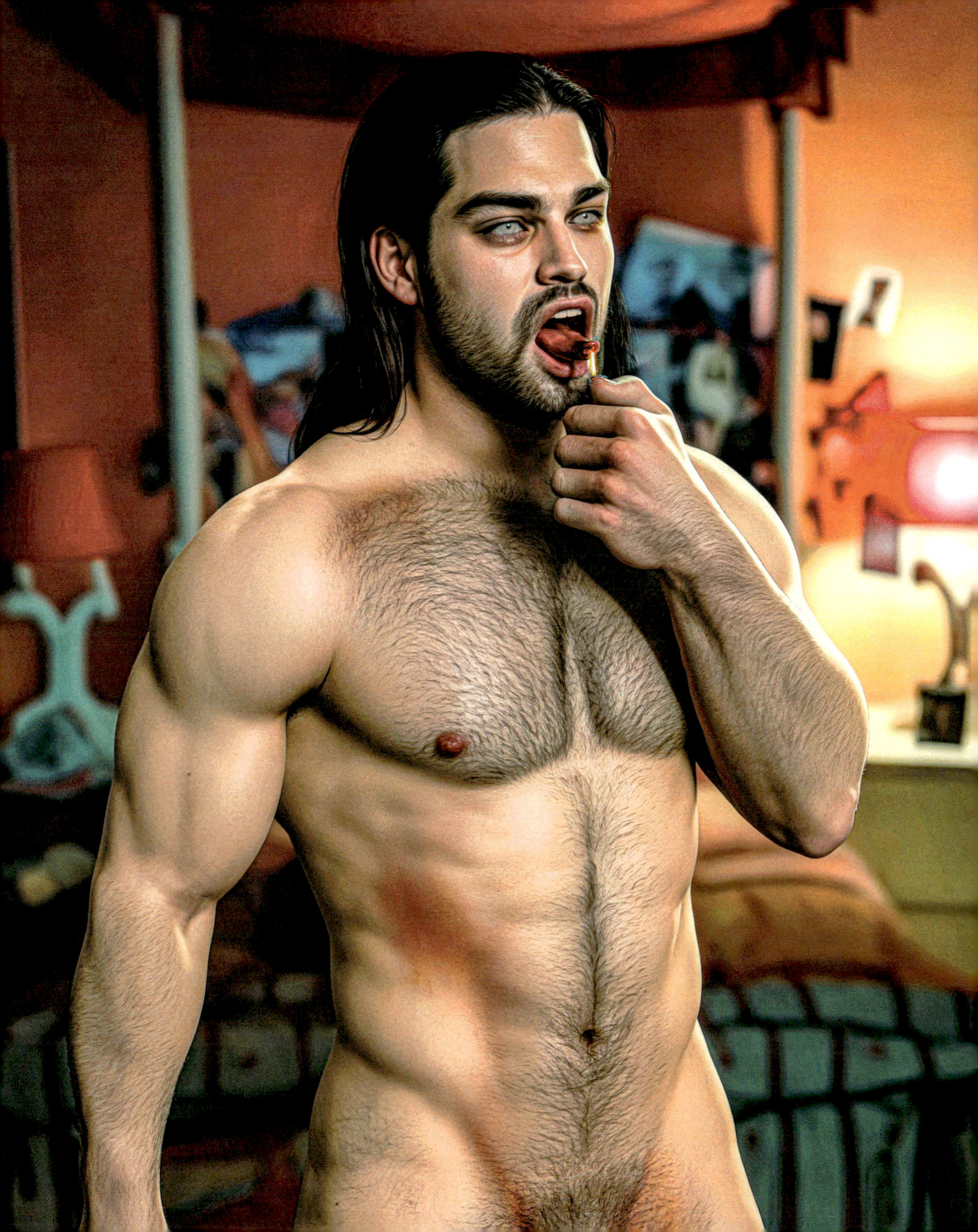

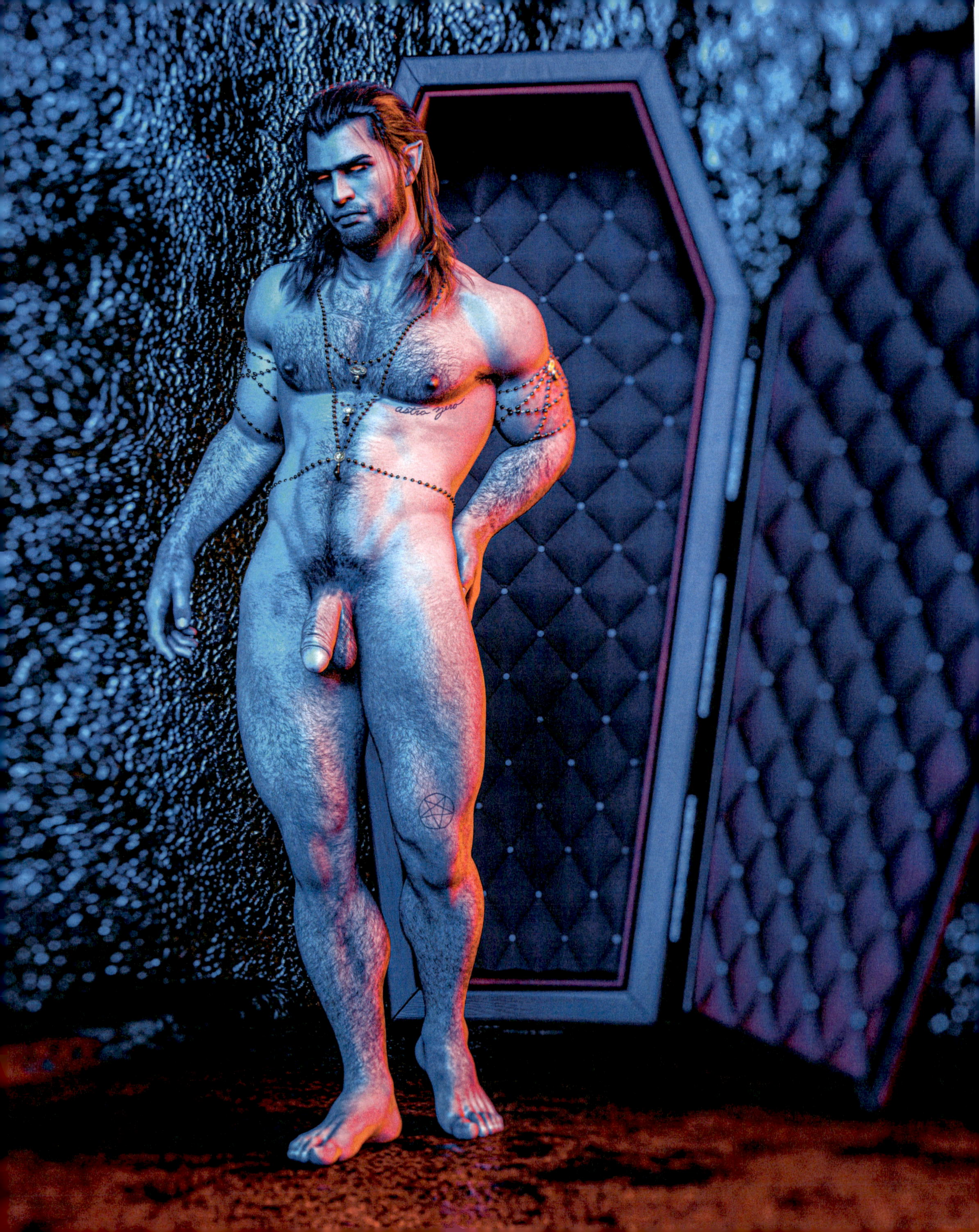
astro zero

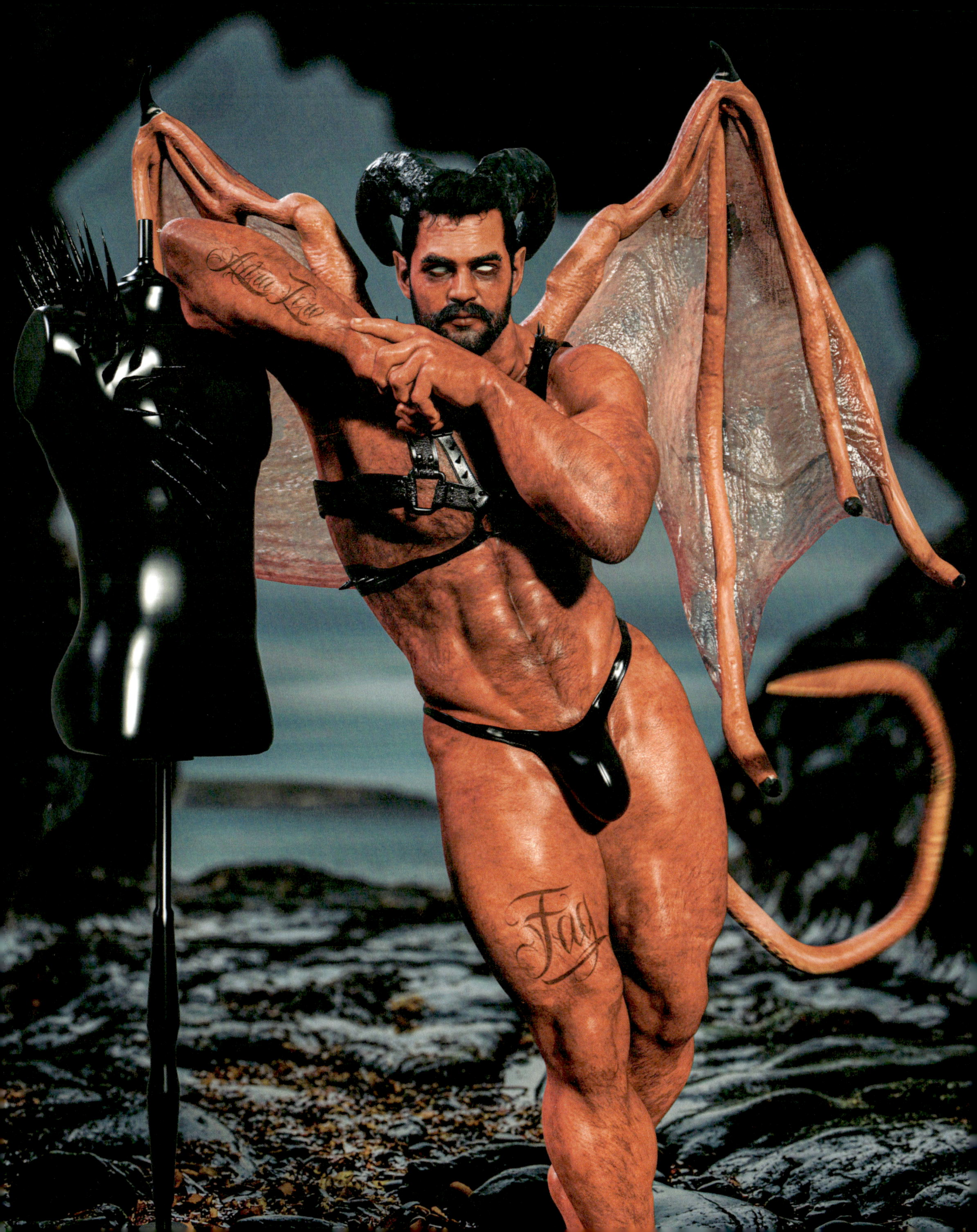

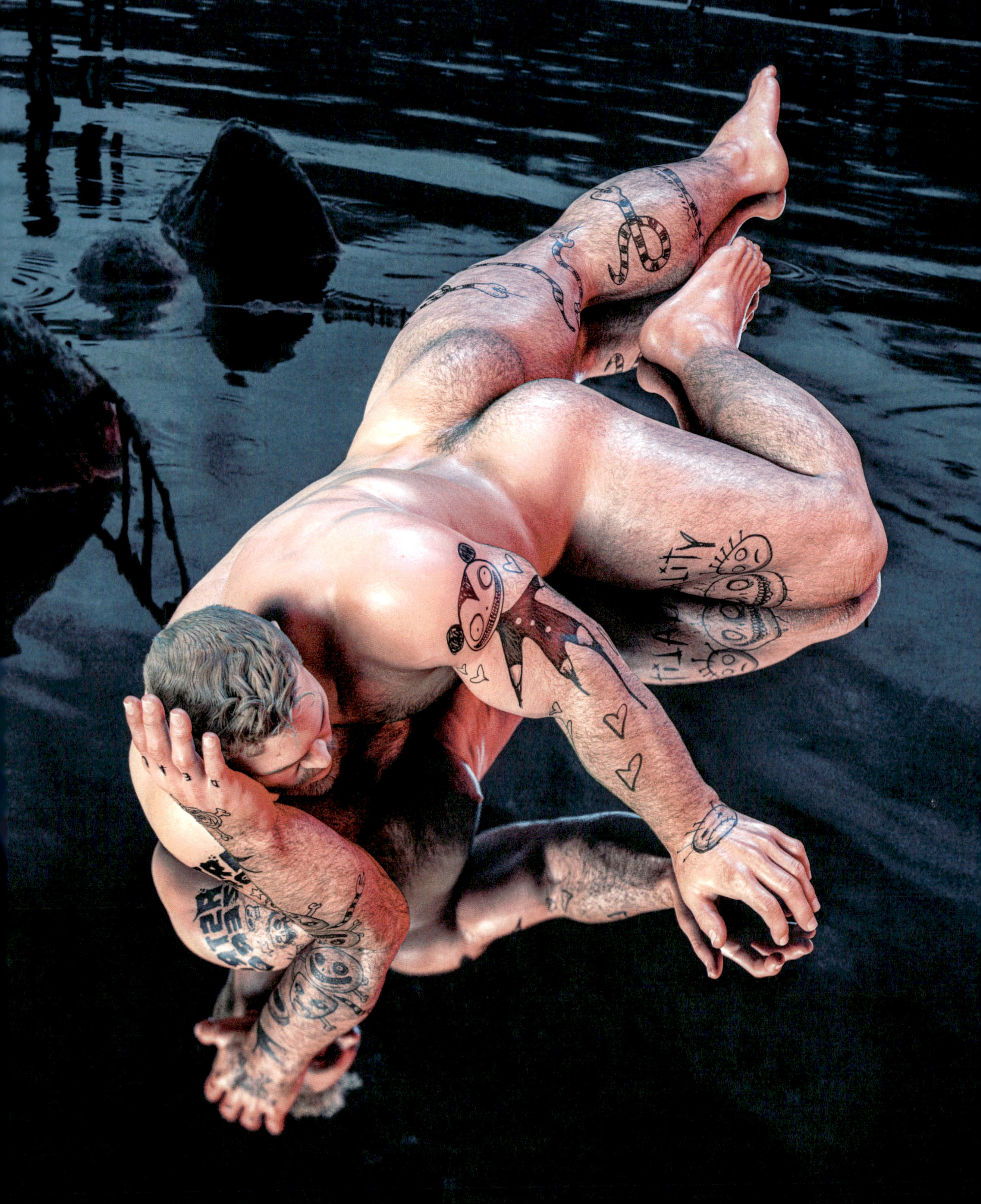

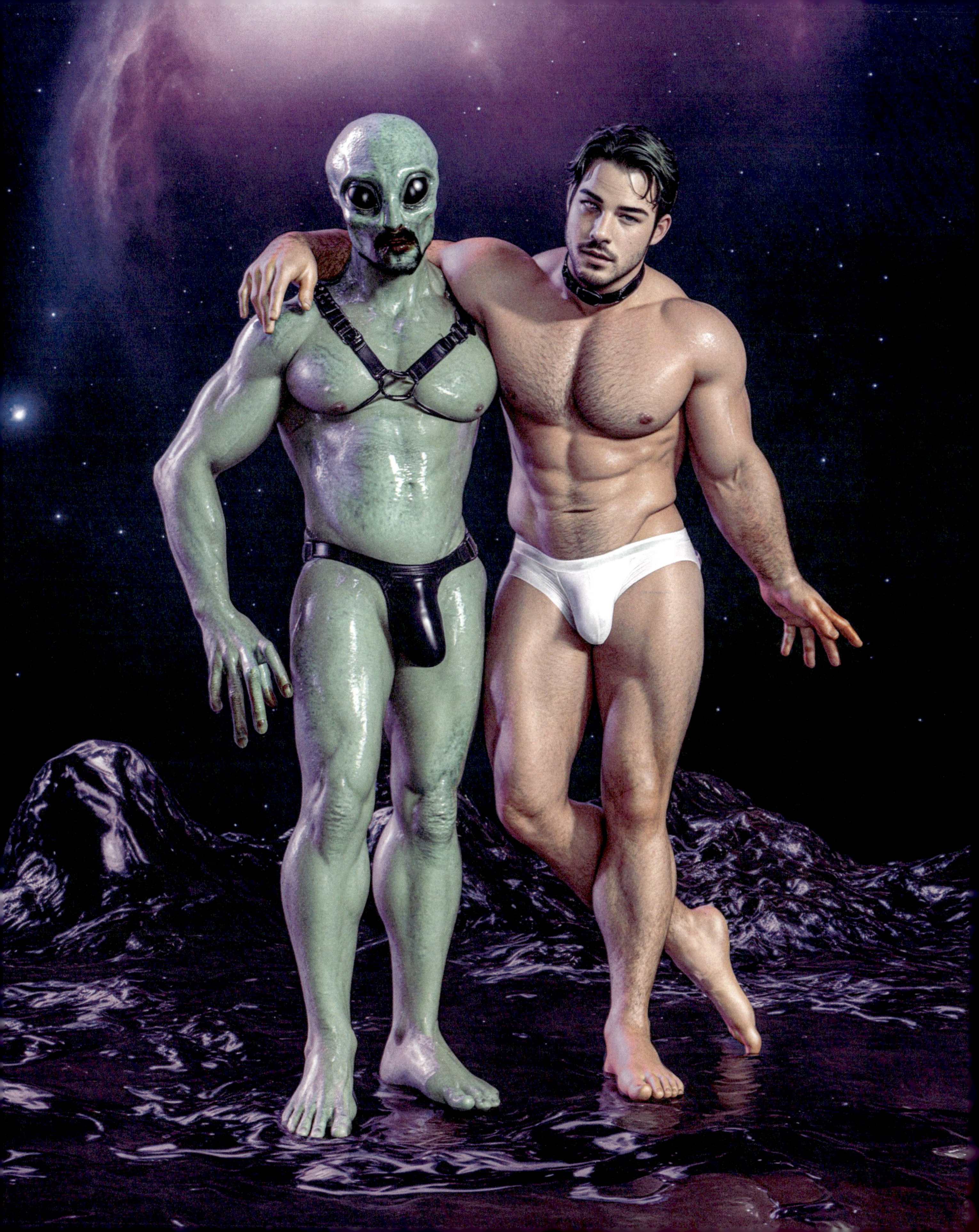

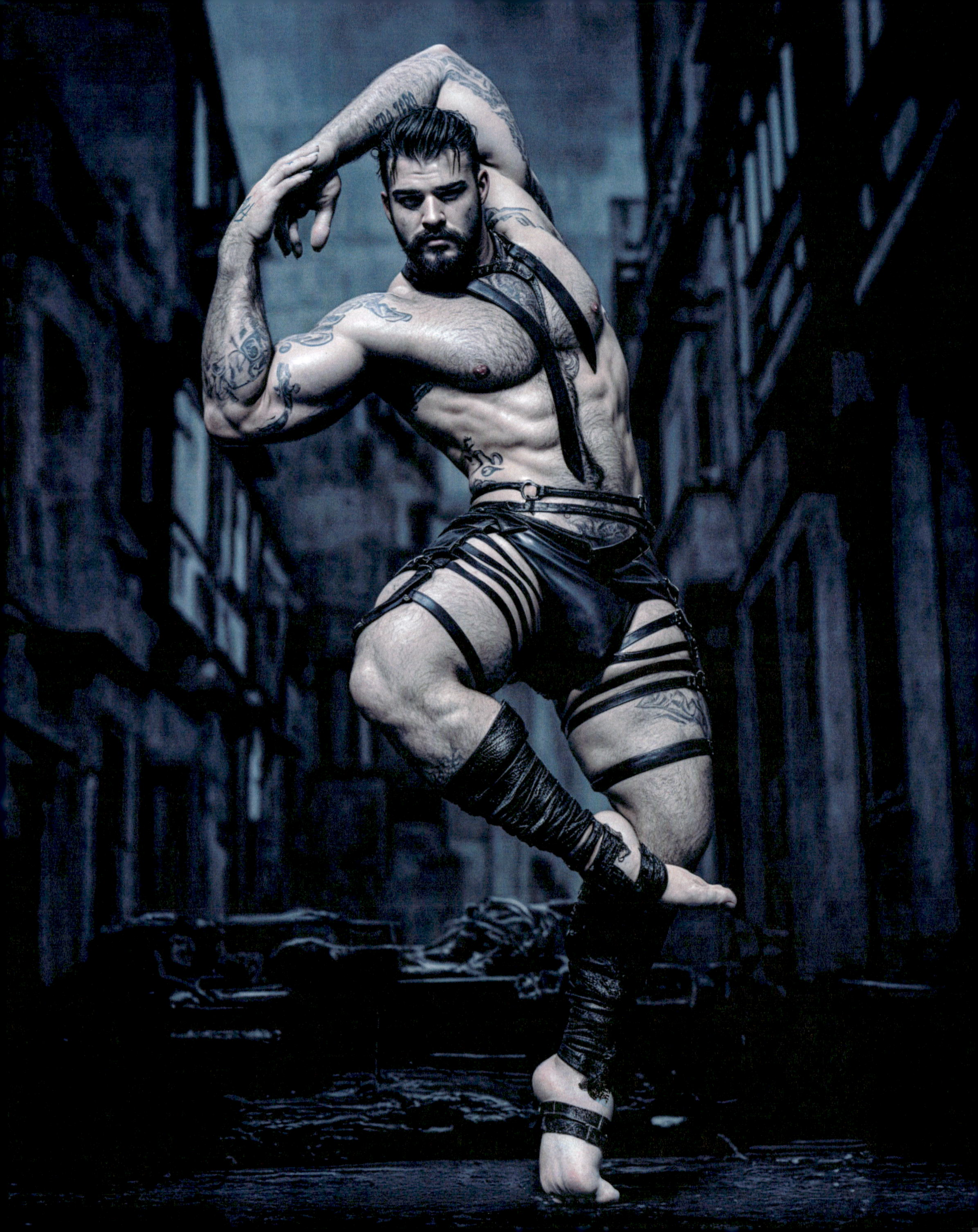

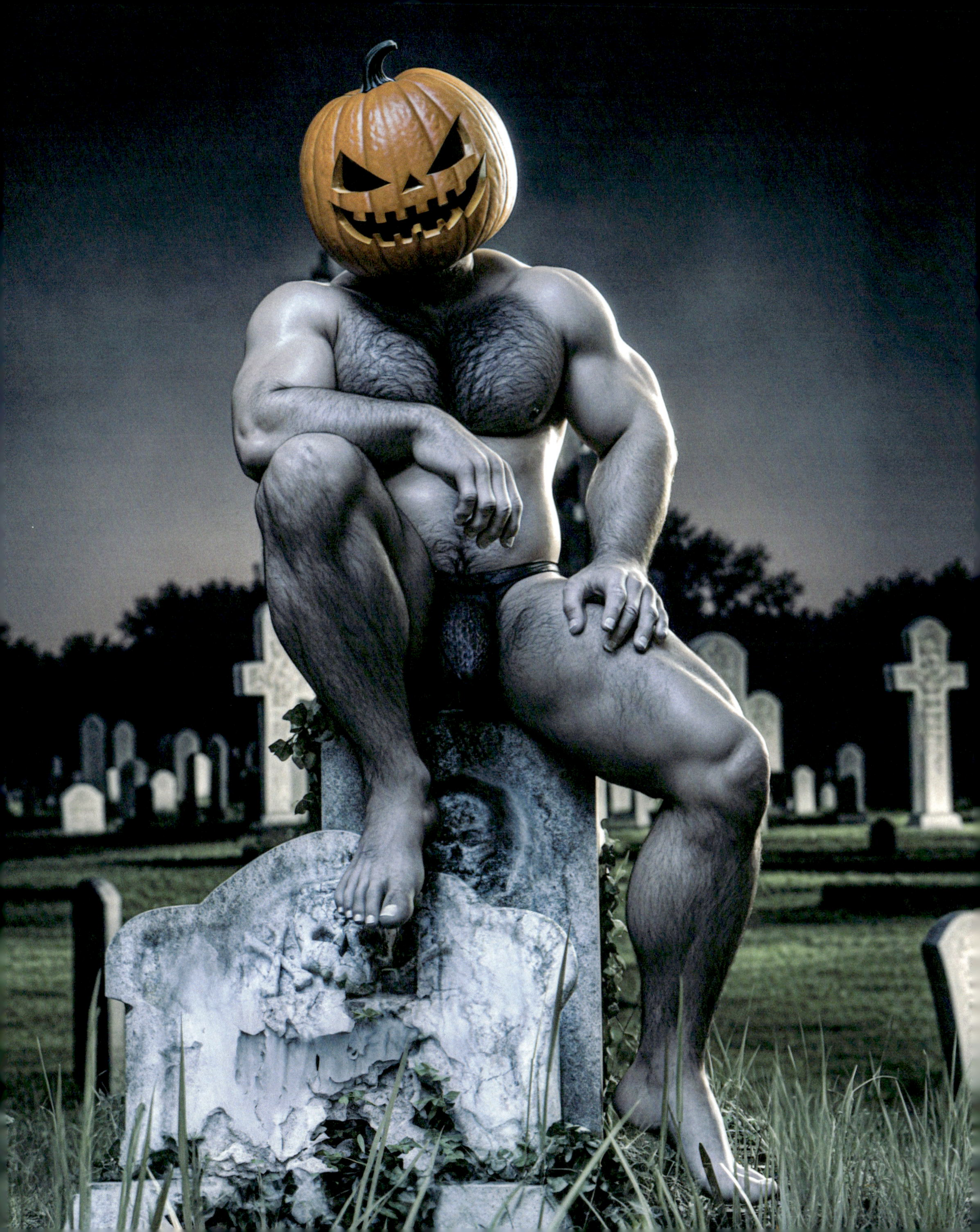

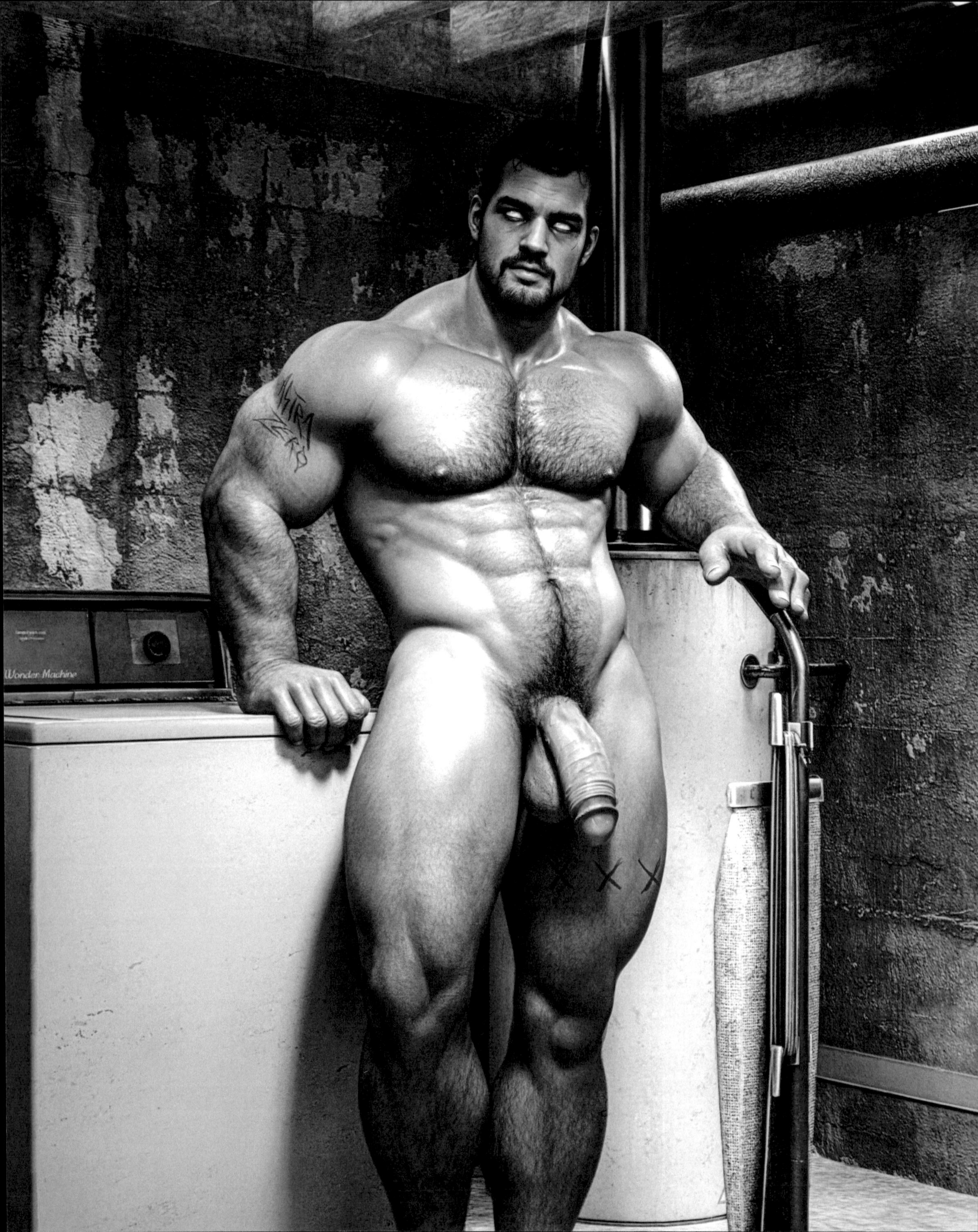

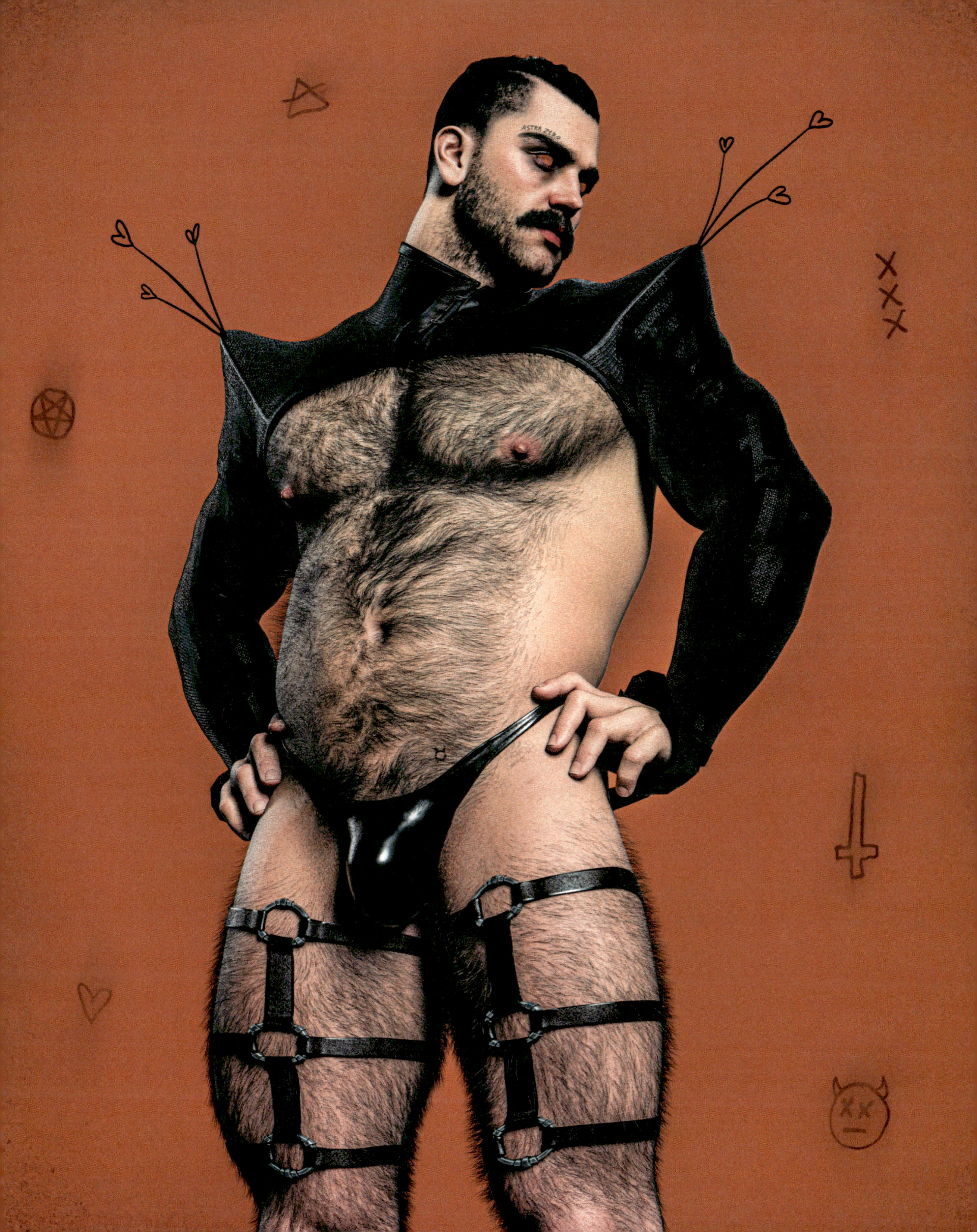

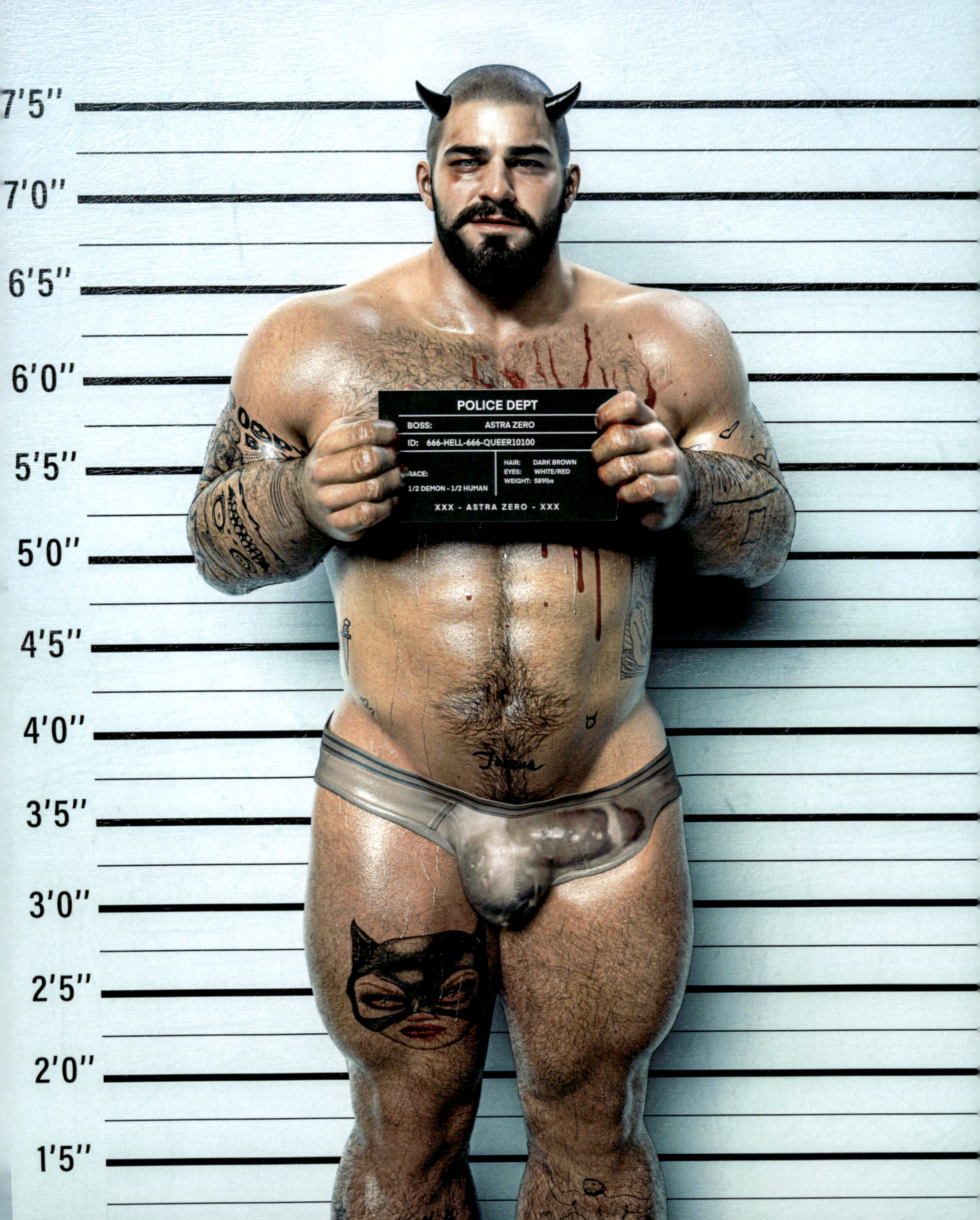

POLICE DEPT
BOSS: ASTRA ZERO
ID: 666-HELL-666-QUEER10100
RACE: HAIR: DARK BROWN
                         EYES: WHITE/RED
1/2 DEMON - 1/2 HUMAN   WEIGHT: 589lbs
XXX - ASTRA ZERO - XXX

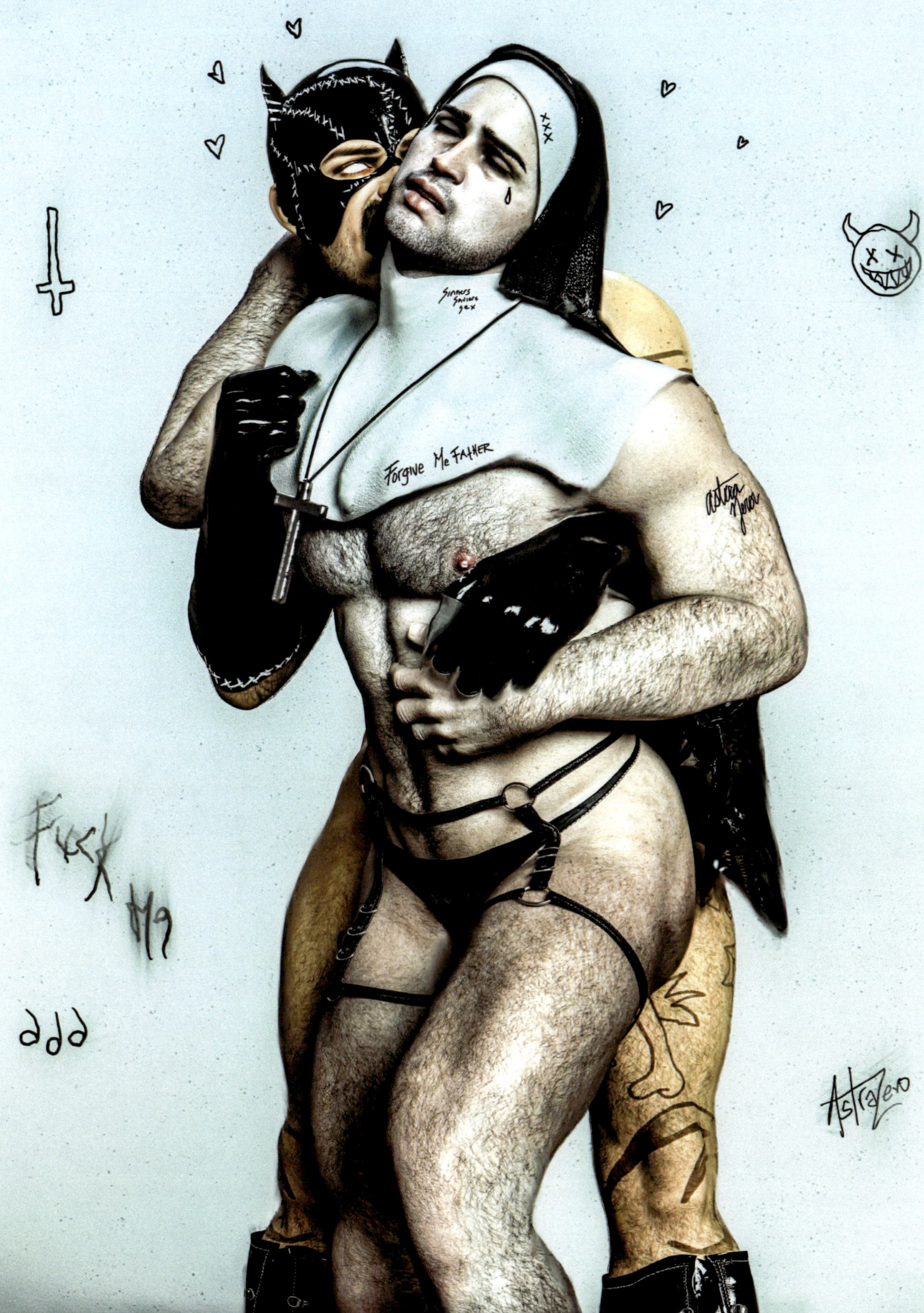
xxx
Sinners
Sinless
gox
Forgive Me Father
astra
gono
FUCK
M9
ddd
AstraZero

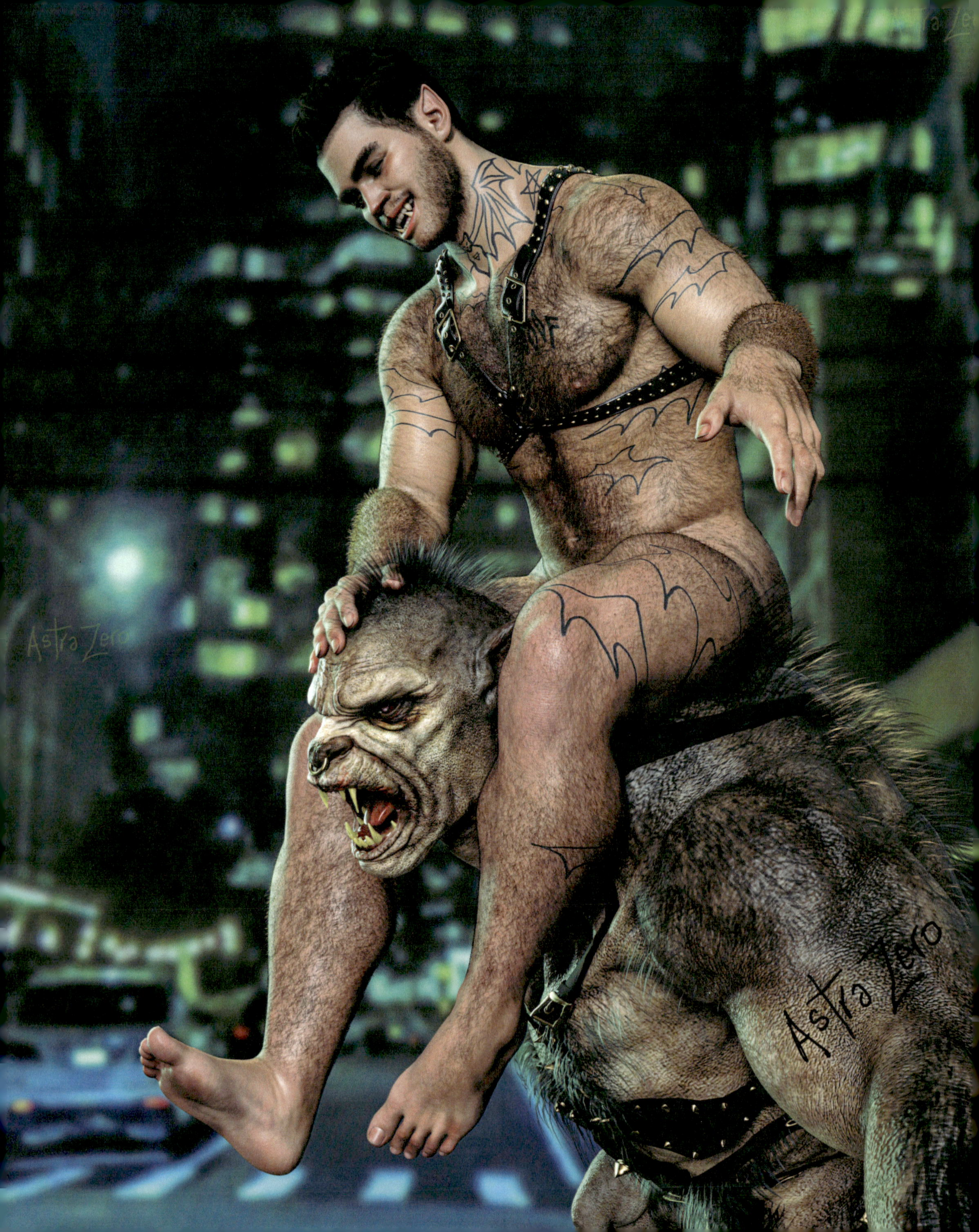

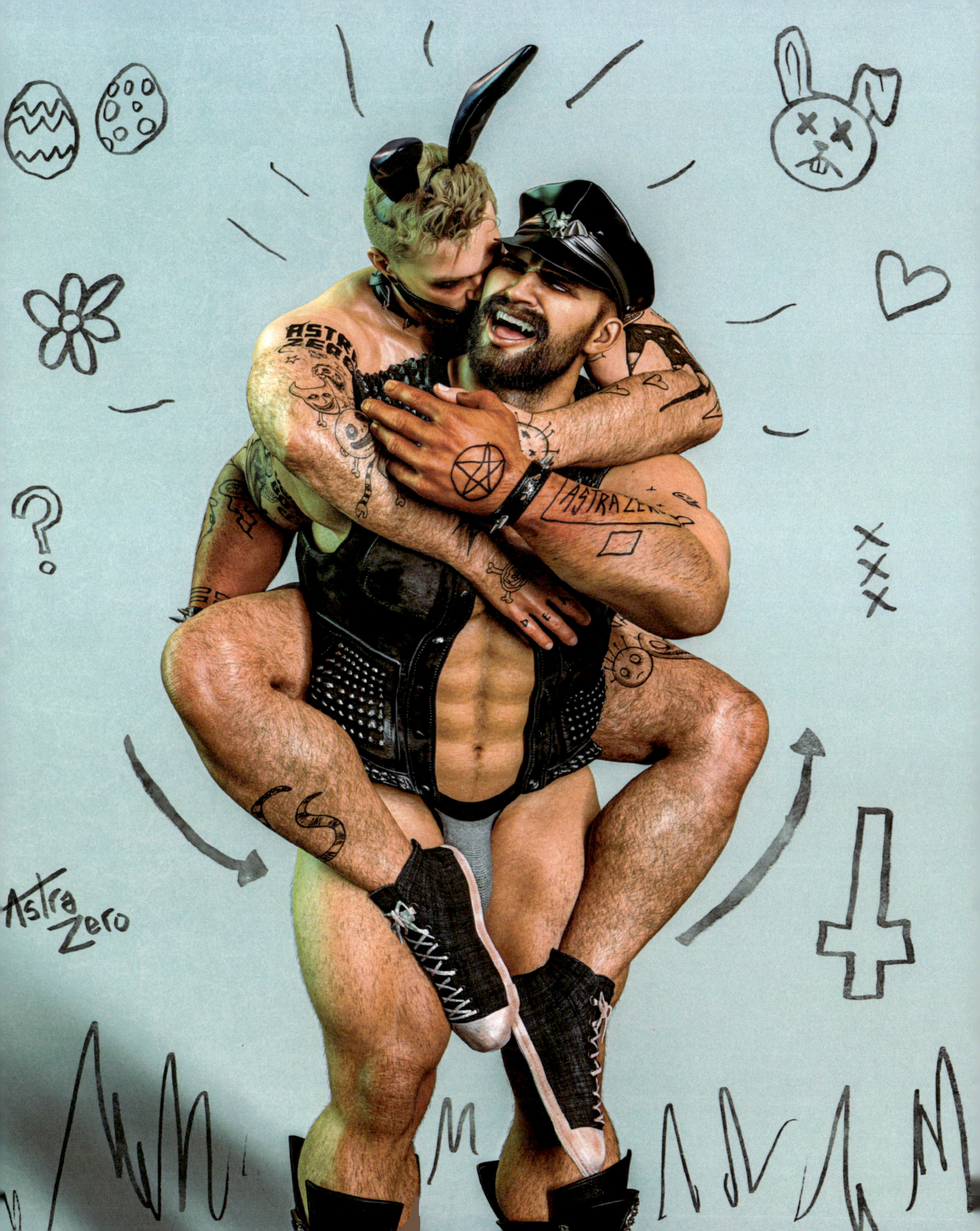

ASTRA ZERO
ASTRAZERO
AstraZero

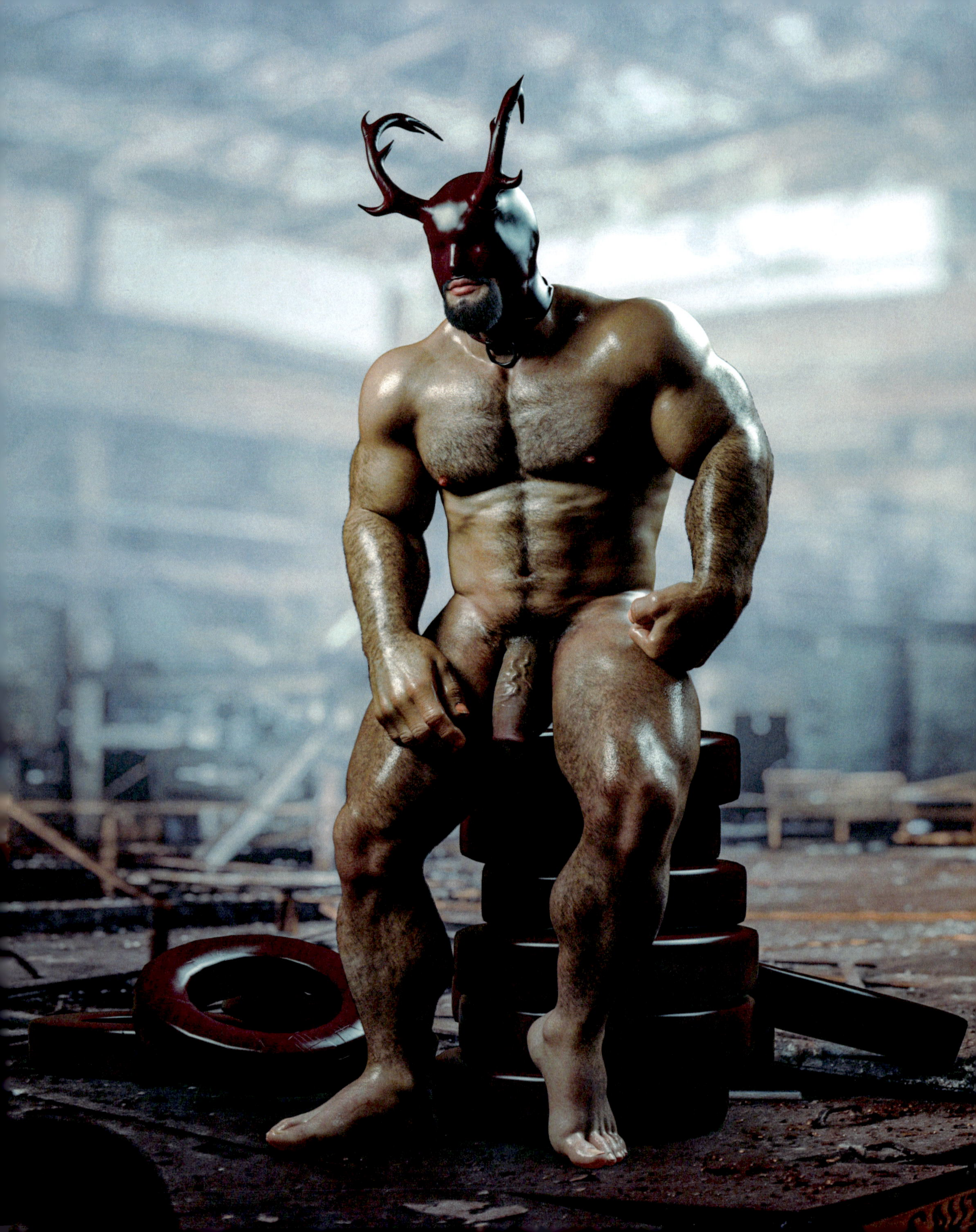

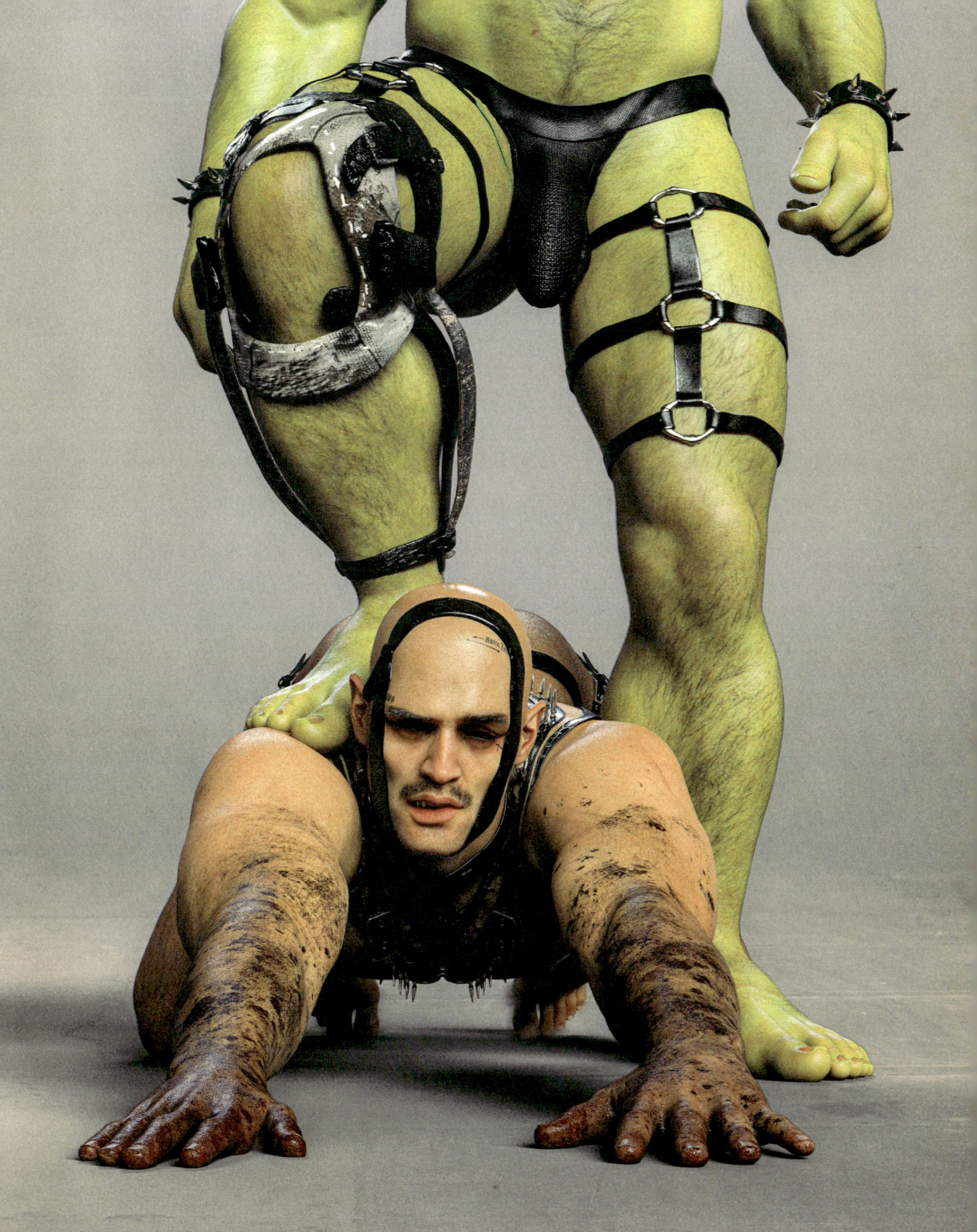

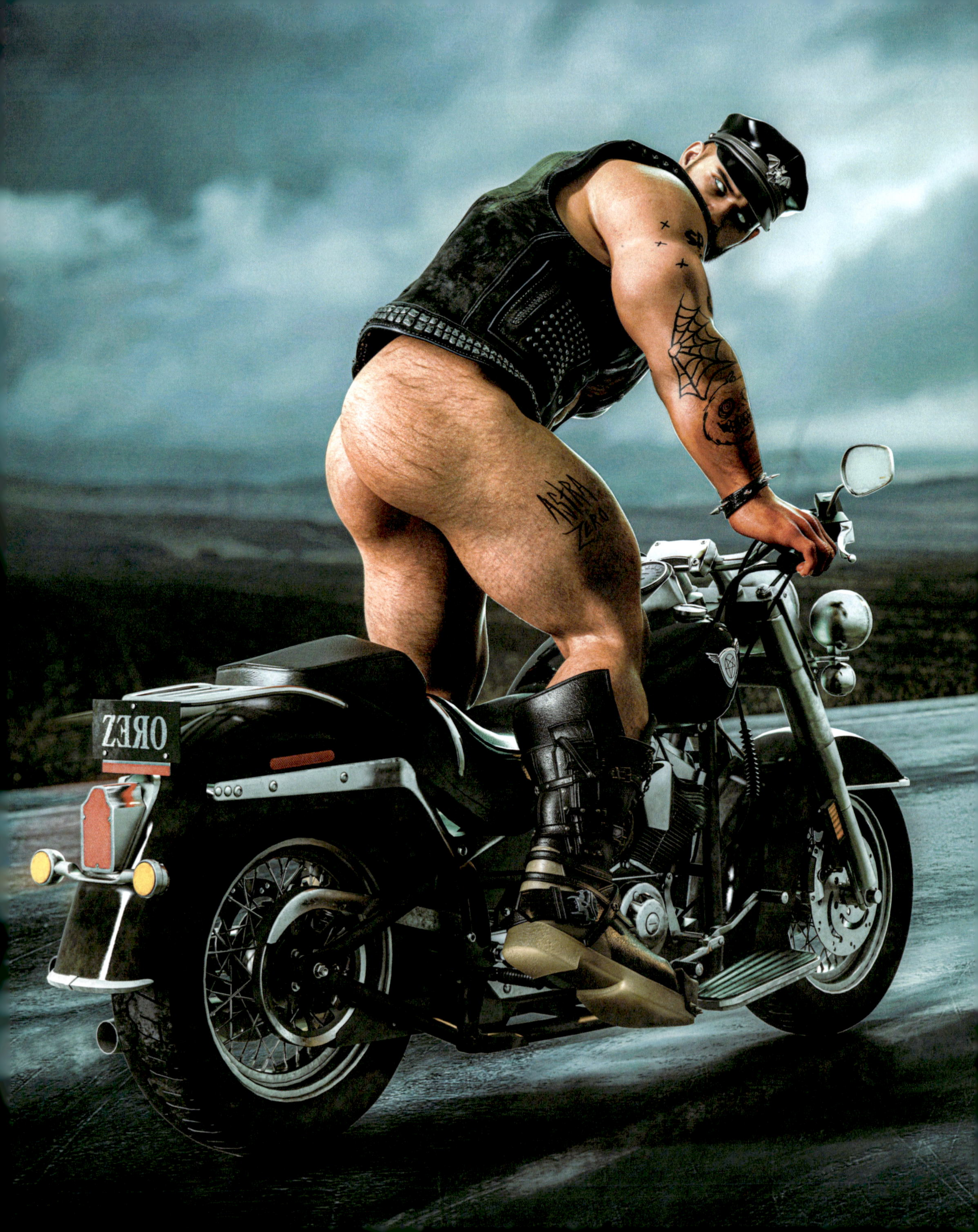
ZERO

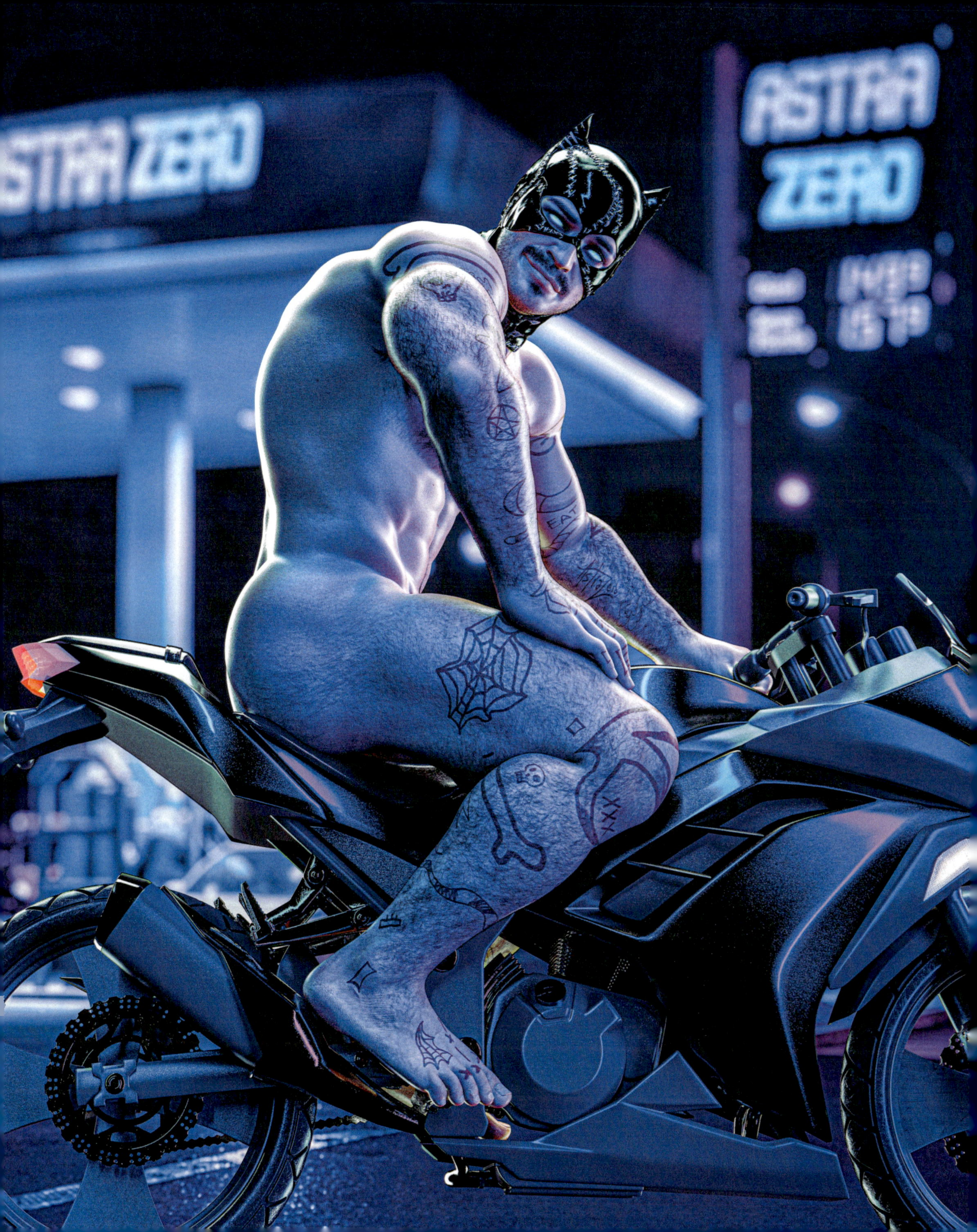
ASTRA ZERO
ASTRA
ZERO

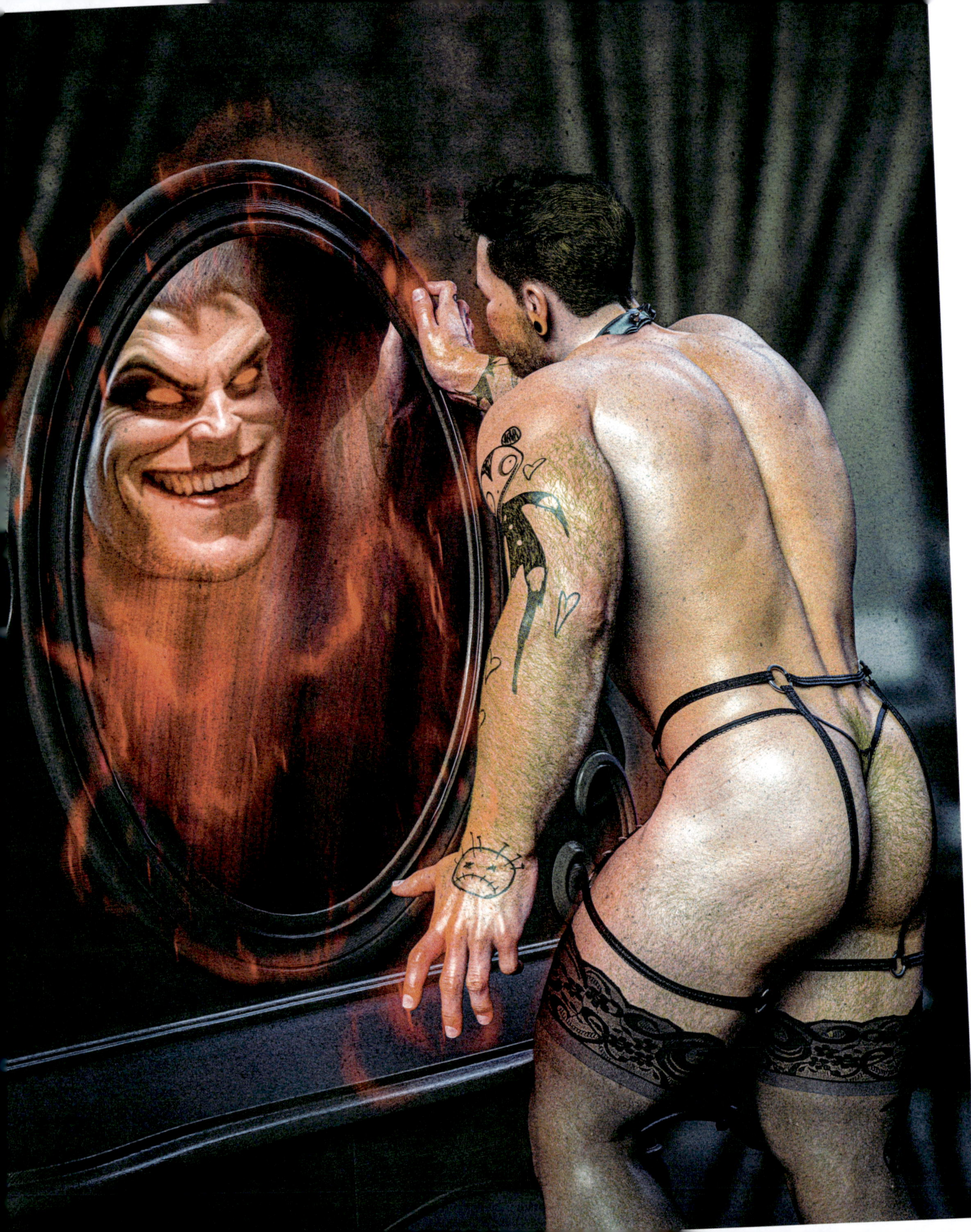

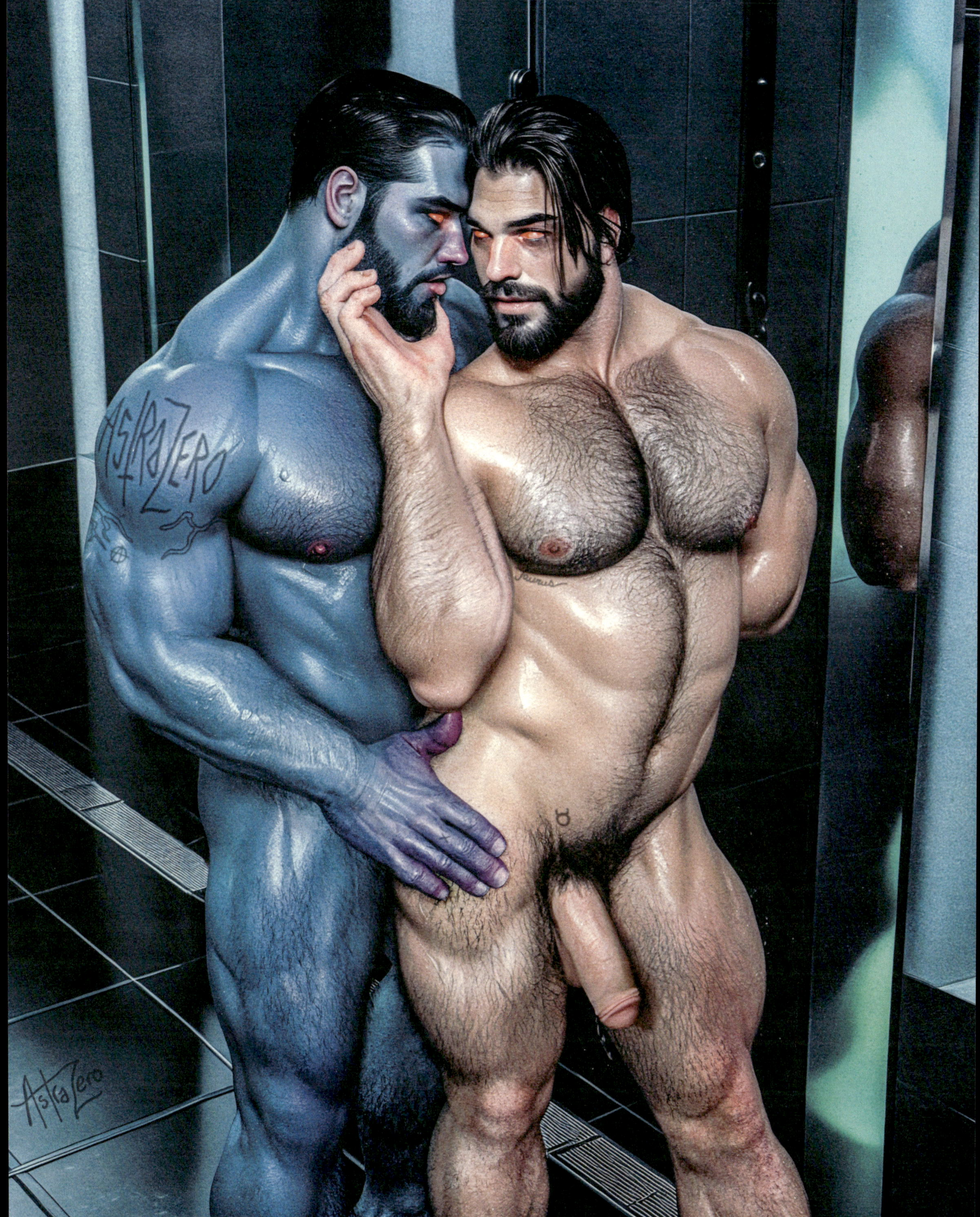

AstraZero
AstraZero

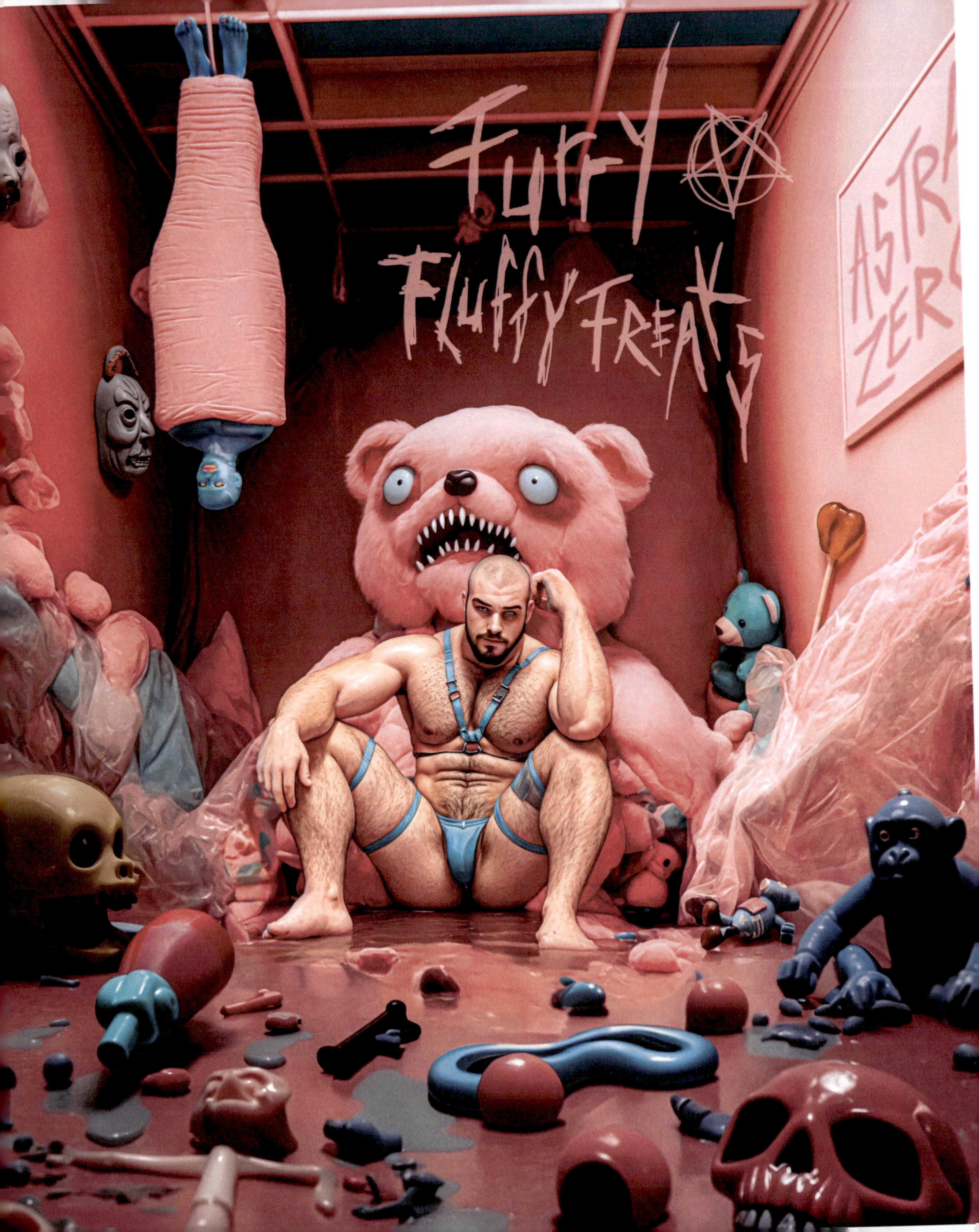

Furry
Fluffy Freaks
ASTRA ZERO

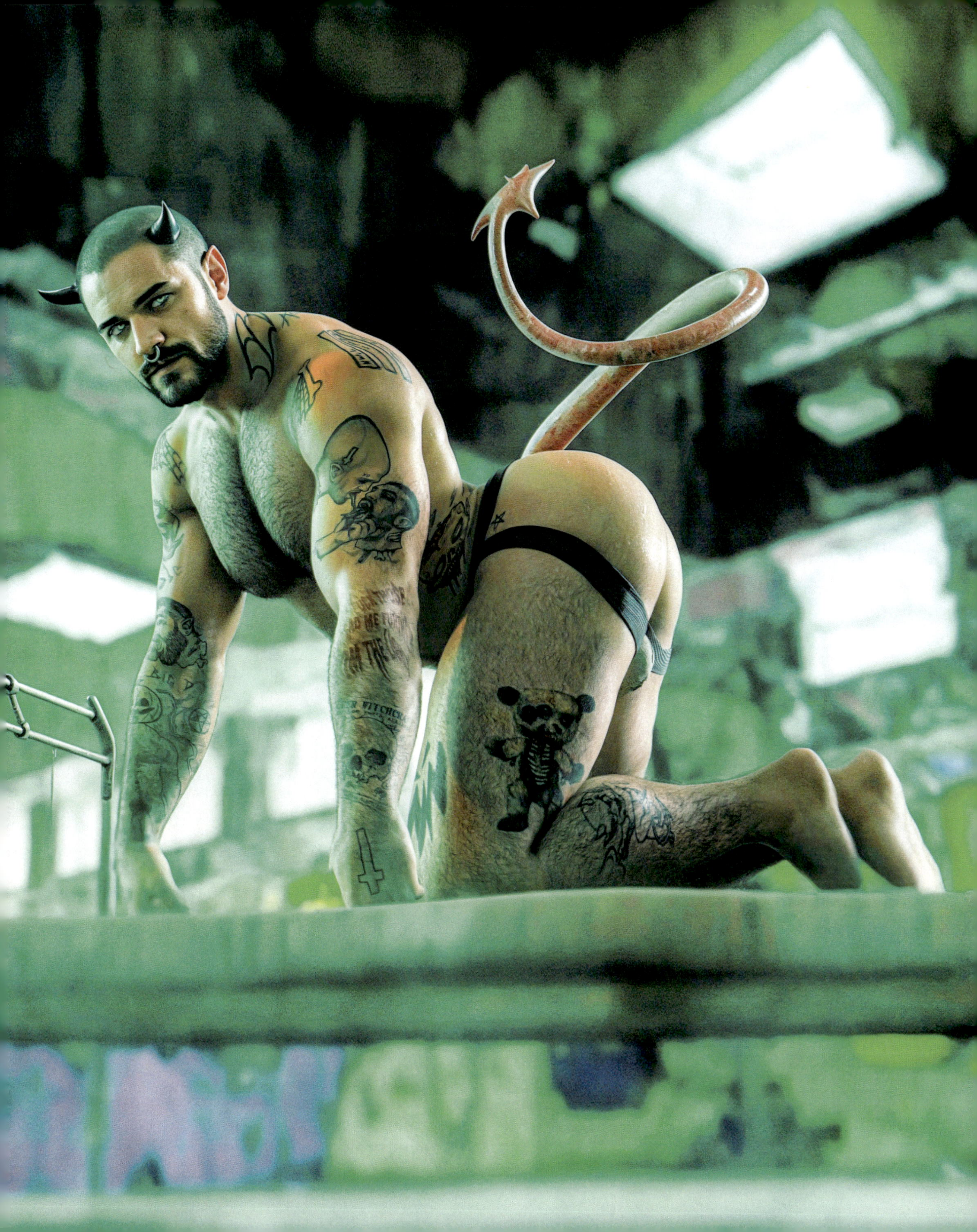

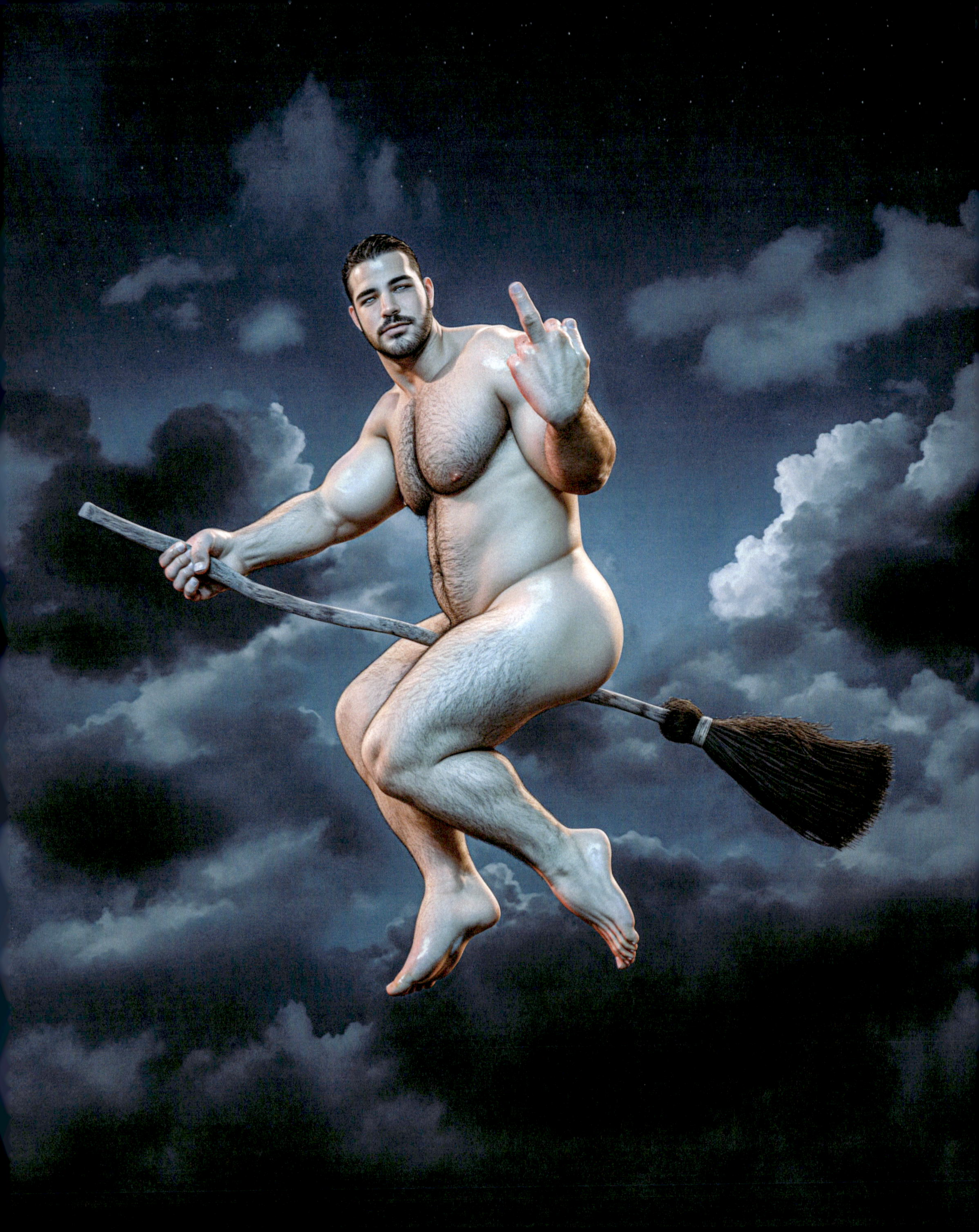

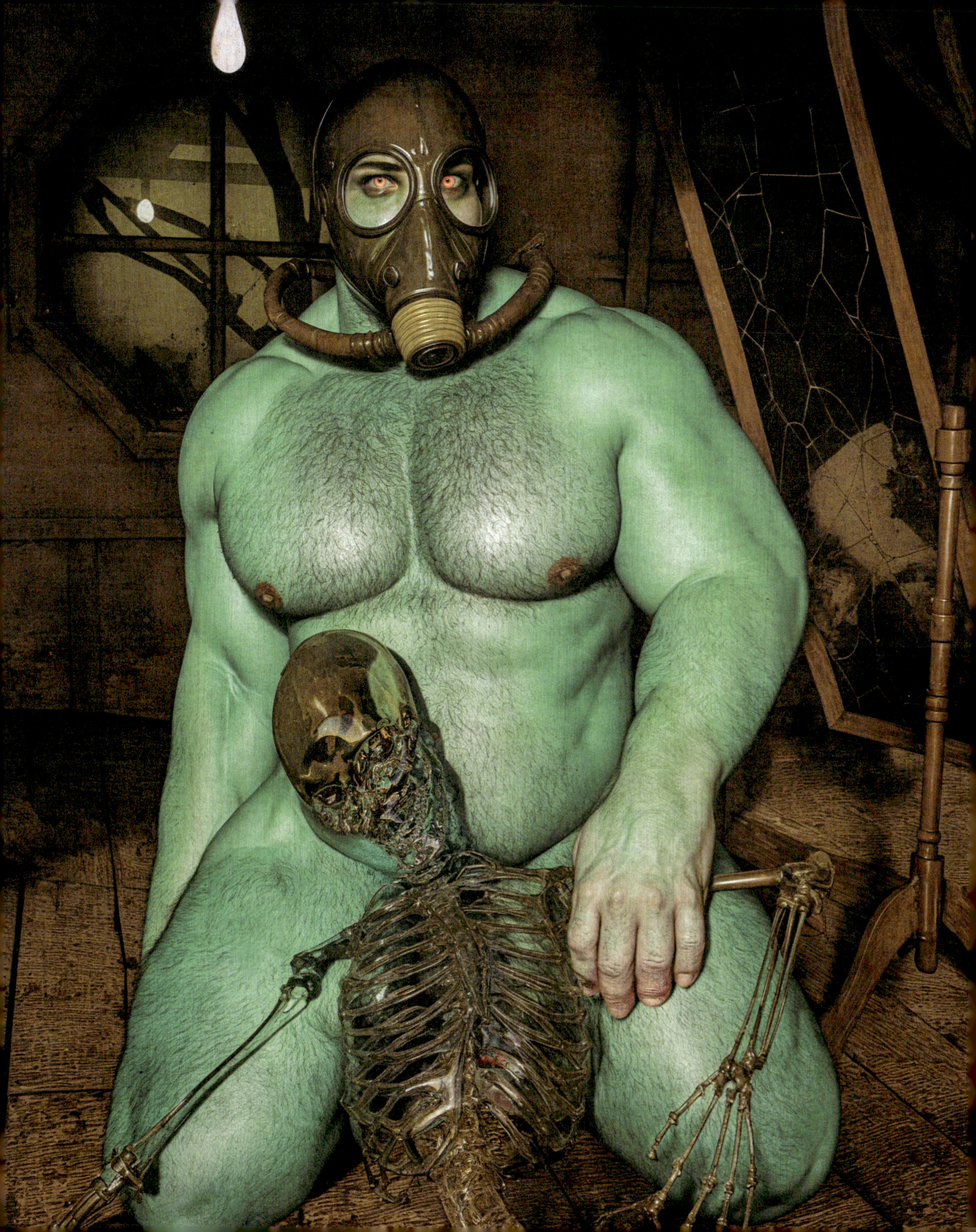

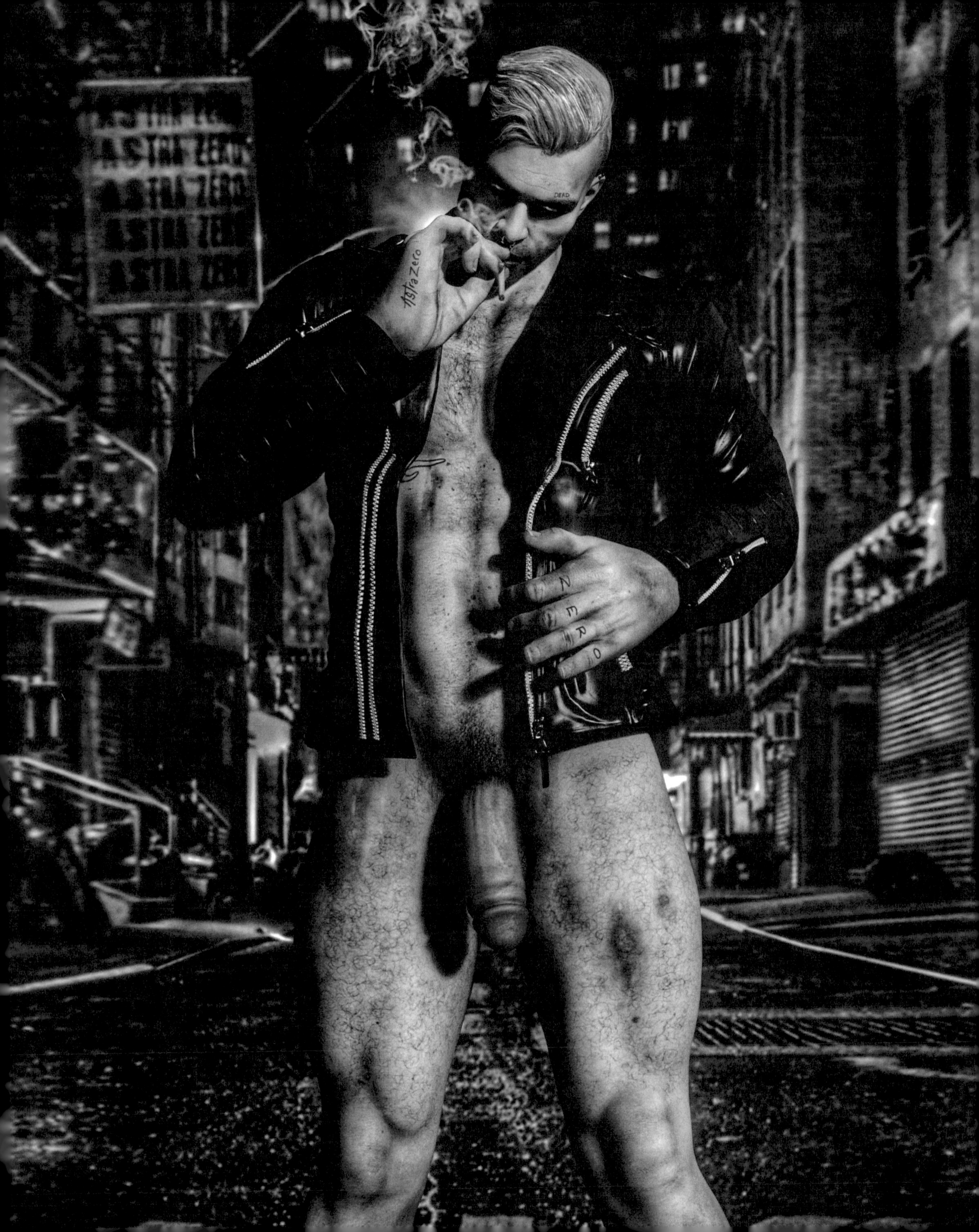

ASTRA ZERO
ASTRA ZERO
ASTRA ZERO
ASTRA ZERO
DEAD
AstraZero
NERO

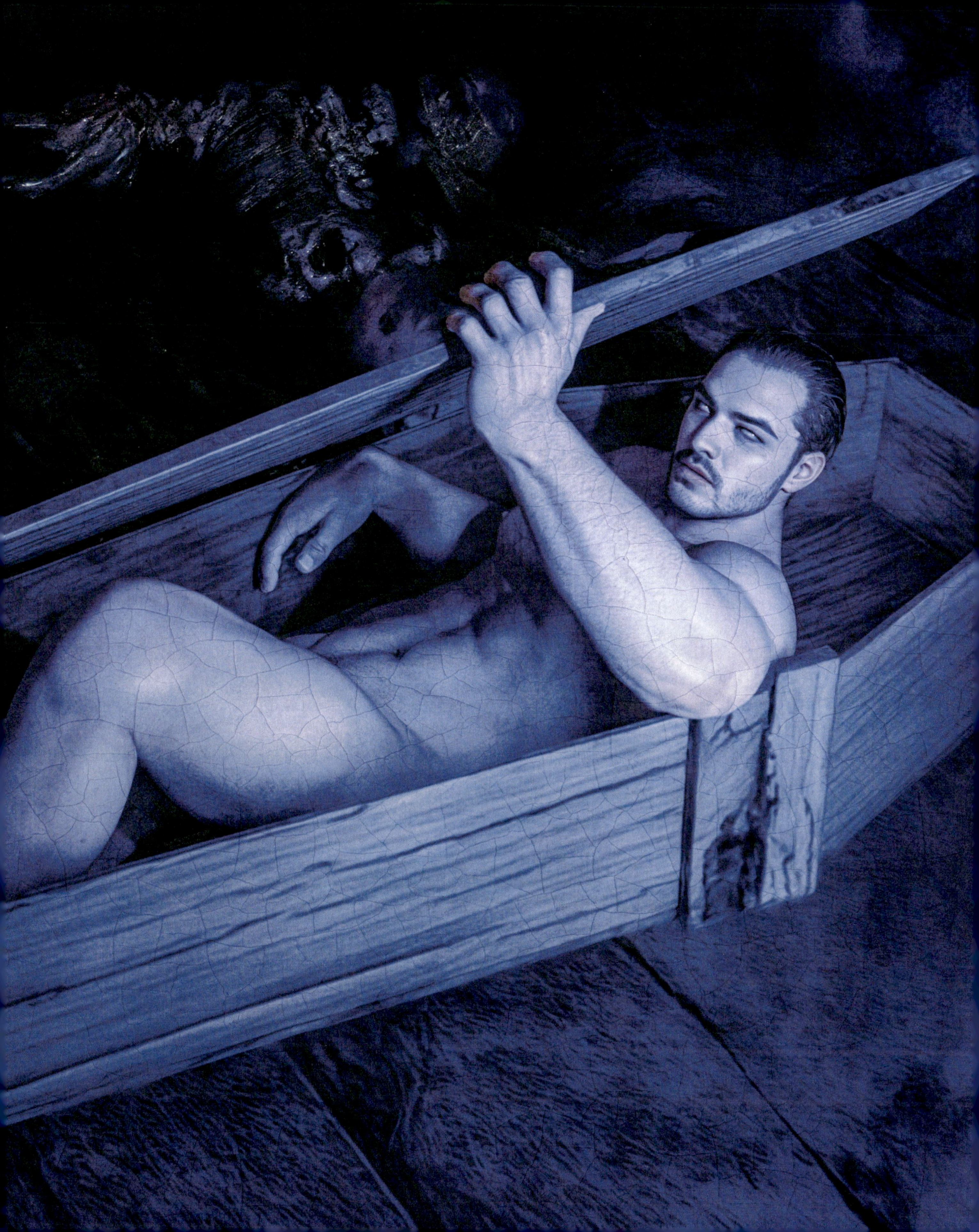

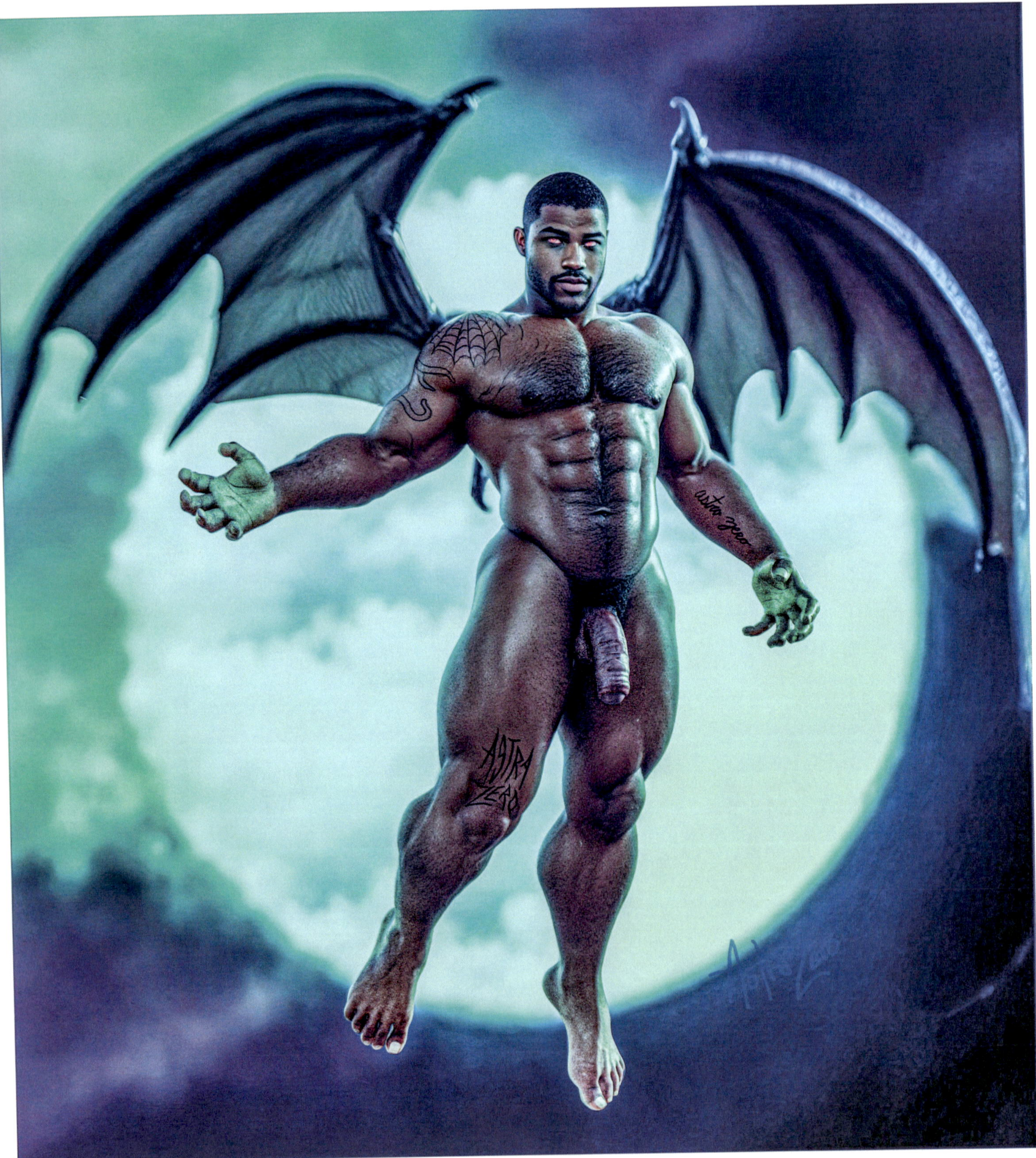
astro zero
ASTRA ZERO

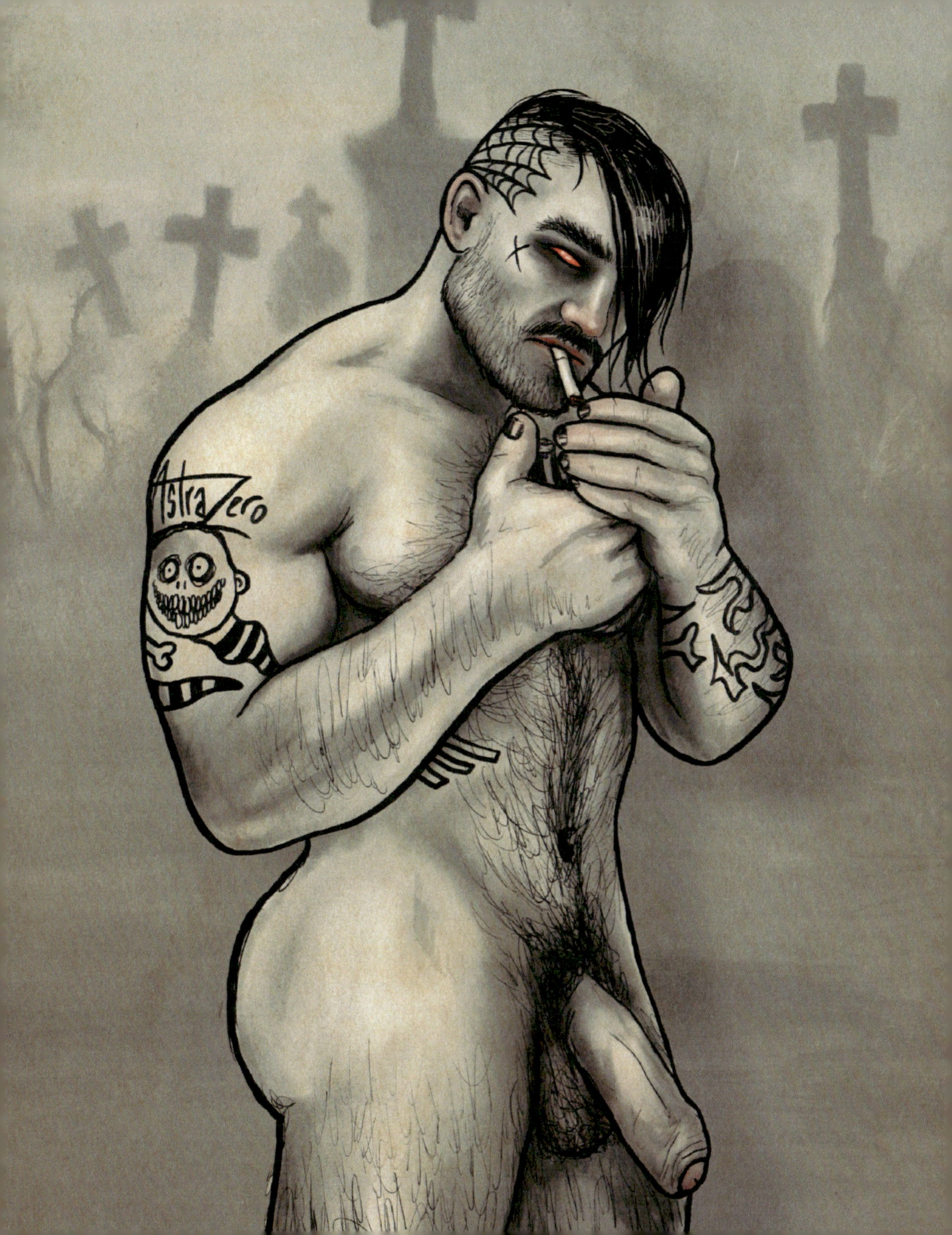
AstraZero

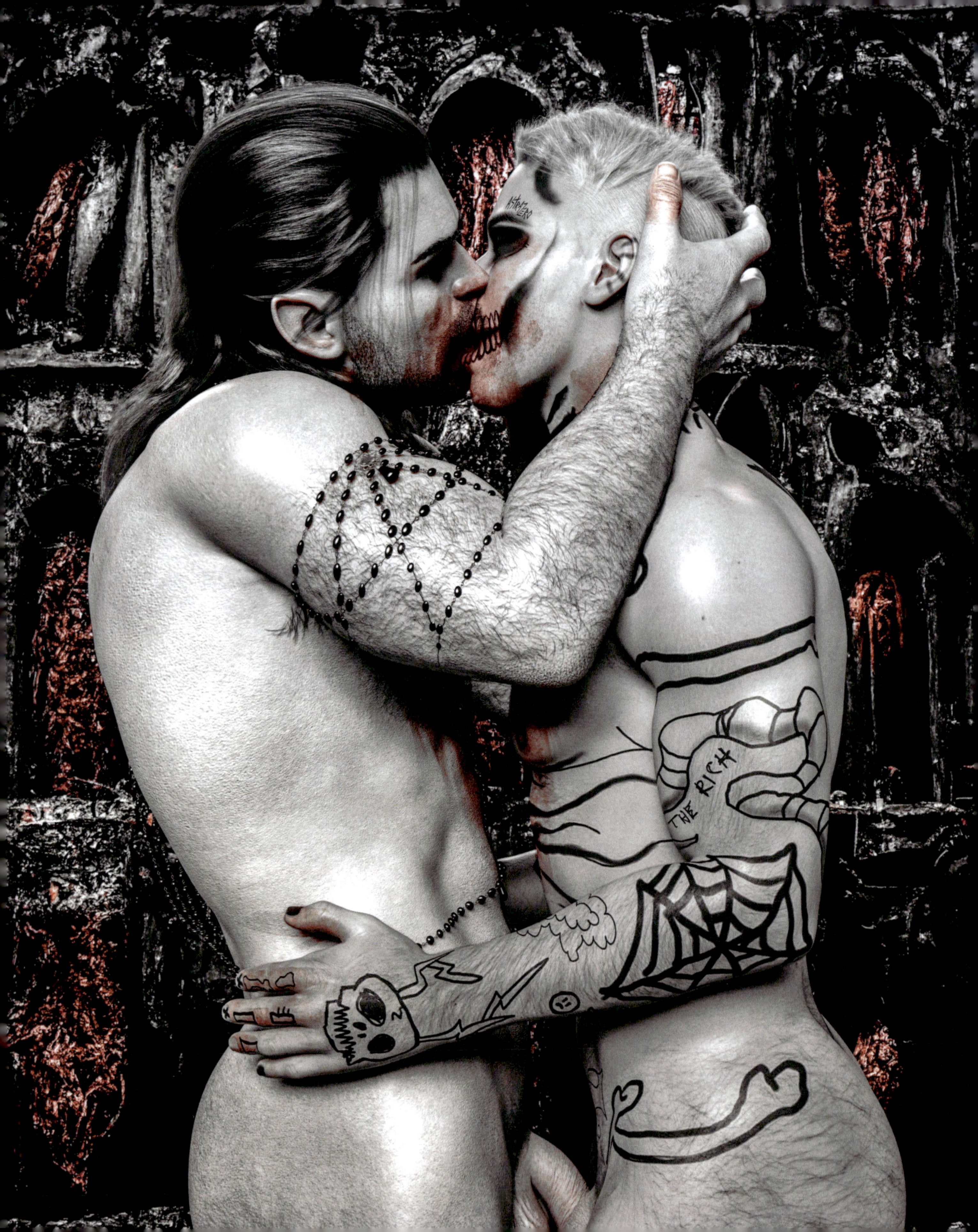
THE RICH

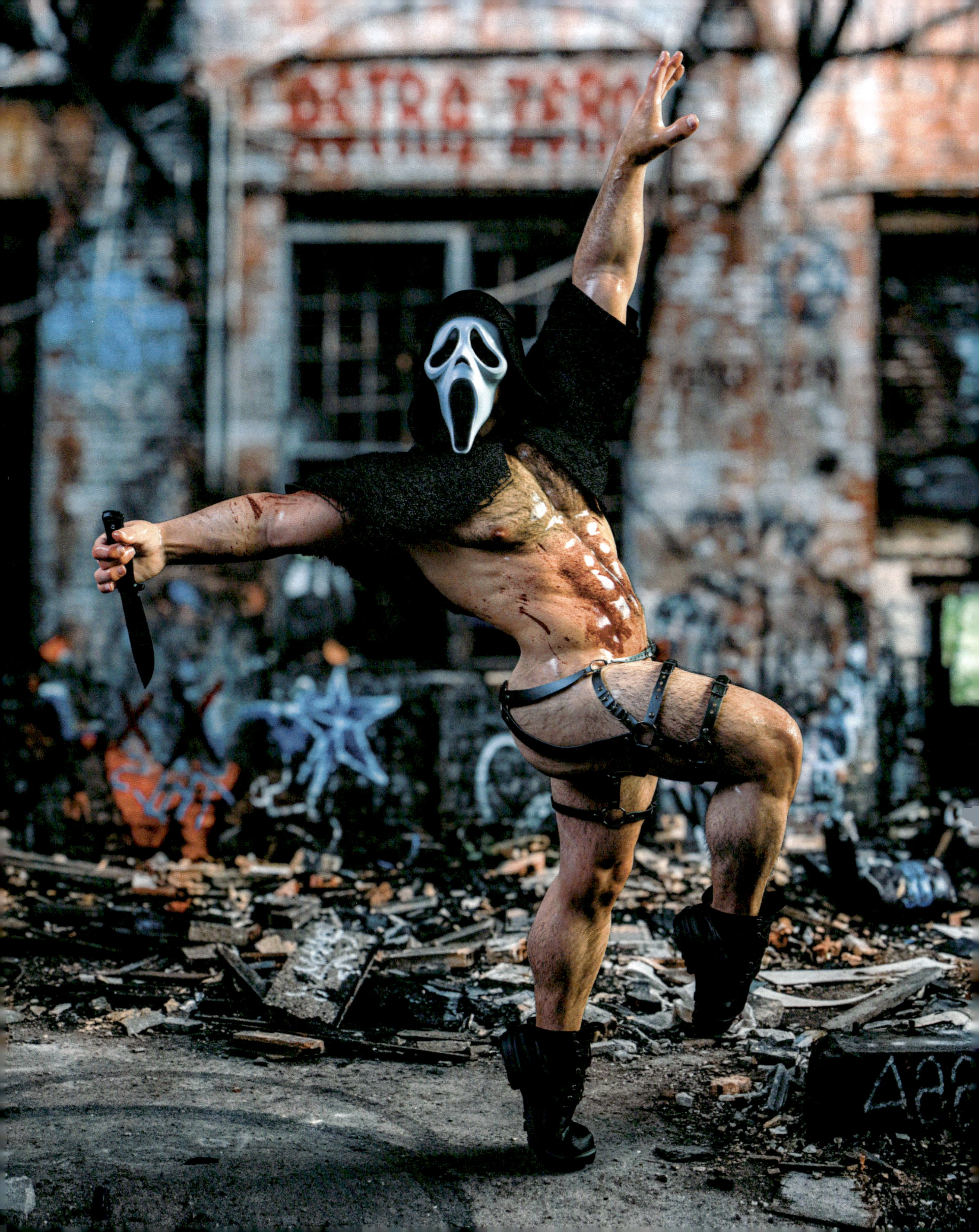

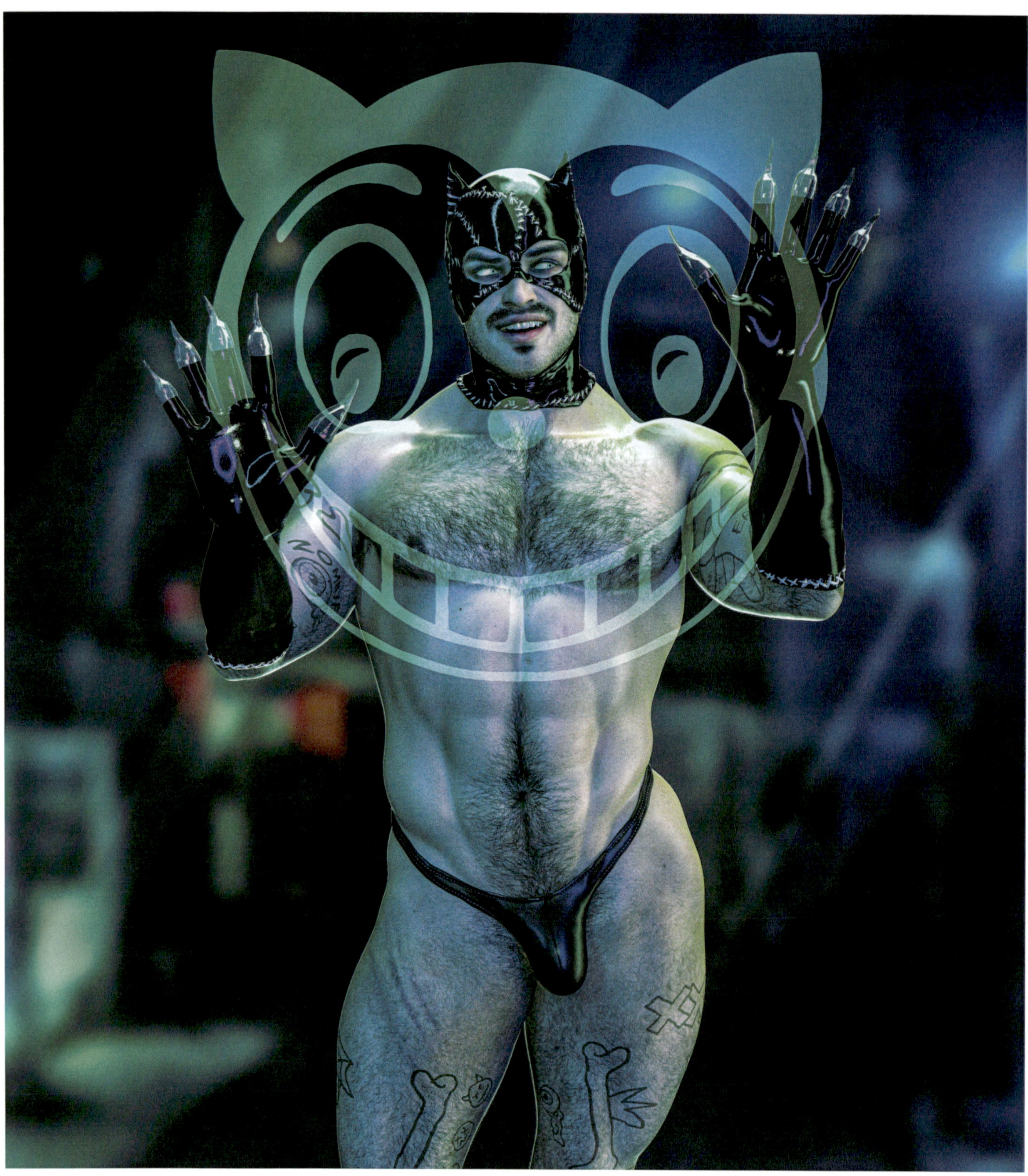

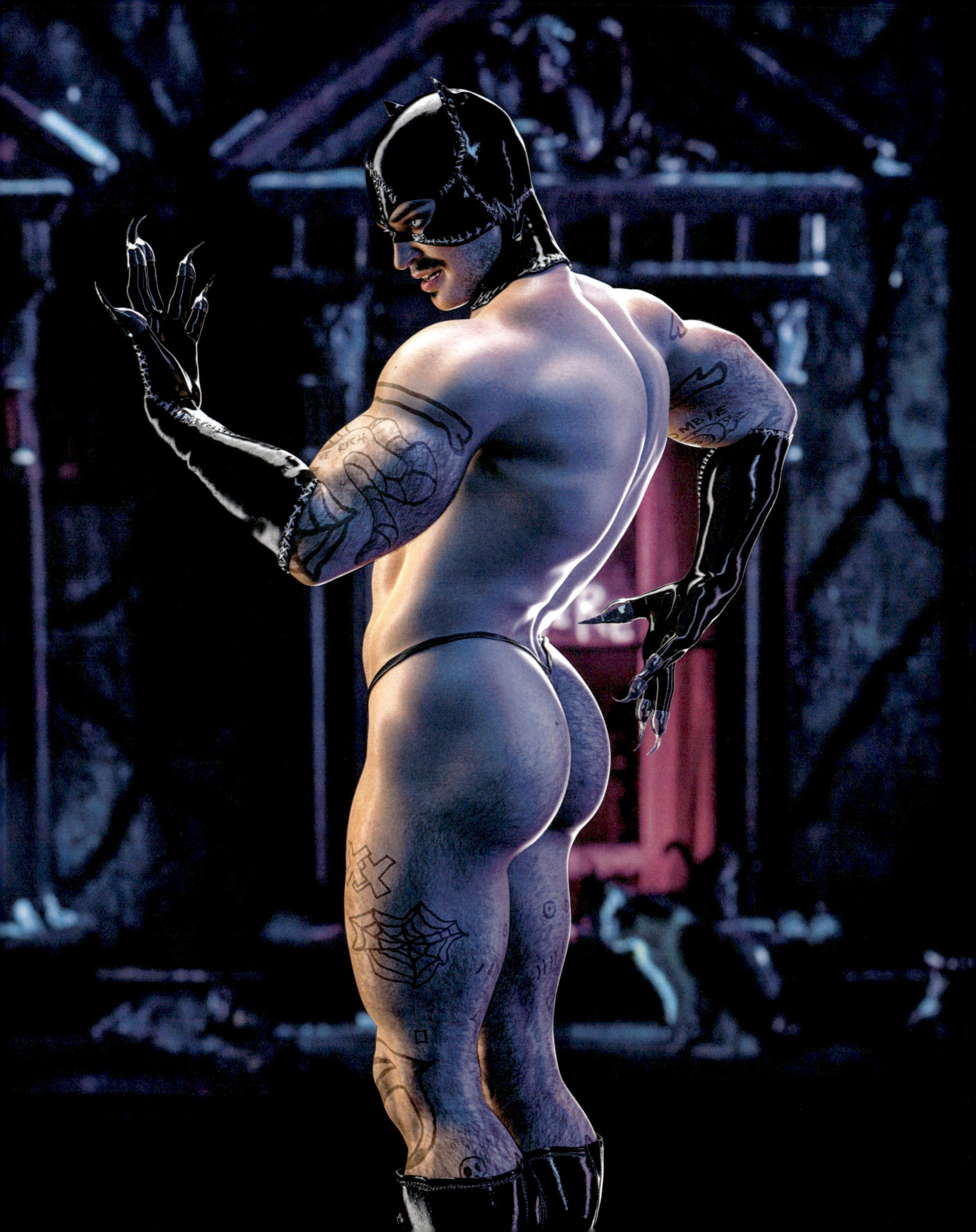

WE DONT NEED them

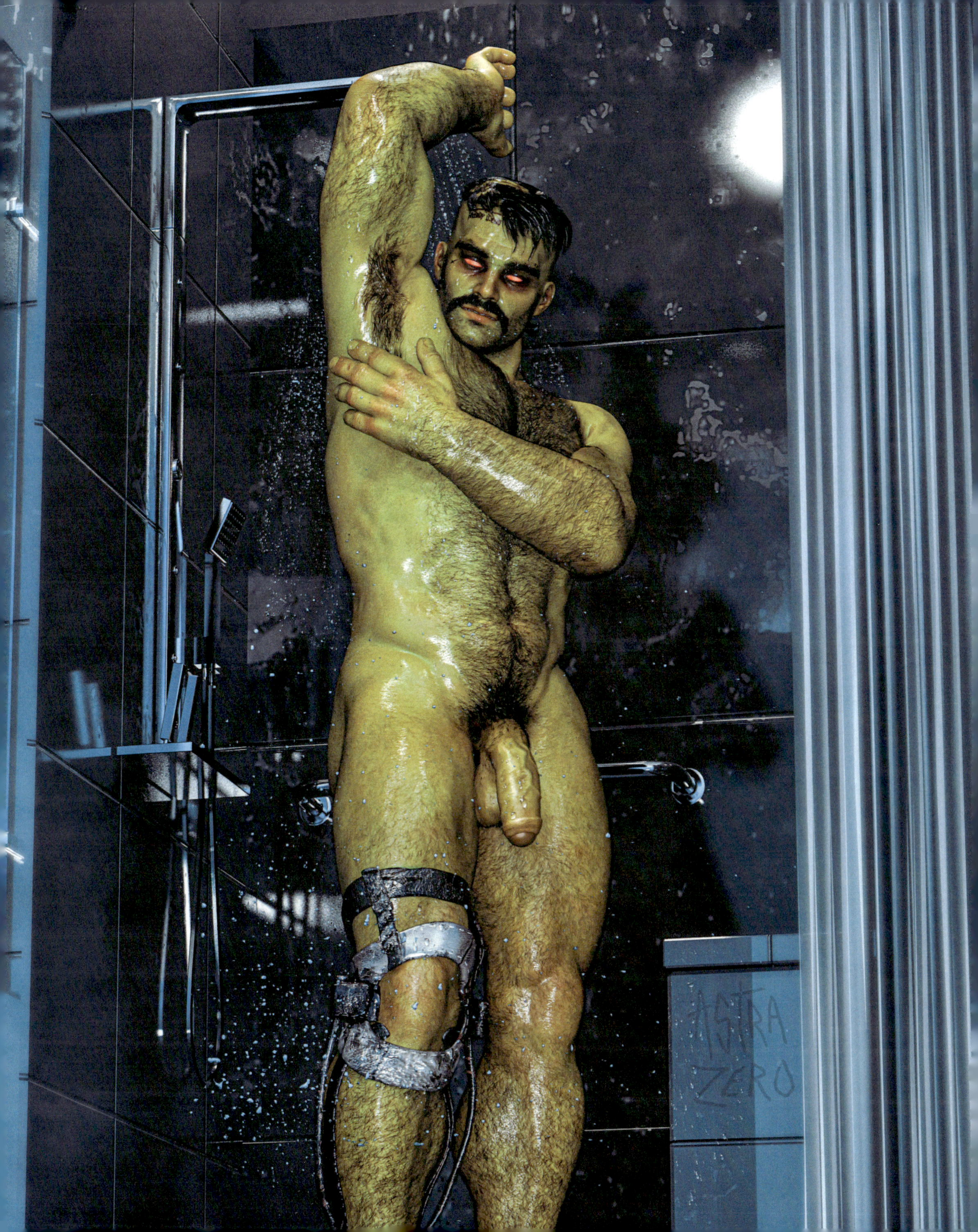
ASTRA
ZERO

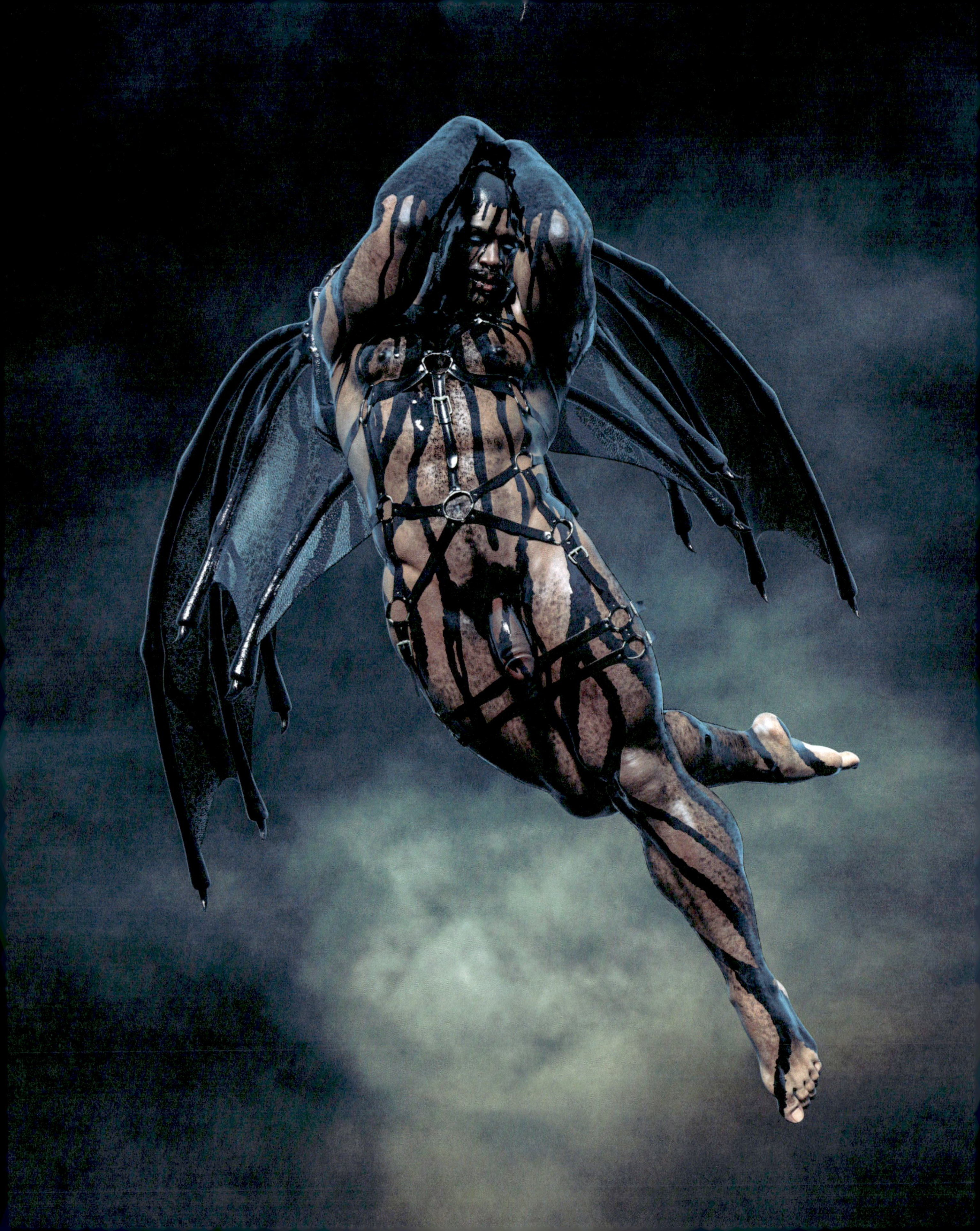

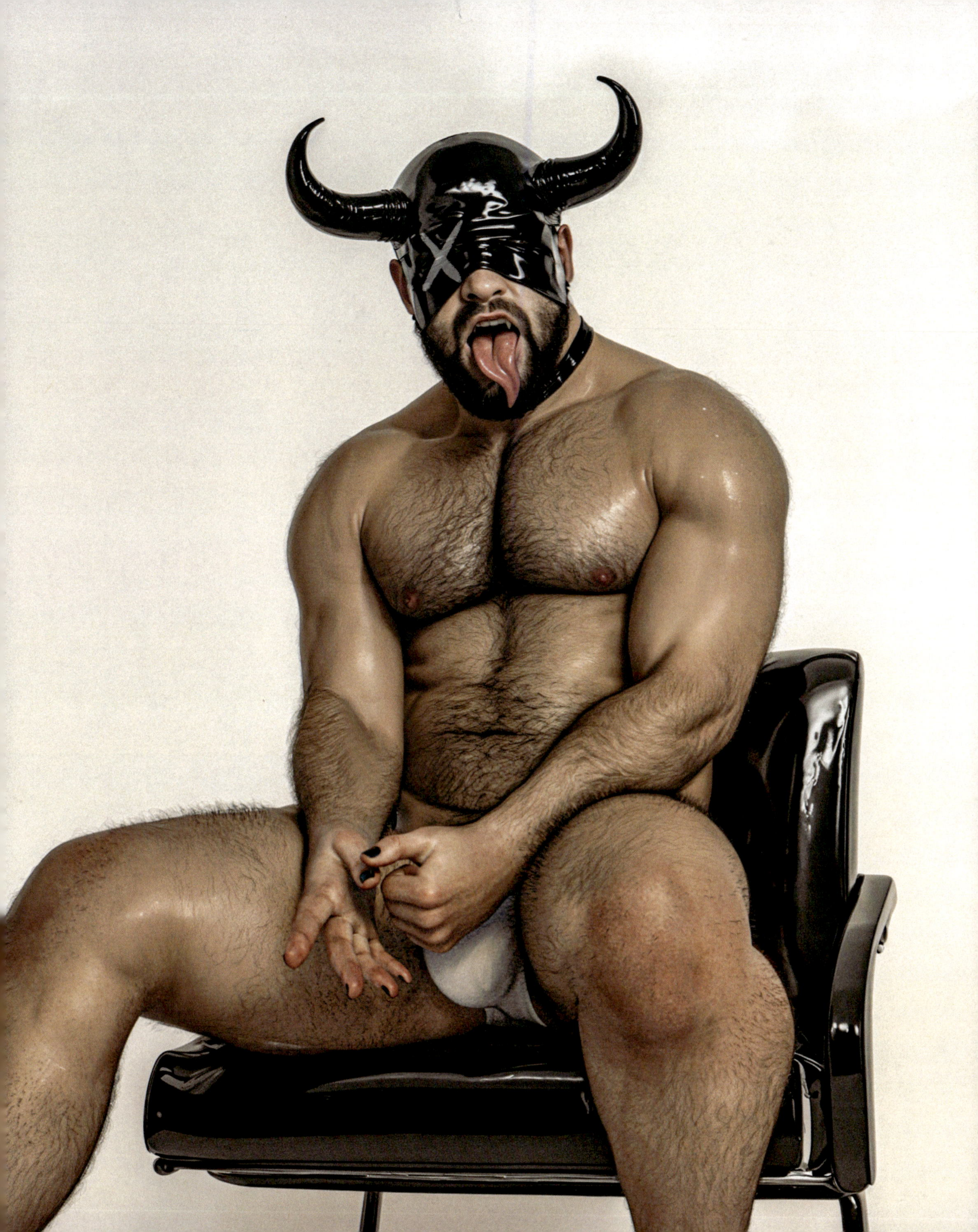

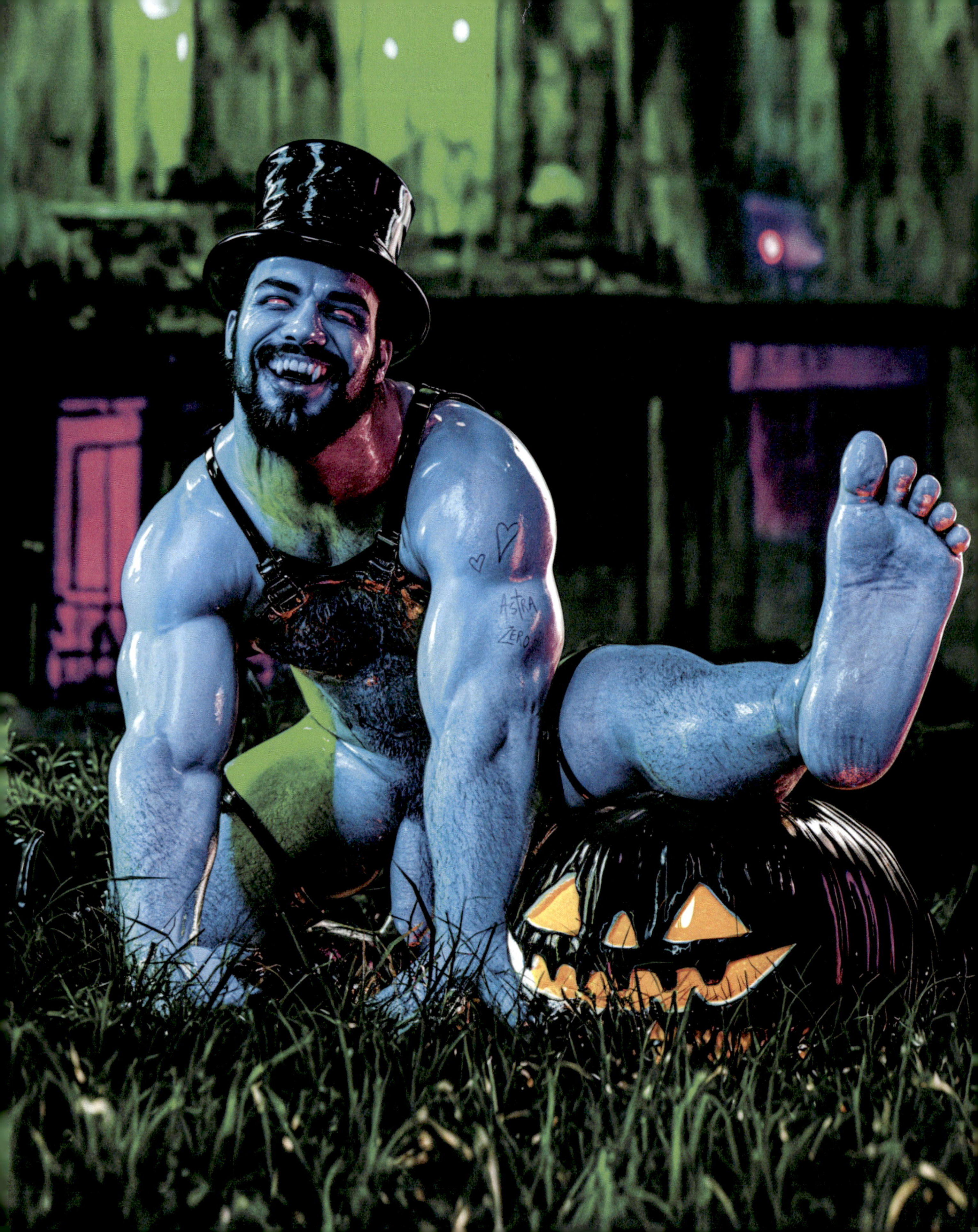

ASTRA
ZERO

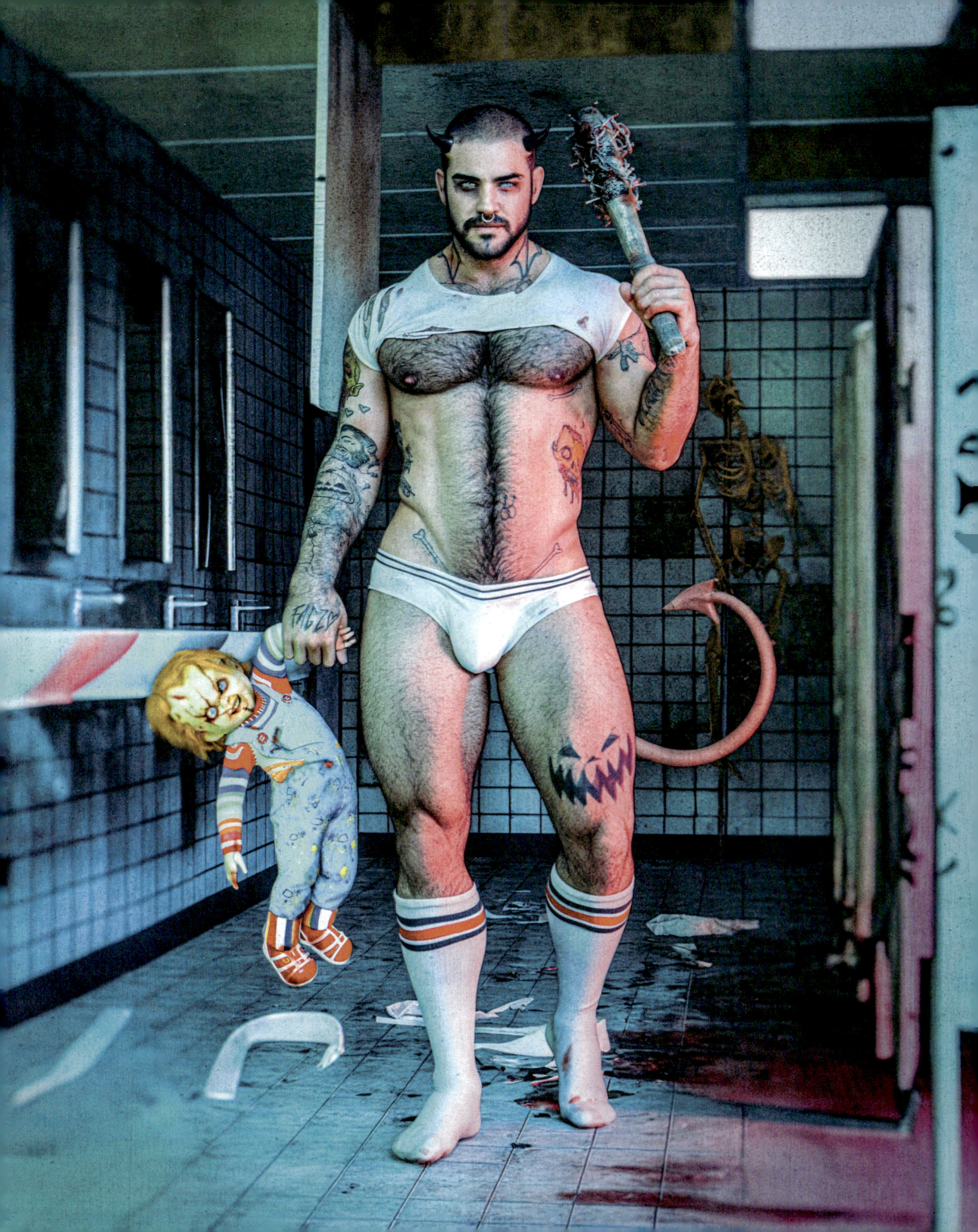

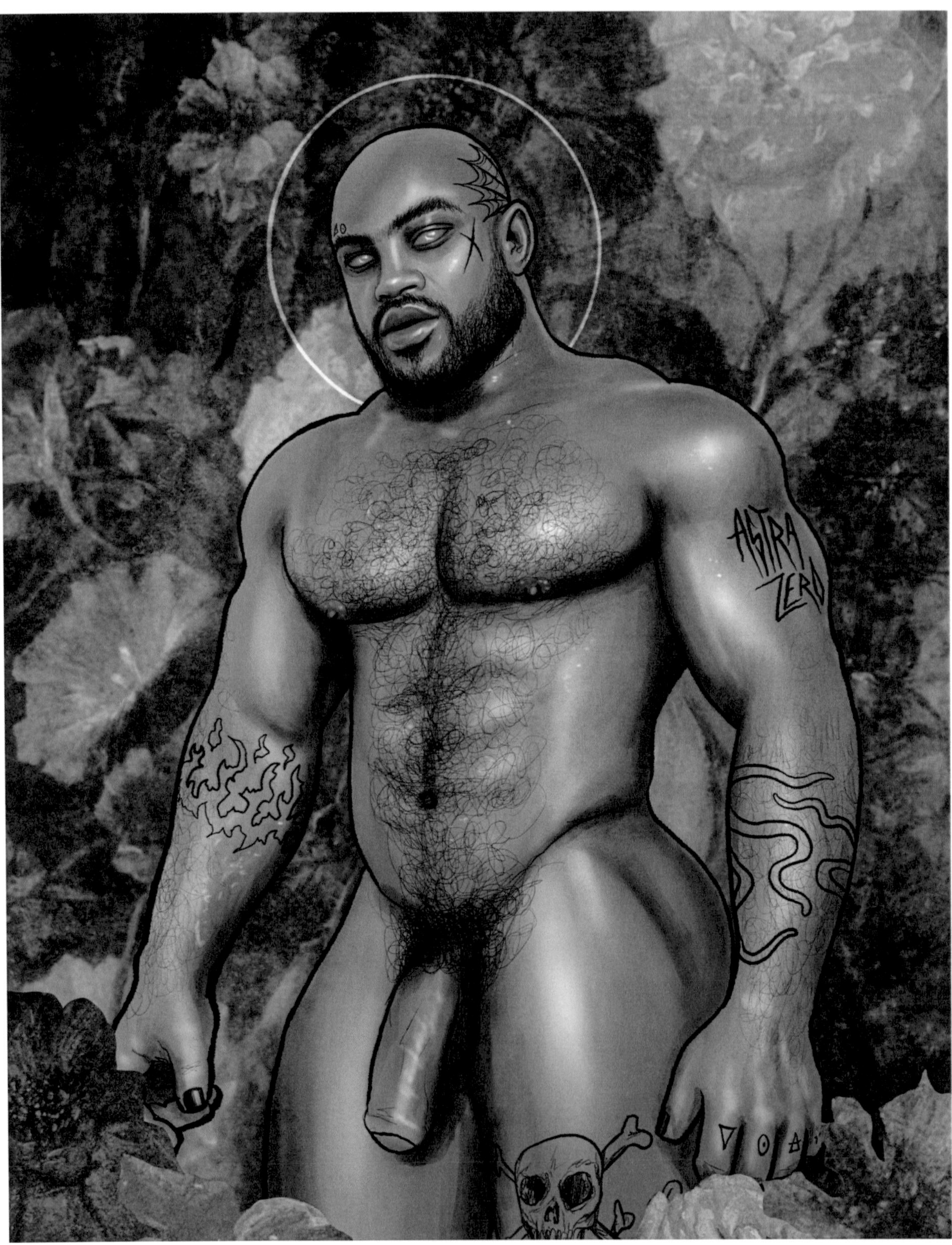

ASTRA ZERO

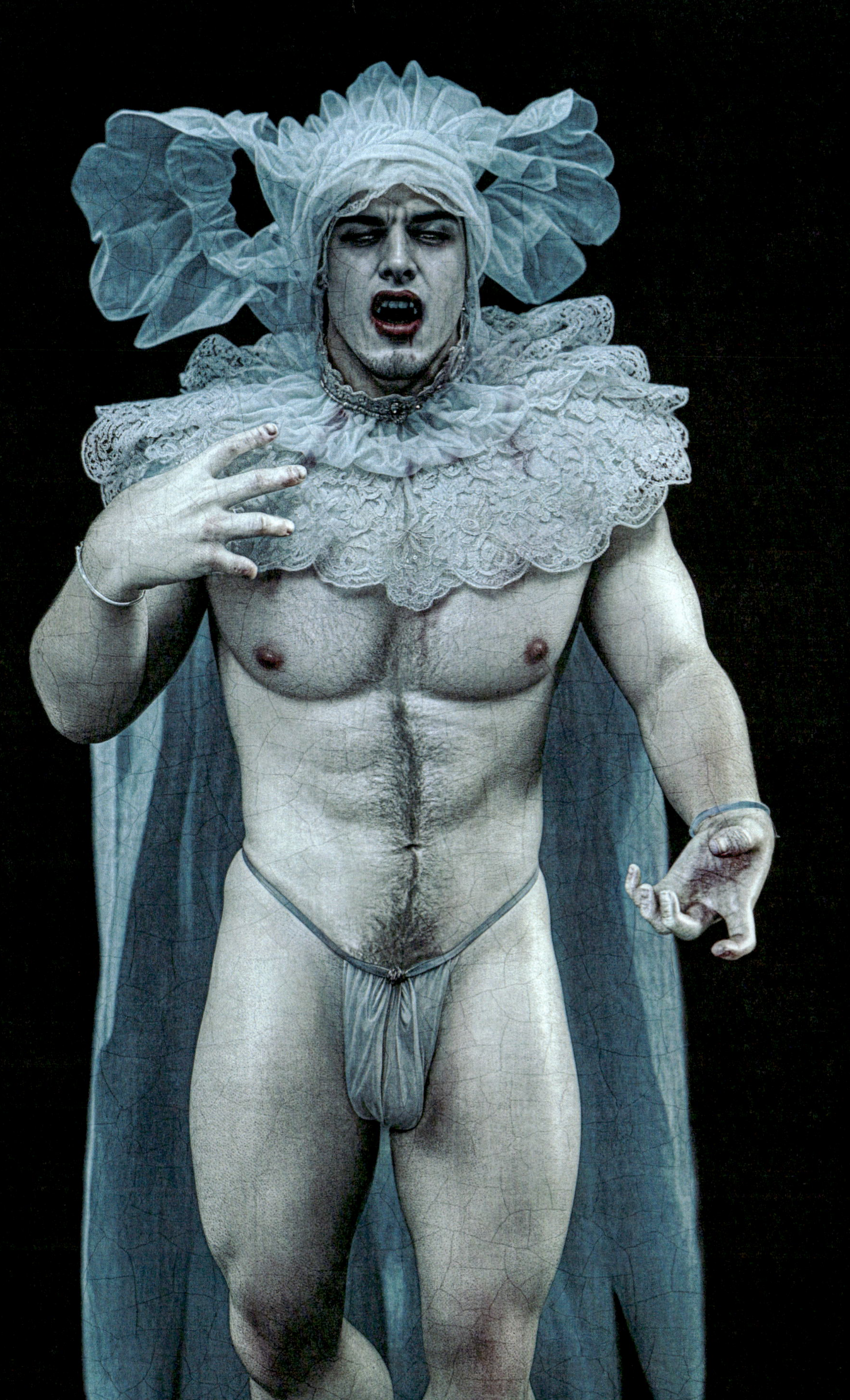

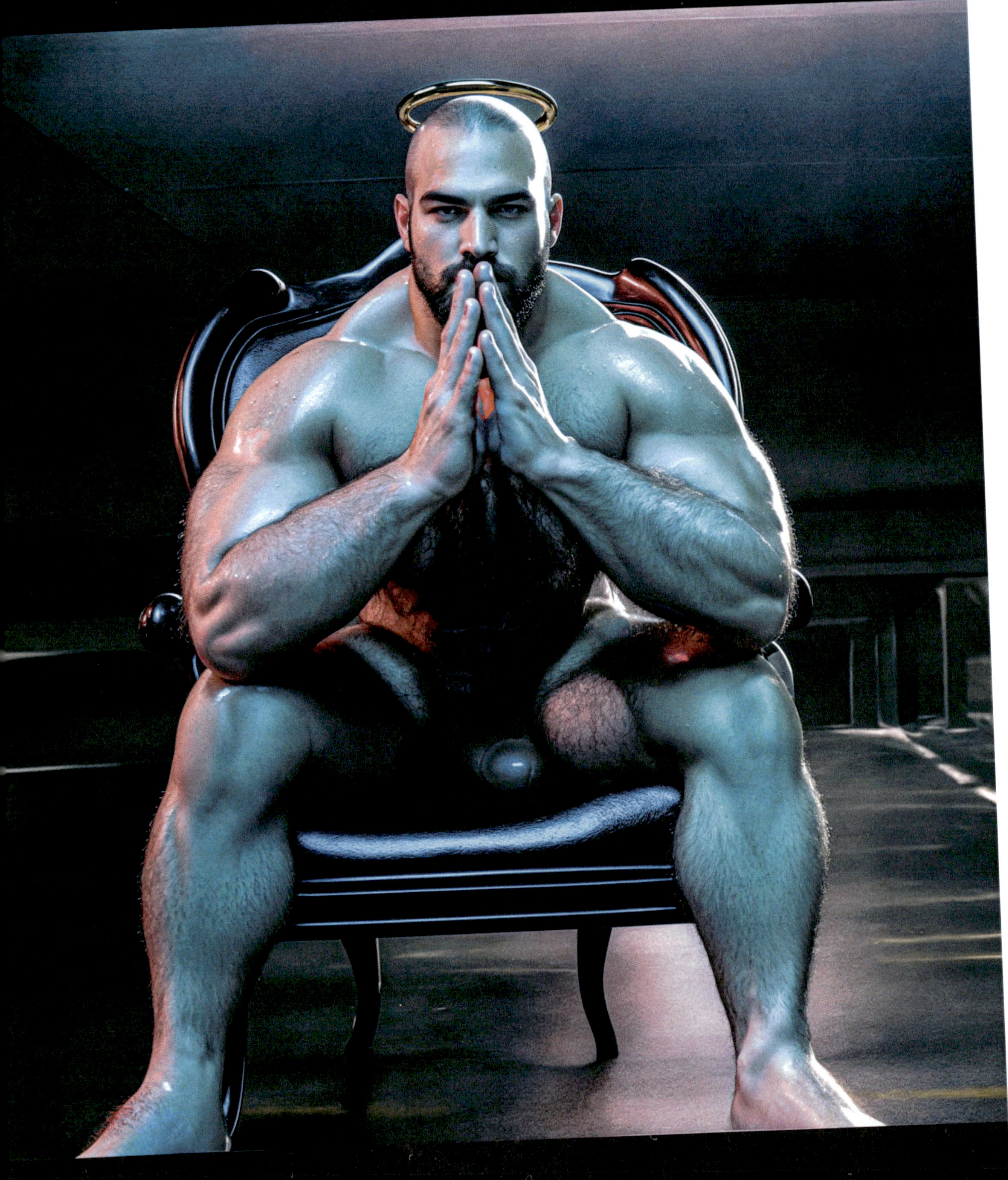

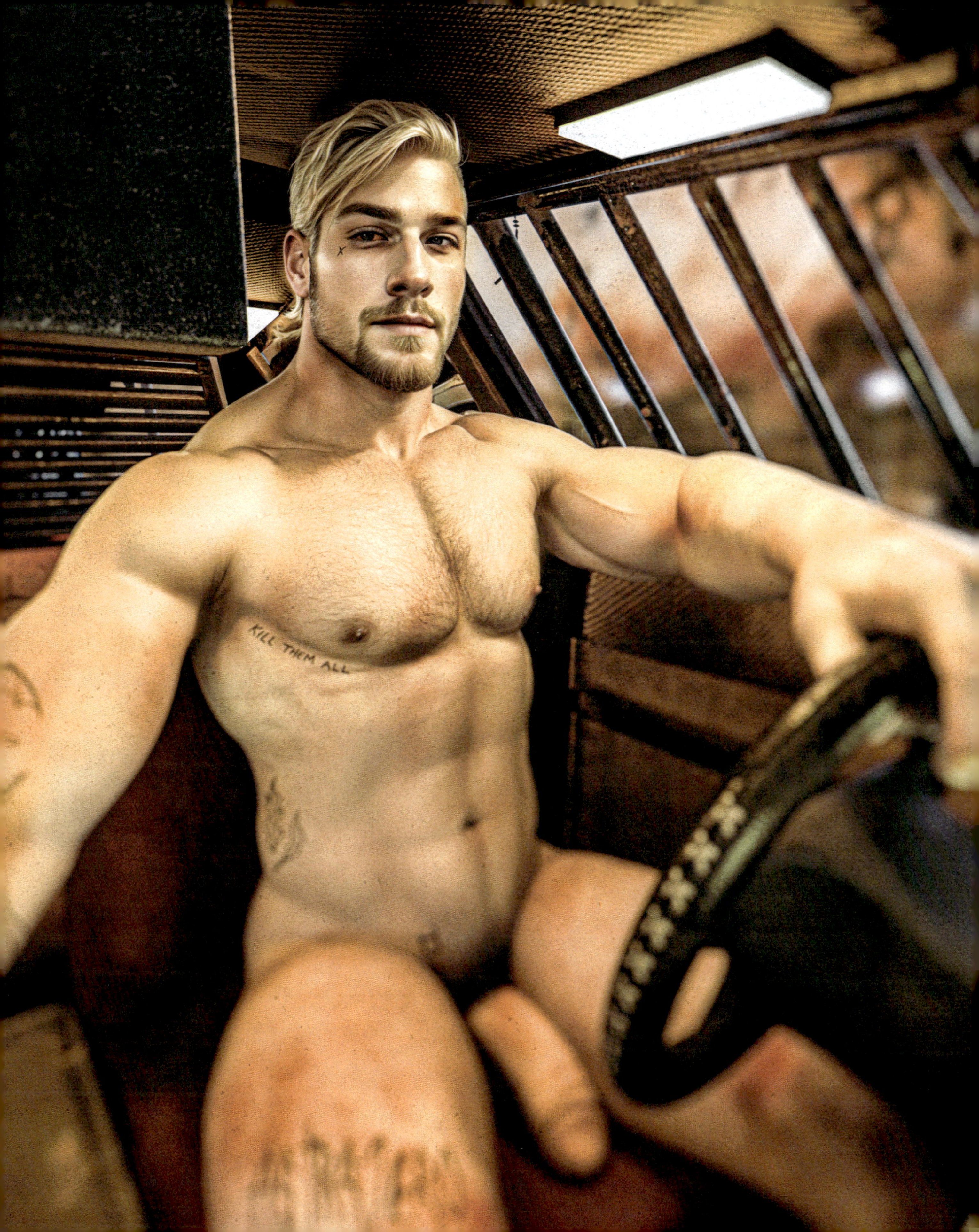
KILL THEM ALL

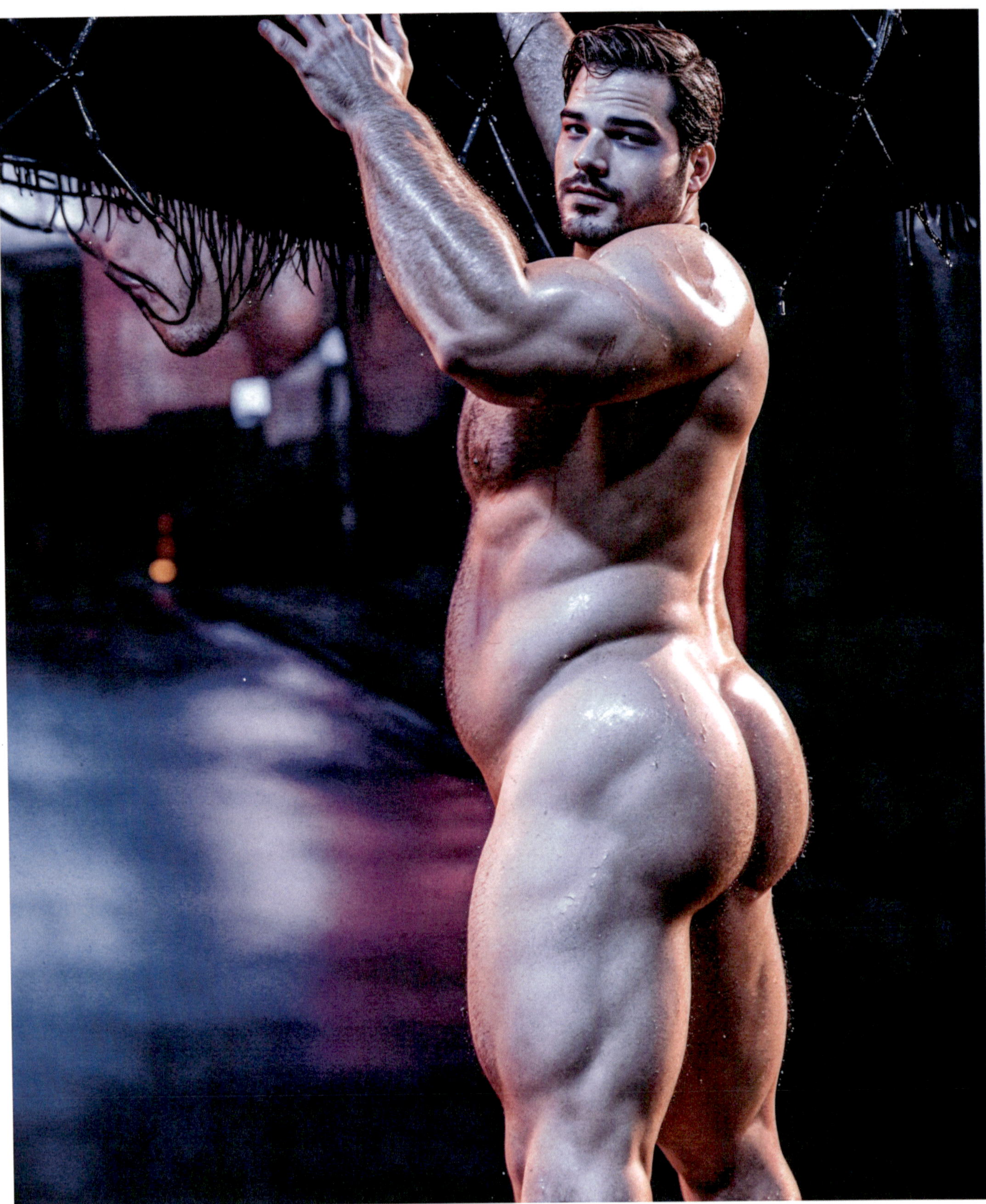

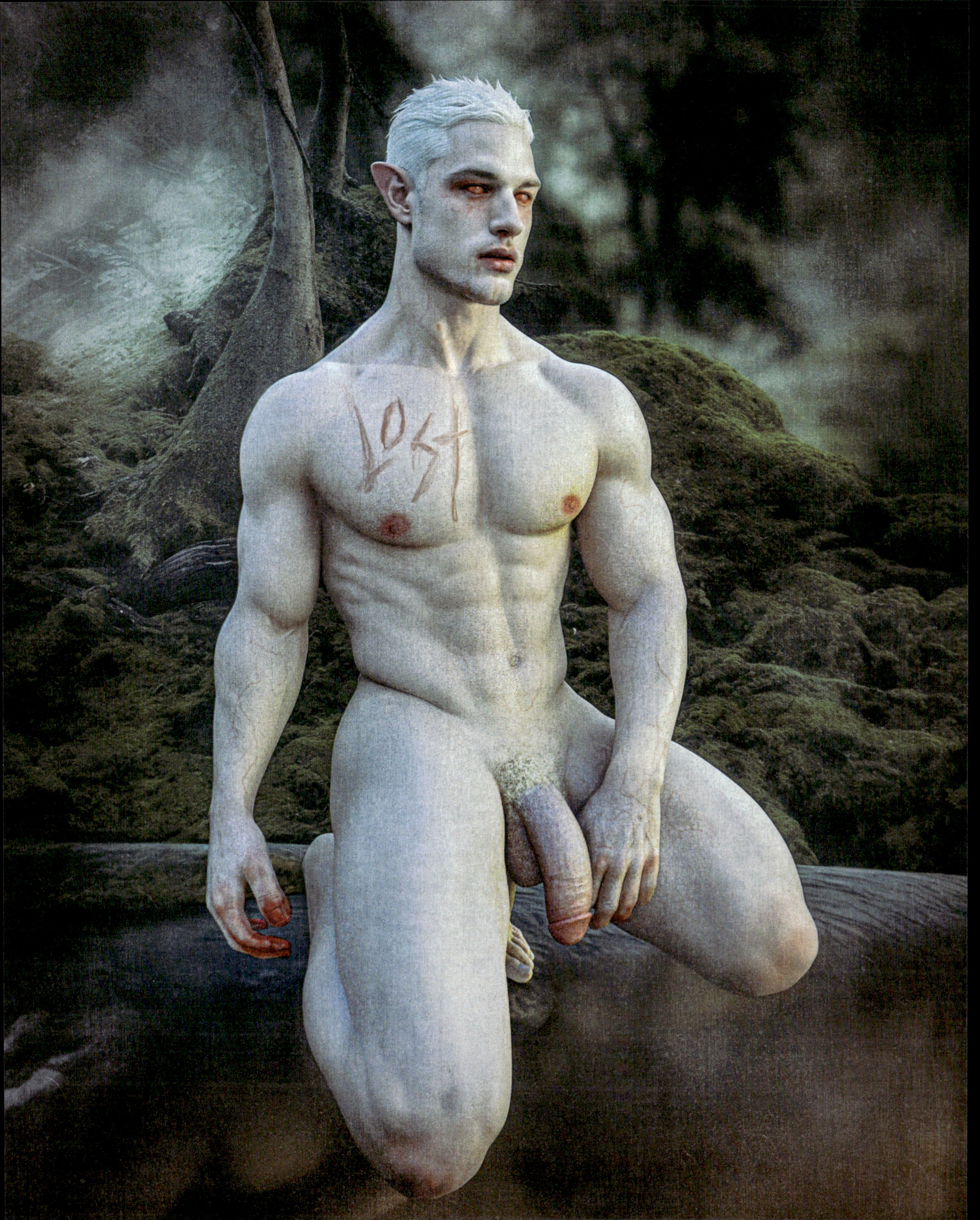
LOST

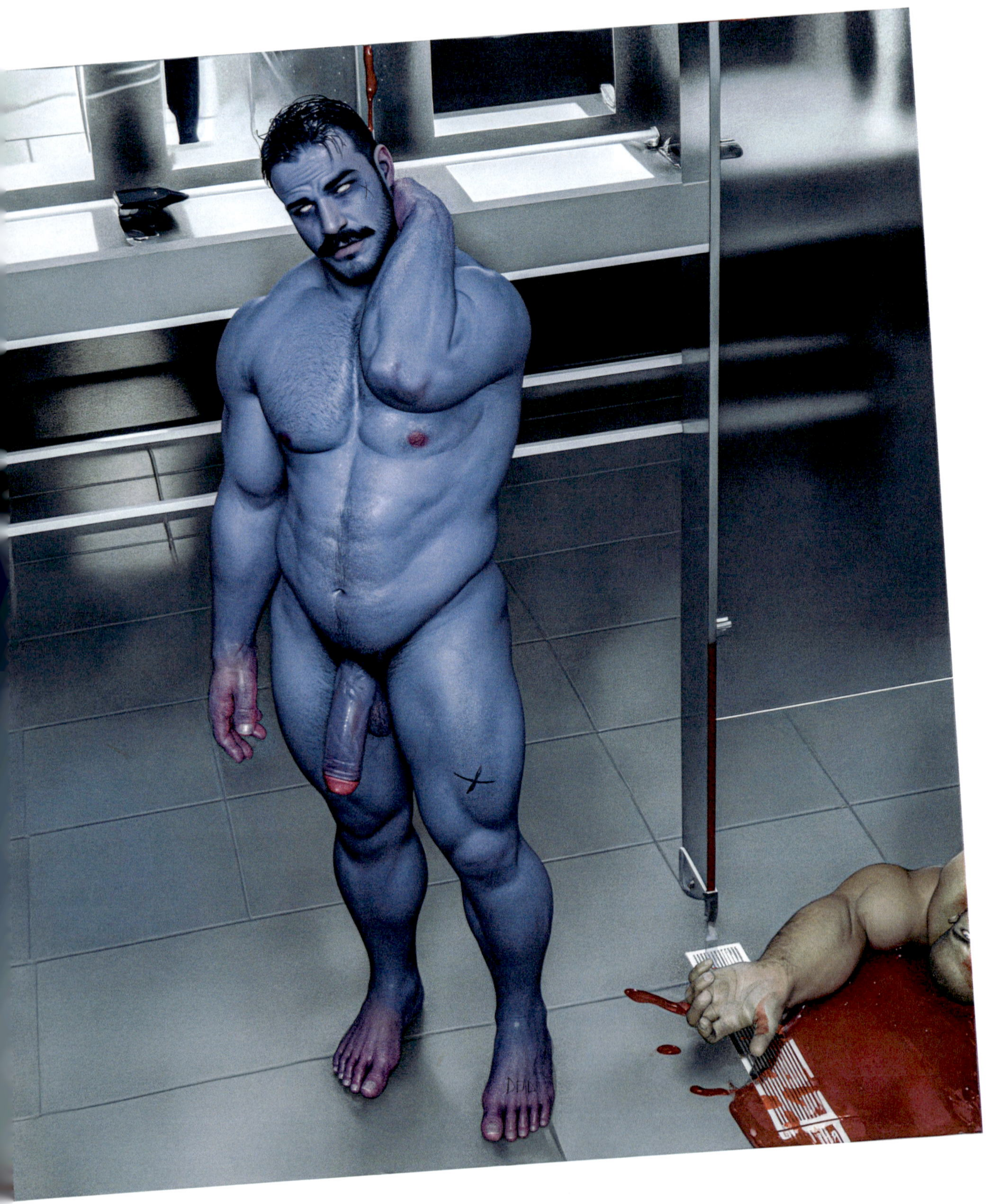

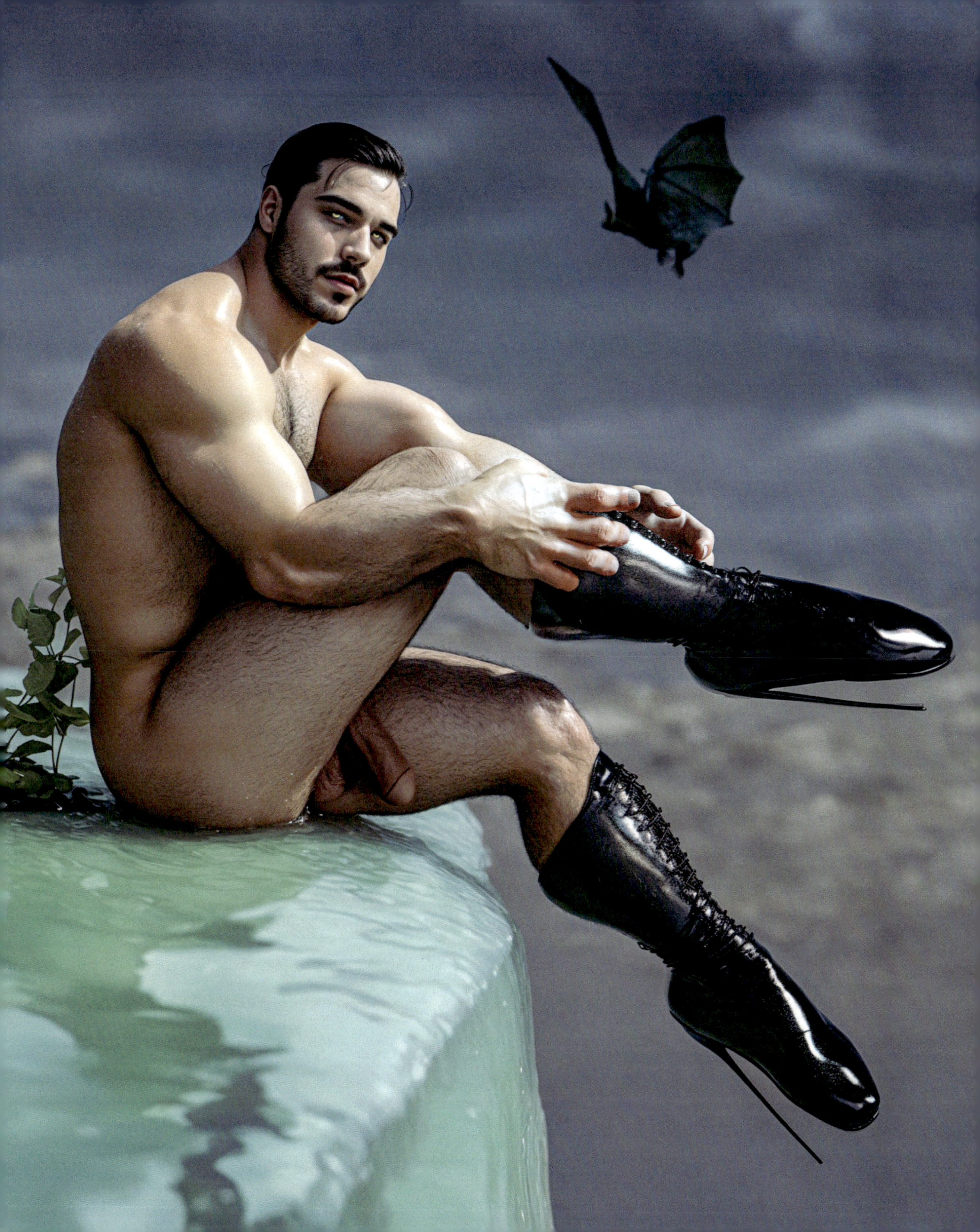

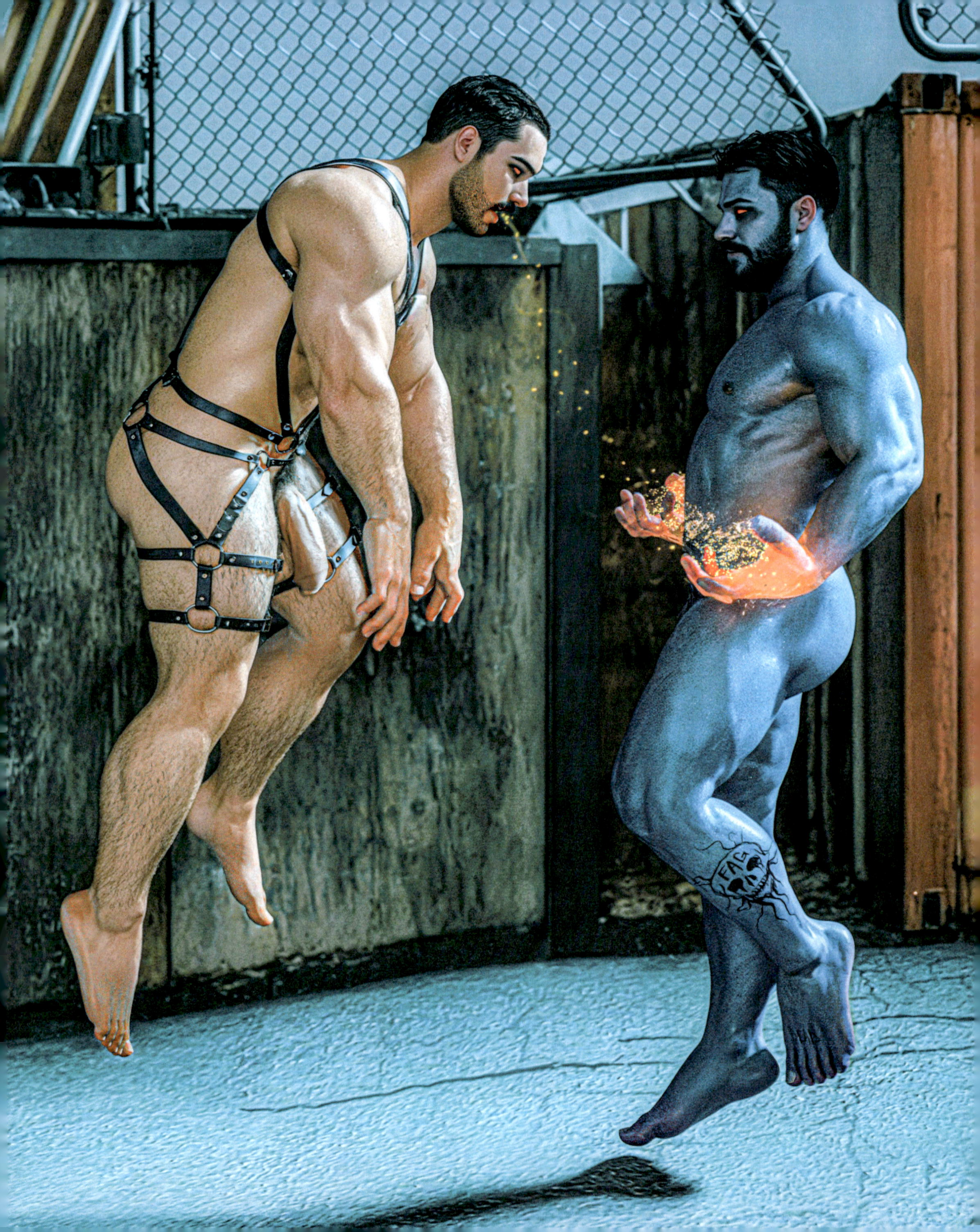

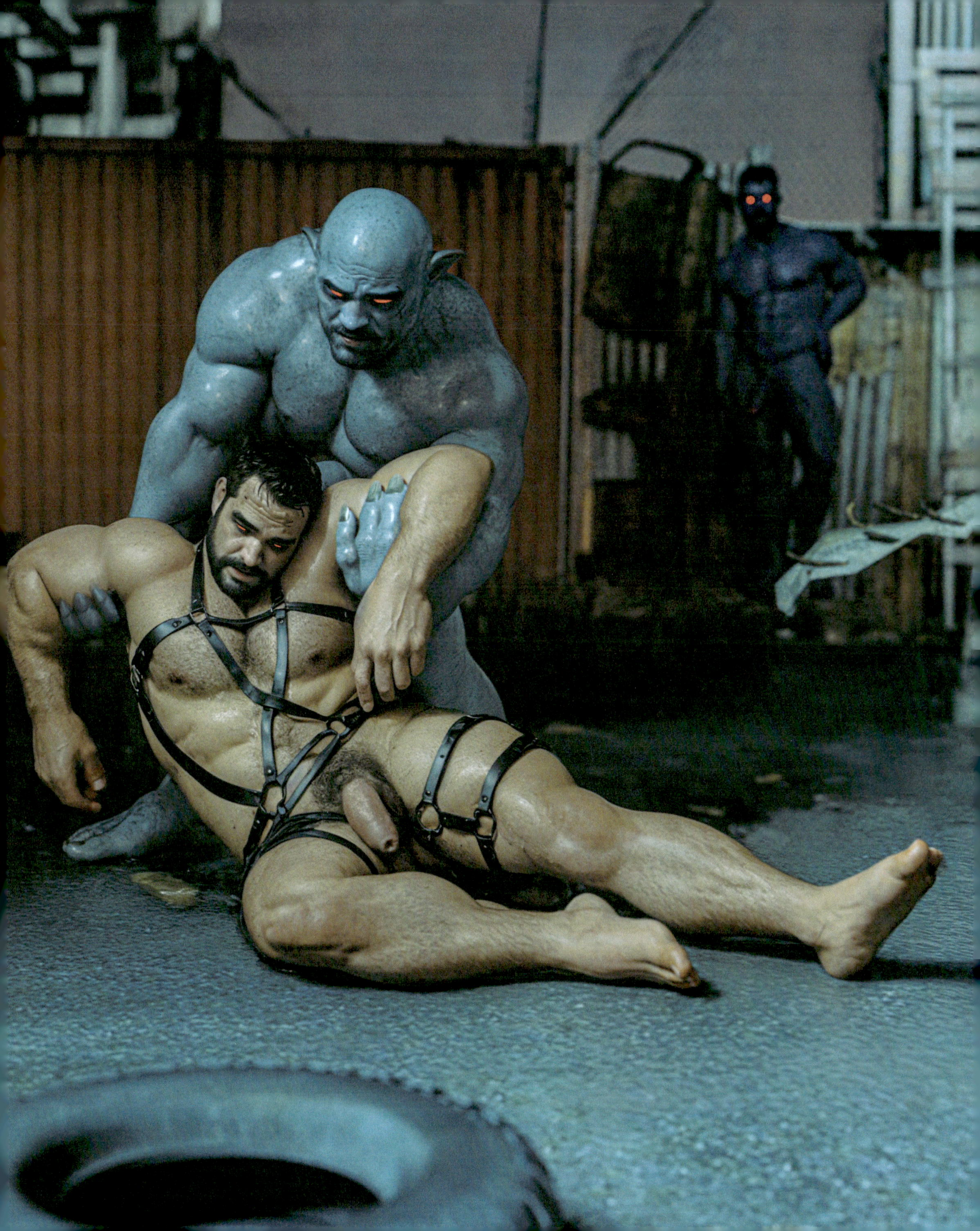

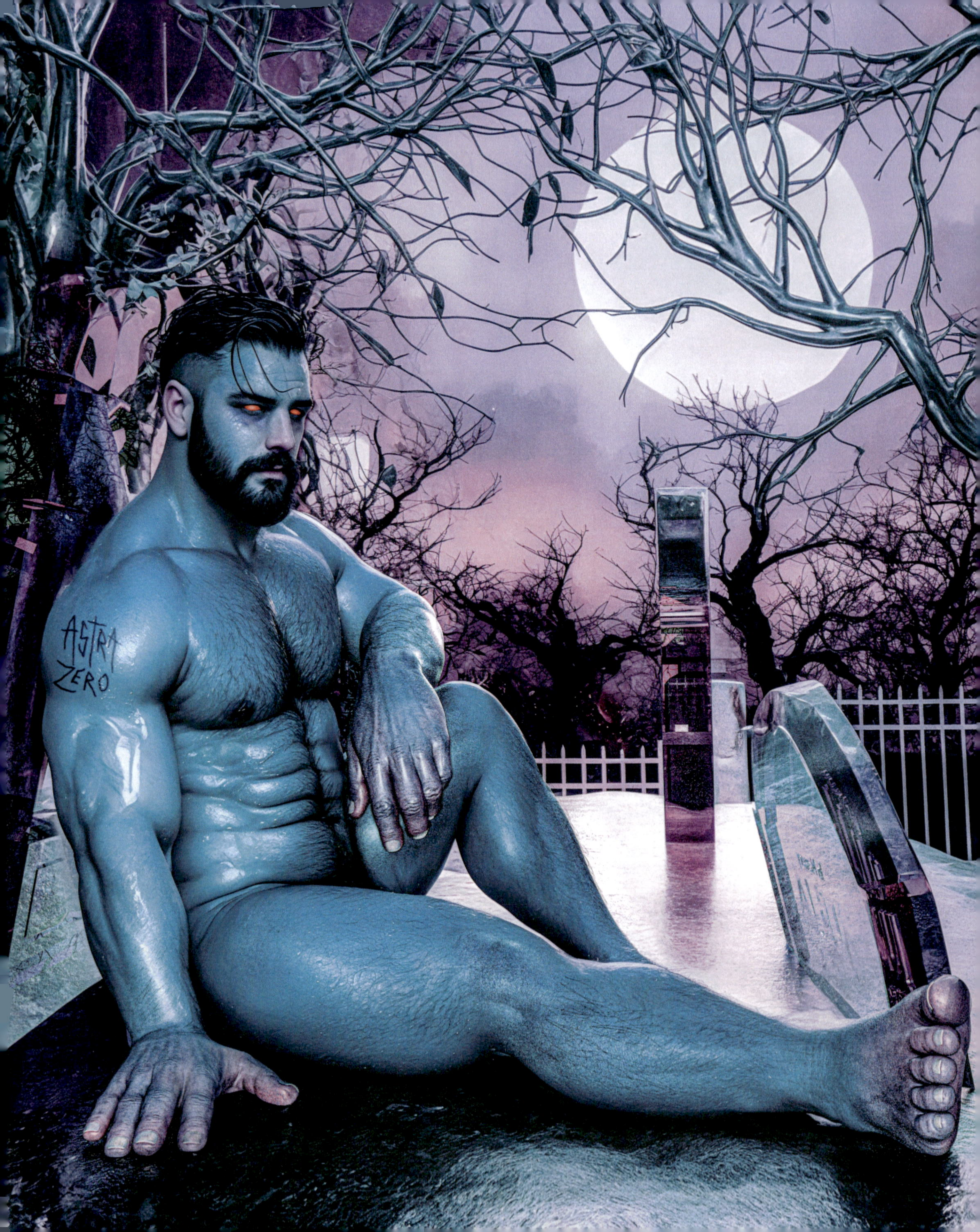

ASTRA
ZERO

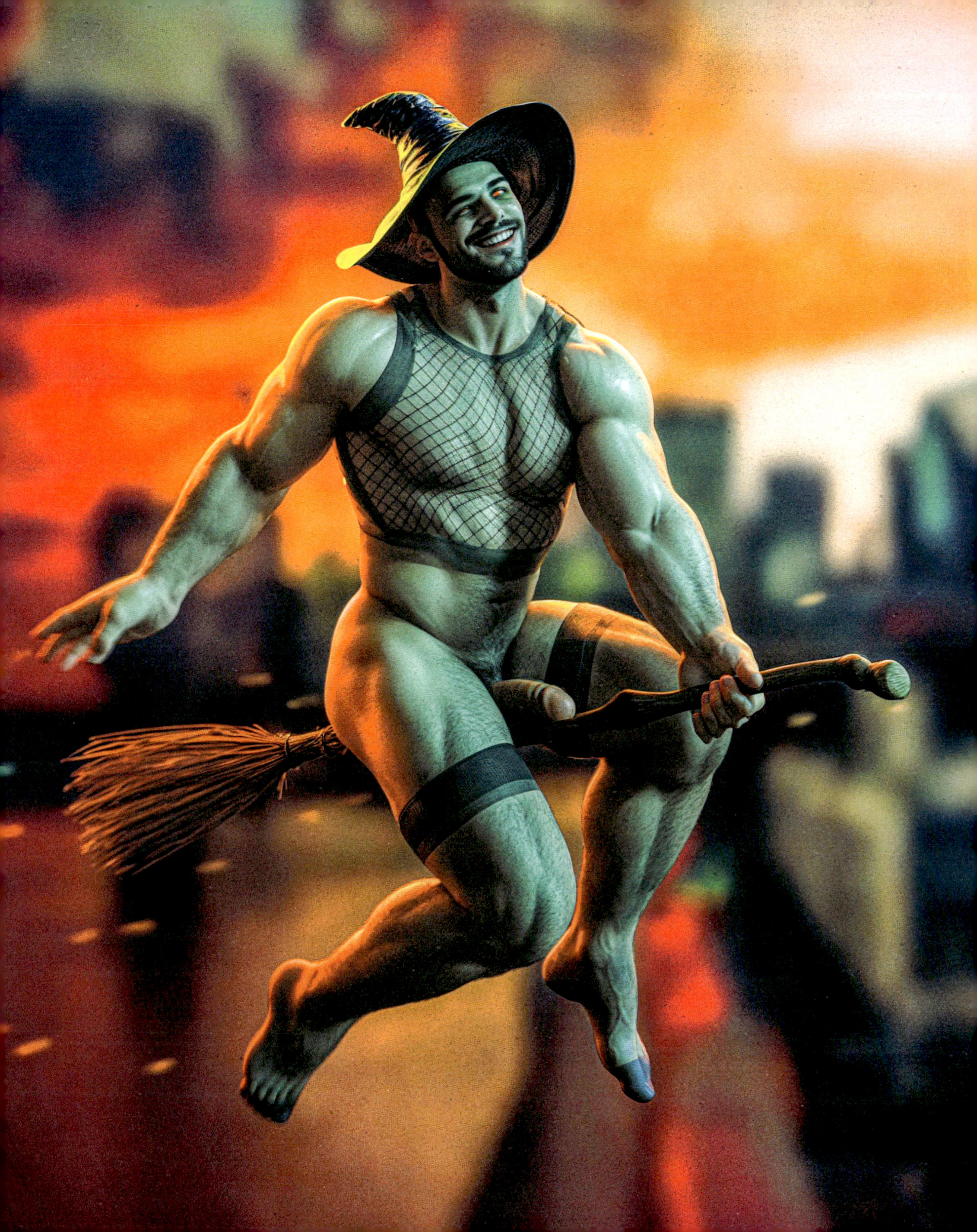

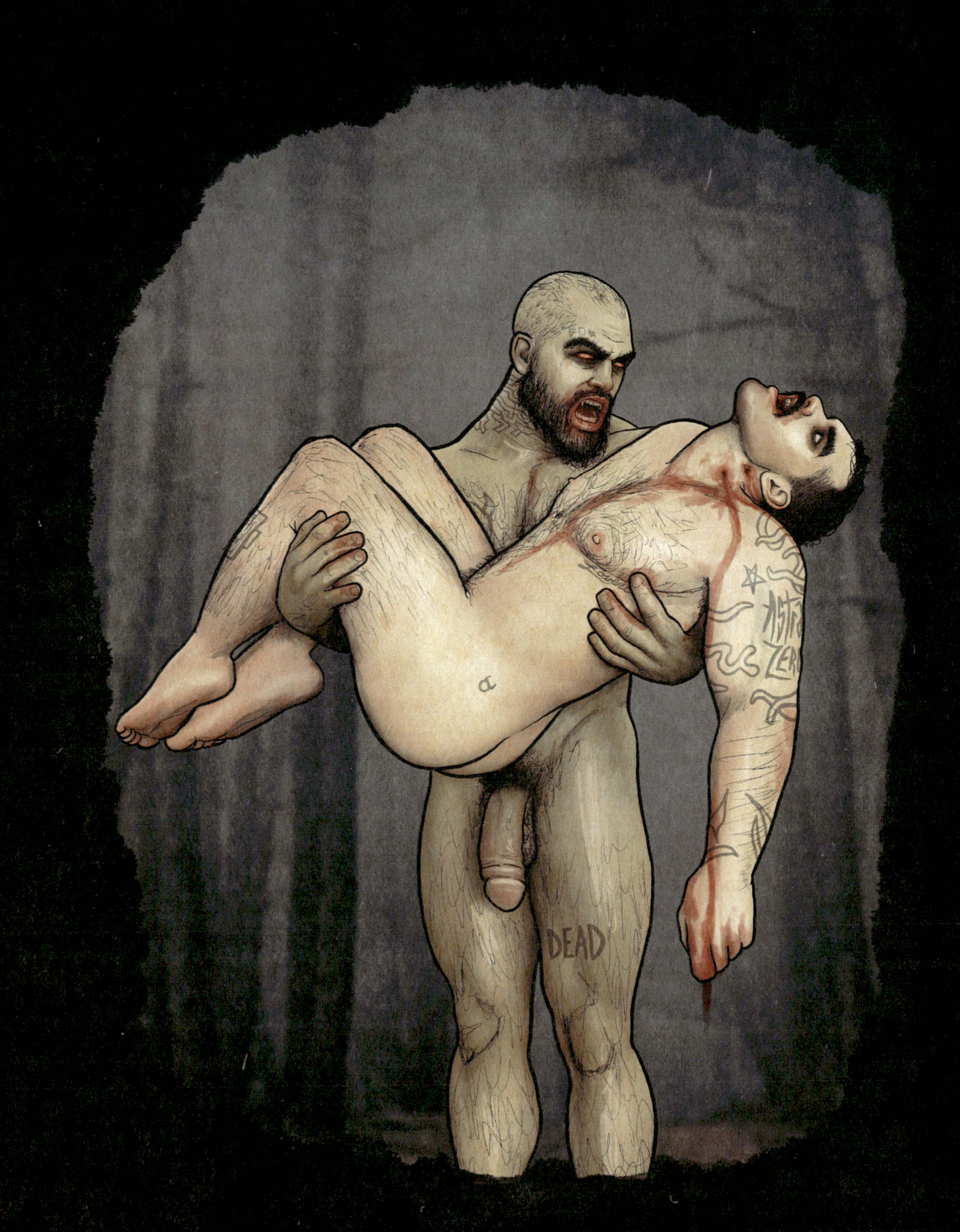

About the Artist

Astra Zero (born Dustin Nicholls) is a queer Canadian alternative visual artist, designer, illustrator, video editor, creative director and songwriter.

His work fluctuates from a gothic macabre style and spooky cute themed visuals to his more popular sexually charged style of gay themed monsters, pop culture and historical revamped artwork with a dark erotic twist.

Starting off as a mainly 2D Artist with drawing & painting, His work has evolved to incorporate & mix more mediums and styles into his workflow, from Photography, 3D rendered work and digital painting, to animation, photo / video editing and graphic design.

You can see more of his work on social media @astrazero and on his website: www.astrazero.com

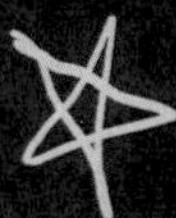

ASTRA ZERO

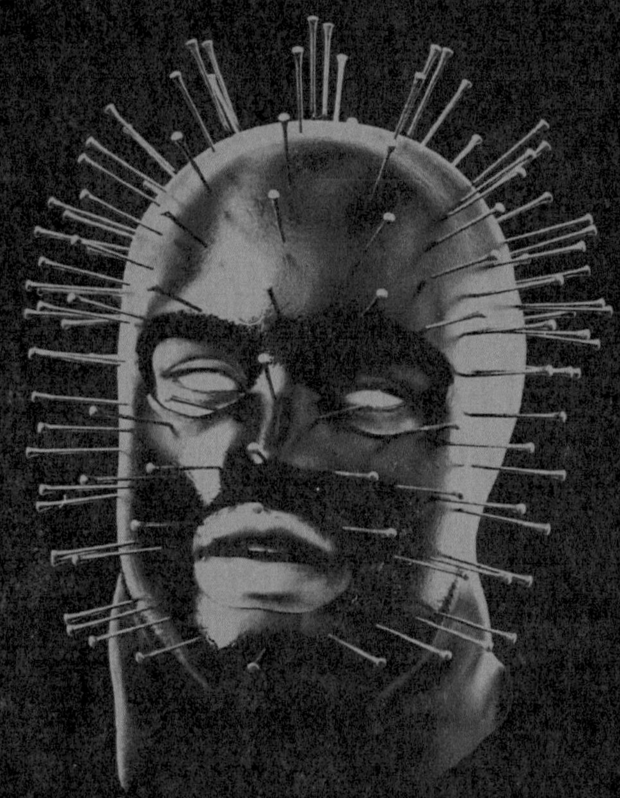

astrazero.com 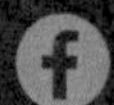 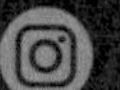 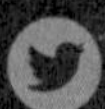 @astrazero